THE CITY

on

THE HILL

THE CITY ON THE HILL

a

History

of the

Harrisburg

State Hospital

by

Ernest Morrison

Thomas Sinclair lithograph of the Pennsylvania State Lunatic Hospital, 1851.

... What is really being praised is not the establishment of the Harrisburg State Hospital but the existence of enlightened and humane concern for fellow human beings ...

John B. Logan *

*on the occasion of the presentation of historic documents marking the 125th anniversary of the hospital in 1976.

PREFACE

Americans were becoming accustomed by the 1840s to the idea that it was the responsibility of the state to provide for the mentally ill. The issue at that time was over the form that the state's care should take and how that care should be paid for—whether or not large, centralized, state-run hospitals or dispersed county facilities, then currently in vogue, were the appropriate arrangements.

In a sense this debate has continued to the present day. Prior to the middle of the nineteenth century, facilities were almost always local ones. After 1851, central state hospital care for the mentally ill gradually became the norm. Then, during the 1960s, there was a return to the idea of a dispersed local system of delivering health care to these individuals. This book, then, in addition to being a history of the Harrisburg State Hospital, traces these national trends and their impact on the local scene. As the first state mental hospital and as the one adjacent to the seat of state government, its story has come to represent Pennsylvania's shifting attitudes on the care of its mentally ill.

In studying the available material for the one hundred and forty years since the hospital's founding, a reader is struck by the dedication and concern of those involved with the care of the mentally ill. In reviewing the reports, the letters and the medical notes of the doctors and superintendents; and in talking with the nurses, the attendants and the administrators of the hospital at Harrisburg, the professional attitude and humane intentions of those who have been connected with it become apparent. Today we possess better treatment possibilities, but no greater sensitivity.

At the same time one cannot help but be struck by the feeling of resigned helplessness that must have existed in earlier years—when people were faced with a lack of modern medical knowledge and treatments. The cases involving epileptics, often children, who were considered as mentally diseased individuals beyond any regimen of care and the general inability to help tubercular patients are especially distressing to read. For these individuals, then, hope or Divine providence were the only available curatives. There are also stories of poignant cases among persons other than the patients. State Senator Joseph Konigmacher, a friend of Pennsylvania's poor as well as its insane, is certainly one of these.

One interesting sidelight to a study of the history of mental illness is that, while the twentieth century may have given their use a few new twists, voluminous quantities of statistics were being collected and used to support social and political views early in the history of nineteenth century asylum keeping. From the very earliest years a wide variety of patient information was gathered at the Harrisburg State Hospital separately for each sex: the reason for admittance, place of birth, occupation, length of time insanity had been manifest as well as detailed records of the receipts and expenditures on the farm, the garden, the piggery and the hennery. The hospital superintendents, moreover, used this data to support their appeals to the legislature for increased appropriations by showing "need" as well as to prove that "results" were being achieved by the institution. The legislature, later, became sophisticated enough to use the same data to show that the asylum population had become "chronic" in nature.

The casual reader may question the need for chapters on "moral treatment" and on the treatment of the insane prior to the nineteenth century and especially why there is a separate one on Thomas Kirkbride, the superintendent of the Pennsylvania Hospital for the Insane at Philadelphia. It is impossible to understand the founding of the Pennsylvania State Lunatic Hospital at Harrisburg without first understanding the background (both the popular and the legislative mind that led to that establishment), and then without knowing something of moral treatment. And to appreciate, to assess properly the significance of moral treatment, it is necessary to understand the history of the treatment of the insane prior to the nineteenth century. Lastly, without knowing something of Kirkbride it is impossible to know John Curwen, the first superintendent of the Pennsylvania State Lunatic Hospital.

While several biographies have been written about Dorothea Dix—in some she is considered "forgotten" and in others overpraised—her important role as a "publicist" in the founding and early support of the Pennsylvania State Lunatic Hospital is hopefully placed here in better perspective. At the same time the roles that individuals such as Thomas Kirkbride, Luther Reily, Joseph Konigmacher, Jacob Haldeman, and a succession of superintendents, physicians and staff, from John Curwen on, have played in the development of the hospital are brought together for public view for the first time.

Dix, Curwen, and Kirkbride would, in the words of Earl Bond, a Kirkbride biographer, "rejoice at many of the advances made in psychiatry since their day; the discovery of promising treatments for general paralysis, for dementia praecox and attacks of depression and excitement; ... the better understanding of the complex forces in the mind that has come from Freud." But they "would wonder why we had not made better use of our knowledge and our resources." Earl Bond's answer was that "we are better scientists than Kirkbride and his friends, but not better people."

Throughout the text the work of a number of Pennsylvania architects is discussed. These were not consolidated into one substantial sketch, as they might have been, since this was peripheral to the purpose of the book. It should be noted, however, that the several building phases and the wide variety of structures erected at The Pennsylvania State Hospital—which range from the earliest designs in 1841 to those sixty years later—offer a laboratory for the shifting modes of nineteenth-century architecture. It was during this period that, in the words of Norman T. Newton, American architecture "endured successive eclectic 'revivals' ... borrowing freely from different foreign types and styles." A review of the bibliography will provide, for the interested reader, several sources of material for further study of the work of Strickland, Haviland, Hutton, and Dempwolf.

Lastly, this history of the Harrisburg State Hospital has been written for the general reader. For this reason, use of statistical lists and charts has been kept to a minimum. The book, then, is not a tome for reference, but a story to be read for enlightenment, even pleasure.

Occasionally during interviews former physicians, nurses and staff members at the Harrisburg State Hospital would mention that it had been "fun" working there. This seemed, at first, to be a peculiar term to describe what, to the typical outsider, appears as a hostile place. There was, moreover, frequent talk of hard physical work, but never of "burnout." Today the word fun has negative connotations; of cheap amusements rather than of lasting pleasure, a succession of meaningless thirty-second film images instead of an afternoon on the porch reading a book.

The period from 1851 through the great depression of the 1930s was a different time; a harsher, but also a gentler age. Heavy manual labor, for both men and women, was a way of life. Hours of duty were long. Periods of relaxation, moreover, were less frequent and simpler, but probably more refreshing and more fulfilling. People took pleasure in their work as well as in a simple, long walk around the grounds with a friend. An individual could be content with a life of thirty or forty years of service in a single demanding job that, as John Curwen put it, required him or her "to soothe the fretful, to calm the excited and noisy; to comfort the timid and complaining; to restrain those inclined to mischief; and to bear calmly, without provocation or resentment, the reproaches and taunts which may incessantly pour into their ears. ... " All of which, he went on to state, called for the "exercise of patience, forbearance and good nature, with a great deal of that gift which we call tact and management."

It is to these men and women then that this book is dedicated; those whose spirit still lives in the rooms and halls of the many buildings of "The City on the Hill," whose spirit still walks on the hillsides about those buildings.

* * * *

The book's Glossary is not intended as a source for general medical terminology. It is provided, rather, as a guide to unusual words or meanings, or those that were used as vernacular expressions among the patients or hospital staff or of medical terms, once in common usage, that are now obsolete. Words such as "lunatic" and "insanity," against which some people recoil with shock, are used throughout the text as they were historically. When in earlier days such words were in common use, they were not depreciatory. In this history then the institution is called the Pennsylvania State Lunatic Hospital until the time in 1921 when its name was changed to the Harrisburg State Hospital.

The bibliography consists of books that are available in most major libraries and of interest to the general reader. For the researcher such primary sources as correspondence and hospital annual reports that were used in the preparation of this book are available at The Pennsylvania Hospital in Philadelphia, The Pennsylvania State Archives and The Dauphin County Historical Society in Harrisburg.

Among the manuscript sources used were: the Harrisburg State Hospital's Annual Reports, the Commissioners and Trustee Meeting minutes, John Curwen's Journal, John Curwen's and Jerome Gerhard's Letter Press Books—all at the Pennsylvania State Archives; John Curwen's Correspondence with Thomas Kirkbride and Kirkbride's Student Notebook at the library of the Pennsylvania Hospital in Philadelphia; selected issues of *The Pennsylvania Medical Journal* at the Pennsylvania Medical Society; and the Harrisburg State Hospital's Oral History file, housed in the hospital's Dix Museum.

Other manuscript materials located at the Pennsylvania State Archives and Pennsylvania State Library included: the *Minutes of the Commissioners of the State Lunatic Hospital and Union Asylum For the Insane;* June 9, 1845-January 19, 1853; the *Minutes of the Board of Trustees of the Harrisburg State Hospital,* 4 volumes; the *Legislative Journals of the Pennsylvania House of Representatives;* the *Legislative Journals of the Pennsylvania Senate;* and the *Minutes of the Executive, Local and Visiting Committees of the Board of Trustees of Harrisburg State Hospital,* 1851-1924.

The writing of this history of the Harrisburg State Hospital is the result of the vision of the Historical Committee of the hospital, especially Edith Krohn and Joan Leopold of the hospital staff. Without their enthusiasm and interest and the assistance of committee members such as Robert Eaton, the son of former Superintendent Hamblen Eaton and Mrs. Julius Anderson, the wife of Julius Anderson, a prominent former hospital physician, this story likely would have gone untold.

The assistance of the staffs of the Pennsylvania State

Archives and the Pennsylvania State Library, and the many doctors, nurses, and administrators of the Pennsylvania State Hospital (both past and present)—far too numerous to mention individually but all helpful beyond belief—must be acknowledged. Caroline Morris and Barbara Bernoff of the Library of the Pennsylvania Hospital in Philadelphia also were helpful in making available the correspondence of John Curwen while Elizabeth Moyer, the oral-historian, always seemed to find new and interesting people to interview. Warren Wirebach of the Dauphin County Historical Society, who recommended areas for investigation and came up with days-saving research materials such as that on Joseph Konigmacher, and Alfred White, who made valuable suggestions about the manuscript, and Jane Batt, who proofread the final mauscript, also must be recognized. All this help I deeply appreciate.

Lastly, without William E. Goodman, who has labored so long and faithfully in preserving much of this material and in keeping alive the spirit of "The City on The Hill," this book would not be what it is.

TABLE OF CONTENTS

Page

I Five Thousand Years of Darkness 1

II "Moral Treatment" 7

III Thomas Kirkbride 14

IV Pennsylvania Survey and Memorial 23

V Dorothea Lynde Dix 31

VI Founding of the Pennsylvania State Lunatic Asylum 42

VII John Curwen 65

VIII Early Years 73

IX Civil War and the Second Decade 94

X Decline of "Moral Treatment" 108

XI Many Members But One Body 122

XII A New Hospital Rises 138

XIII The City on the Hill 156

XIV The Last Fiefdom 192

XV Return to the Community 214

XVI The Present and the Future 225

Appendices

A. Chronological Chart 234

B. Hospital Officers 236

C. Construction Journal and Hospital Grounds Schematic 239

D. Glossary 244

E. Admissions Data 248

F. Act of 1845 252

Bibliography 257

Index 260

LIST OF ILLUSTRATIONS

Frontispiece — Thomas Sinclair lithograph of the Pennsylvania State Lunatic Hospital, 1851.

	Page
Dorothy Lynde Dix, 1802-1887.	54
1863 Harpers drawing of Camp Curtin with the Pennsylvania State Lunatic Hospital in the background.	55
Interior of Kirkbride Building, male side, about 1900.	56
Interior of Female Nine show close living arrangements, about 1890.	57
"Dr. John" Curwen, first hospital superintendent, 1851-1881. and Jerome Z. Gerhard, superintendent from 1881-1891.	58
Pennsylvania State Lunatic Hospital Band, 1885.	59
View of hospital from the Laundry Tower, about 1900.	60
Male and female attendants, about 1900.	61
Female 9 & 10 building with Laundry Tower and Machine Shop on the right.	62
Kitchen in old building with cart being readied to transport food to one of the hospital buildings, 1890s.	63
Ice House and pond, first snow of the season, October 30, 1925.	64
Italianate entrance of the new Administration Building constructed during Henry Orth's superintedency.	178
New Administration Building with the Old Kirkbridge Building in the background, about 1895.	179
Addison Hutton's architectural floor plan for the Chronic Insane Building, 1900.	180
Interior of old Laundry, about 1910.	181
Interior of Female One showing one of the day areas, about 1910.	182
Henry L. Orth, hospital superintendent, 1891-1919. and Edward M. Green, hospital superintedent, 1919-1934.	183
Aerial view of hospital in winter, about 1930.	184
Physical therapy on the female side of the hospital, 1930s.	185
Patients shoveling snow off the hospital underground, 1950s	186
Howard K. Petry, hospital superintendent, 1934-1954 and Hamblen C. Eaton, hospital superintendent, 1954-1969.	187
Dix Museum, erected in 1853.	188
Hospital ravine with stone bridge	189
Chapel, built in 1913 by John A. Dempwolf.	190
Poplar Drive, approaching the site of the old ice house.	191

Photographs of the Chapel and Poplar Drive, courtesy of the Museum and Historical Commission of Pennsylvania. Remaining photographs courtesy of the Harrisburg State Hospital and the Pennsylvania State Archives.

I

FIVE THOUSAND YEARS OF DARKNESS

Throughout human history civilization has taken steps forward—often hesitant, occasionally determined; along with sometimes larger, even more frequent ones backward. Five thousand years ago the Pharaohs first started building pyramids. Since that time, fields of endeavor such as government, philosophy, the arts (both the practical and the fine), and the sciences all have seen such waves of advancement and retreat. Progress has been measured from discovery to discovery. One of the few areas, however, in which there was little change until recently and certainly no real advance, was in the treatment of mental disease. As Thomas Graham has said: "To try to write the history of psychology as a succession of forward steps would be a misguided effort."[1]

The Bible contains many stories of men and women being possessed by devils or evil spirits. In one case Jesus cast them out of two men and into a herd of swine. The melancholia of King Saul in the Old Testatment was even attributed to an "evil spirit" sent by God. Saul's cure, moreover, was accomplished by David's harp playing. Thus the ideas of demoniacal possession and of music's therapeutic ability are old ones.

For the ancient Egyptians, also, the care and treatment of the insane, the retarded, and the epileptic were based on the notion that they were possessed by demons. The "healing" of such individuals was therefore an exclusive right of the priesthood. Their methods of cure consisted of elaborate, secret, mystical ceremonies. Greece, like Egypt, had her healing temples—more than 300 such shrines have been identified—places devoted to invoking ritual purification from the gods.[2]

With the rise of scientific inquiry during the Age of Pericles, however, medicine started to free itself gradually from religion. A few Greek physicians and philosophers were able to make a beginning in the direction of more reasonable treatment of the insane. It was the Greeks, for example, who located the brain as the center of intellectual activity. They also made some crude attempts to classify the various afflictions and to formulate a few specific remedies.[3]

It was Hippocrates, the "father of medicine," who first stripped medicine of its supernatural trappings.[4] In writing of epilepsy, known in ancient Greece as the "sacred disease," he said: "The Sacred disease seems to me to be no more divine and no more sacred than other diseases; but springs from natural causes like other diseases." He also rejected incantation as cure. "They who first attributed this disease to the gods seem to me to have been just such persons as the conjurers, purificators, mountebanks and charlatans now are."[5] And in one of the remarkable statements for the age, Hippocrates claimed: "Men ought to know that from the brain, and from the brain only, arise our pleasures, as well as our sorrows, pain and grief ... and by the brain, too, we become mad or delirious, and filled with fears and terrors ... "[6]

Although Hippocrates and one or two other Greek physicians, such as Asclepius of Prusa, practiced advanced ideas for treatment of the mentally ill (controlled diets, massages, bathing and exercise), they were the exception. Most Greek doctors kept their mental patients locked in dark rooms; reasoning that this was conducive to peace of mind. It was about this time, too, that physicians starting the odious and frequently harmful practices of blood-letting and purging—means of therapy that would continue in use for several thousand years.[7]

A few physicians in the centuries following the birth of Christ advanced sentiments of humane treatment for the insane, but by the year 200 AD the rise of Christianity and the fall of science were complete. Most Roman doctors advocated the use of chains, flogging, and the application of terror and torture. All the evidence suggests that this was the pitiful lot of the mentally afflicted up until the nineteenth century. In the thirteenth century, for example, Peter of Spain, a prominent physician, who became Pope John XXI, prescribed that a liquid made from the liver of a vulture be drunk for nine days the moment an epileptic fell into a fit. And in sixteenth-century England, the recommended method for "gathering the remembrance of a lunatic" was to beat and cudgel him until he had regained his reason. Even so great and gentle a person as Sir Thomas More believed in scourging as a remedy for insanity.[8] The word "Bedlam" (a corruption of "Bethlehem") was the name of a hospital founded in England in 1247. It became a symbol for centuries of sanctioned cruelty to the mentally ill.[9]

The years following the last Crusade in the thirteenth century, moreover, saw the rise across Europe of a large class of wandering poor and "deranged." One Benedictine abbot, who wanted more Inquisitors to deal with deluded females, wrote: "Many suffer constantly from the most severe diseases and are not even aware that they are bewitched ... Man and beast die as a result of the evil of these women."[10] And it was in 1487 that, with the endorsement of Pope Innocent, the *Malleus Maleficarum* was first printed. This book, which dealt with the theological basis for witchcraft, also included sections on "judicial proceedings" and on "the methods by which the works of witchcraft may be successfully annulled and dissolved."[11] Thus, abuse of the insane had official justification as the purging of evil from the body.

The Medieval period also saw both the comic and tragic aspects of madness enter the human psyche in the form of Art and Literature. We have *Tristan and Isolde,* Erasmus's *Praise of Folly,* the writings of Cervantes and Shakespeare (where madness is allied with death and murder), and the paintings of Peter Brueghel and Hieronymus Bosch. Both Bruegel's and Bosch's work is filled with images of fools as well as bizarre and fearsome monsters. One medical historian, Fielding Garrison, has called the seventeenth century "the age *par excellence* of medical delineations in oil painting. Velasquez for example devoted a dozen canvases to dwarfs, four to court fools and three to idiots.[12]

While all of these works were ones of the imagination, Bosch's "Ship of Fools" was named for a boat that actually plied the rivers of the Rhineland and the Flemish canals with its cargo of madmen. Medieval cites such as Nuremberg regularly disposed of their unwanted insane by turning them over to the sailors who sailed the rivers of central Europe.[13]

* * * *

The early colonists brought with them to America all of the awe, the fears, the superstitions concerning insanity—both the religious and the practical—that were rampant in Europe. Demoniacal possession was the usual explanation for the disease's cause. The witchcraft crazes of colonial New England, in which dozens of individuals lost their lives, were based on this presumption. In Salem in one year alone, 250 persons were tried—fifty were condemned; nineteen were executed; and three others died in prison or of torture. As Deutsch claims, not only were many of the accused clearly mentally ill, but so too were some of the accusers.[14]

Medicines used to treat the mentally ill were also as primitive in Colonial America as they had been in Medieval Europe. Among the many recipes for curing a cough, an "aitch" or a "bruse," that William Penn brought to America in his *Book of Phisick* was one for "convoltion feets" (epileptic fits). It read:

> Take young Callo Crowns or Rooks before any feathers grow, and dry them in an oven entire and beat them to powder and give the patient as much as will lie on a groat [an English coin] quickly in a spoonful or two of white wine five or six mornings.[15]

As Independence approached, a variety of methods were in place in Colonial America for handling the mentally ill. The more violent cases were usually treated as if they were common criminals—the pillory, the jail, the whipping post or the gallows was their fate. The "harmless" ones were either handled as paupers or else permanently housed in kennel-like structures—often in the town square. The tax records and the town meeting minutes of many communities, for example, show one time assessments of the town's citizens to build "little houses" to permanently incarcerate one of their "deranged" brethren. Non-resident "Indian stragglers and crazy people," of course, were simply driven out of town medieval style—"warning out," it was called.

No less onerous by today's standards was the common practice of "selling off" paupers and the insane to the "lowest bidder"—for their "care" and whatever labor the buyer could wrest from the individual. The object, of course, was to get the individual off of the community's welfare list. Entire families, including young children, were sold off in this fashion (to different buyers in some cases). The term of servitude was usually for one year, when the unfortunates would be resold. When this method was unsuccessful, dumping of the mentally ill on another town was sometimes resorted to. The individual would be spirited at night to a distant community, left standing in the town square, confused, unable to recall the next morning where he came from or how he got there.[16]

The centuries-old practice at Bedlam of exhibiting the "lunatics" for a fee continued in most American mental institutions, even to the end of the eighteenth century. It was quite common, for example, for the inhabitants of Philadelphia to entertain their out of town guests in this manner. While sightseers at the Pennsylvania Hospital usually just gazed, some would try to goad the patients into violent rages. Later, when asylums were erected specifically for care of the insane, the fences erected around them were to protect the patients from this practice, more so than to keep them from escaping, as was popularly believed.

And at the Pennsylvania Hospital Benjamin Rush, who published the first book on psychiatry in America in 1812, and is sometimes thought of as an early advocate of "moral treatment," believed that mental disease was caused by "excessive action" in the blood vessels. He, therefore, regularly prescribed physical remedies such as bleeding and purging, shock treatments of alternating hot and cold baths, and blistering (of the shaved head) to pacify his violent patients.[17]

* * * *

While there were a few isolated exceptions prior to the dawn of the nineteenth century, this then was the bleak history of treatment for the mentally ill during the five thousand year rise of civilization. It seems especially fitting that the first halting but significant step on the path to modern psychiatry would be "moral treatment." Its originators would start a revolution of humanity toward the afflicted—one that continues even today. A revolution for which they had little scientific basis other than a few trial experiments on incarcerated "lunatics" by pioneers such as Philippe Pinel in France and William Tuke in England.

END NOTES

1. Graham, Thomas F., *Medieval Minds, Mental Health in the Middle Ages*, George Allen & Unwin Ltd., London, 1967, page 7.
2. Deutsch, Albert, *The Mentally Ill In America*, Columbia University Press, New York, 1937, page 6.
3. Ibid., page 7.
4. Little is known of Hippocrates's life. Our knowledge of him is based on a collection of works (manuals, papers, speeches and case histories) which may have been the work of more than one man.
5. Quoted by Ackerknecht, Erwin H., *Short History of Psychiatry*, Hafner Publishing Co. Inc., 1958, page 10.
6. Quoted by Simon, Bennett, *Mind and Madness in Ancient Greece*, Cornell University Press, Ithaca, 1978, pages 220-221.
7. Deutsch, Albert, op. cit., page 8.
8. Ibid., page 13.
9. There were a few exceptions during the Medieval period. Gheel in Belgium, which was principally a religious shrine devoted to "miraculous" cures, did adopt a family method of treatment for the mentally ill.
10. Graham, Thomas F., op. cit., page 77. Historically women were singled out for attack.
11. Graham, Thomas F., op. cit., pages 77-79. *Malleus Maleficarum* or *Hammer of Witches* was directed mainly against women. The book was the work of two Dominican priests, Henry Kramer and James Sprenger.
12. Garrison, Fielding H., *History of Medicine*, 3rd edition, W. B. Saunders Co., Philadelphia, 1924, page 312.
13. Foucault, Michel, *Madness and Civilization*, Pantheon Books, New York, 1965, page 8.
14. Deutsch, op. cit., pages 33-36.
15. "Extracts from the 'Book of Phisick' of William Penn," article in *The Pennsylvania Magazine of History and Biography*, Vol. XL, 1916.
16. Ibid., page 45.
17. Tomes, Nancy, *A Generous Confidence*, Cambridge University Press, 1984, page 30.

II

MORAL TREATMENT

Beginning in the late eighteenth century, doctors and lay people alike began to debate the mix of therapeutic treatment and environmental intervention that was appropriate for the care of the insane. Since then each generation's resolution of the issue has depended on its view of the basic nature of insanity—whether it is a disease of the mind, or a spiritual disorder, or some varying combination of the two. Which of the views was current, in turn, has depended largely on the understanding of the mind-body relationship prevalent at the time. Do disorders of the mind cause bodily disturbances, or do physical diseases cause mental imbalances?

This argument, however, had little impact on the actual treatment of mental patients until the mid-nineteenth century. The wealthy sometimes would employ the services of a physician or would house their sick family member in the few available private mental institutions, but individuals in the poorer classes either were cared for at home, locked in basement cells of poorhouses or prisons, or wandered from town to town as if animals—usually avoided, often pitied, occasionally taunted and ridiculed, sometimes scorned or even abused.

Prior to the nineteenth century, moreover, belief in the spiritual origin of mental disorders prevailed. The idea of God's wrath was further supported by the lack of any genuine human medicinal or surgical treatments to intervene in the progress of the affliction. Individuals either got better, or got worse, or died—largely on their own.

When the young Thomas Kirkbride entered the University of Pennsylvania Medical School in 1828, his professor, Nathaniel Chapman, expressed the idea in his lectures that the "passions possess an extensive dominion over the body and can afford no slender assistance in producing its varied derangements." In this theory, the emotions never affected the mind directly, but always worked through the body to influence the mind. Believers in this idea held, for example, that psychological factors such as envy, fear, grief, and unrequited love were remote causes of insanity that acted directly on the body and, through the body, on the mind.[1]

As early as the end of the eighteenth century, however, this theory had been disputed by a number of doctors active in the treatment of mental patients at private asylums in France, England and America. Based on their experience, they felt that insanity was the result of physical causes. They believed, moreover, that because mental illness was largely the result of physical causes, such means of intervention as were available to them—blood-letting to deplete the body's internal excitement (for the various "manias") or stimulants, such as liquor and opium (for "melancholia")—should be employed.

By the time of the rise of the asylum movement in the 1840s, physicians, such as Thomas Kirkbride, were beginning to rework these theories again into one in which the mind's disorders caused bodily disturbances. The ideas of Philippe Pinel, who in 1792 had believed that not enough importance was placed on the emotional, or moral, causes of mental disease, were brought to the fore. Through use of the term "moral" Pinel had attempted to convey the importance he accorded to the emotions as motivators of human behavior.

* * * *

It had been during the height of the French Revolution that Pinel, a village doctor of slight reputation, had been placed in charge of the male and female asylums in Paris. The inmates, who were kept chained in irons and were treated like desperate, dangerous animals, had the appearance of wild beasts. Their clothes were rags and their hair matted and infested with lice. Their keepers, often criminals finishing out their prison terms, whipped them into silence. Pinel believed that striking off their chains and treating them with kindness and sympathy would be likely to restore their sanity as well as make the asylum management easier. This idea astounded Robespierre and his aide, Couthon, but, in the frenzy of the Revolution, they instructed Pinel to "do as you please."

At the same time in England William Tuke was working to convince the Yorkshire Quakers to build an asylum for the members of the Society of Friends. To be named "The Retreat," it would be a "place in which the unhappy might obtain a refuge; a quiet haven in which the shattered bark might find the means of reparation and safety." There was great opposition to Tuke's proposal, but in 1796 "The Retreat" opened near York. It was this Friends site that was to become a model for American asylums fifty years later.

The principal objectives of William Tuke were: to provide a family environment for the patients in non-institutional-looking buildings and surroundings; to emphasize exercise and employment as conducive to mental health; and to treat the patients as guests rather than inmates. "Kindness and consideration formed the keystone of the whole theoretical structure. Chains were absolutely forbidden, along with those resorts to terrorization that were still being advocated in varying degrees by eminent medical men."[2]

The work of Pinel in Paris and of Tuke in England became the cornerstones of the "moral treatment" reform movement. It was these two men, who, unknown to each other, in 1792 formulated its principles, systematized its practices, and then dramatized its results. In the first half of the nineteenth century the idea of treating the insane without mechanical restraints was advanced by an ever-widening group of physicians. In England there was John Conolly and Daniel Hack Tuke and in Germany Wilhelm Griesinger.[3]

Moral treatment, then, consisted of removing patients from their homes to a properly run asylum—preferably a calm retreat in the country—which provided the patient with an intimate family atmosphere. A system of humane vigilance was adopted. Coercion by blows, and the use of bars and chains were avoided. The attendants were to act as if they were servants. Noisy individuals were to be tolerated. The convalescing were allowed access to books, music, and entertainment and were given at least limited freedom of movement. The managers' primary role was to convince the patient, through a system of mild punishments and rewards, that the power of the physician is absolute. Through these actions it was believed that "the patient will minister to himself."[4]

This re-interpretation also led early nineteenth-century asylum physicians to substitue a more gentle medical regimen for the "heroic" ones previously in use. The new generation of doctors felt that the copious blood-letting and purging practiced before were too drastic. They argued that the proper mental exercise built a healthy brain, just as physical exercise developed the muscles. They emphasized that patients were more likely to recover in a pleasant, well- organized environment, where they were treated humanely and were given responsibilities and duties that would assist their return to normalcy.[5]

The removal of confinement and physical restraints, except for punishment, the use of social therapies, such as pleasant surroundings (especially gardens to walk in), participation in or attendance at musical or theatrical activities, and the encouragement of reading (through libraries) and social intercourse (afternoon teas), were all part of the moral treatment methods developed. As further reinforcement, good behavior was rewarded, poor behavior was punished.

They continued to use medical therapies, such as the new narcotic treatments (principally morphine), that were beginning to become available, but emphasized quiet living to "awaken into activity the dormant faculties of the mind and ... to dispel delusions and melancholy trains of thought."[6] The new thinking held that the intemperate use of drugs, tobacco, and alcohol, as well as masturbation, sexual over- indulgence and improper diet were all physical abuses of the body that had a deleterious effect on the mind. Among the specific dangers to be avoided were: religious fanaticism, reckless business activities, domestic disharmony, and excessive study.[7]

All these beliefs, moreover, concided nicely with the popularly held view of insanity. These explanations for insanity, as offered by the asylum superintendents, reassured people that the rising rate of mental illness was, along with all the signs of social disintegration they saw about them, a normal result of progress. As Amariah Brigham wrote: "Where people enjoy civil and religious freedom, where every person has liberty to engage in the strife for highest honors and stations in society, and where the road to wealth and distinction of every kind, is equally open to all," it was to be expected that insanity would be on the increase.[8]

These changing attitudes over the nature of mental illness, moreover, not only affected the use of various treatment methodologies, but also the management of asylums. Prior to 1840 most American institutions were run by two individuals. Hospital managers usually would appoint a visiting physician, who confined his attention to the patients' physical ailments, while a lay superintendent had complete charge of the patients' employment, amusement and exercise. The Friends Asylum at Frankford, Pennsylvania, where Thomas Kirkbride spent a year in residency, was run in just this fashion.

* * * *

Although Benjamin Franklin's Pennsylvania Hospital in Philadelphia was the first hospital in America to receive mentally ill patients, the first institution designed exclusively for housing the insane was opened in 1773 at Williamsburg, Virginia. Care there is believed, however, to have been strictly custodial.[9] The Friends Asylum at Frankford was the first hospital designed for care of the mentally ill as a moral treatment facility. The second was erected in 1821 at Bloomingdale, New York, by act of the State Legislature. In the early years both the Pennsylvania Hospital and the New York Hospital had set aside basement "wards or cells for the reception of lunatics."[10]

The Asylum at Frankford was opened in 1817. It was built on a fifty-acre country site, five miles north of Philadelphia, a location selected for its peaceful nature. The building, which could accommodate forty patients, was three stories high. At first, only Quakers (members of the Society of Friends) were admitted, but in 1834 the hospital was turned into a nonsectarian institution.

* * * *

The growing need for the mental health field as a specialty

and the public acceptance of asylums for the treatment of mental illness led to the feeling that the head of such institutions should be a medical rather than a lay individual, and should have absolute authority in the institution. "The most successful institutions in the country," as Pliny Earle wrote, "were those in which the superintendent was least trammeled by superior authority."[11]

This conception of insanity and its treatment became the basis, not only for the superintendent's position within the asylum, but also for a larger advisory role in society. "They believed that their inquiries into insanity had given them knowledge that, if properly applied, could improve the mental health of the whole community." ... This theory, moreover, offered a scientific proof for the ethic of personal self-control that was looked upon as a bulwark against social disorder. Most people held with Isaac Ray, the highly respected superintendent of Butler Hospital for the Insane at Providence, Rhode Island, that: "If men were always correct in their ways, manners and habits, physical and moral, we should have little insanity."[12] "The strength" of moral treatment, then, lay "in its ability to harmonize with the social needs of the period."[13]

No American doctor came to epitomize this revolution in the treatment and care of the mentally ill more than did Thomas Story Kirkbride of Philadelphia. He devoted his life to the principle of moral treatment, to its expostulation and to its expanded use. And when, forty years later, it fell into disfavor with both politicians and younger doctors, he sacrificed his reputation in its defense.

END NOTES

1. Tomes, Nancy, *A Generous Confidence, Thomas Story Kirkbride and the Art of Asylum-keeping, 1840-1883*, Cambridge University Press, 1984, pages 76-77.
2. Deutsch, Albert, *The Mentally Ill in America*, Columbia University Press, New York, 1937, pages 93-94.
3. Garrison, Fielding H., *History of Medicine*, W. B. Saunders Co., Philadelphia, 1924, page 699.
4. Deck, T. Romeyn, *An Inaugural Dissertation on Insanity*, New York, 1811, pages 27-88. Quoted in Deutsch, Albert, op. cit., pages 91-92.
5. Fonerden, John, "The Brain Is Modified by Habits," article in the *American Journal of Insanity*, 1850, pages 59- 61.
6. Brigham, Amariah, *Remarks*, pg 26, T. Romeyn Beck, *Inaugural Dissertation on Insanity*, New York, 1811, quoted in Deutsch, *The Mentally Ill in America*, page 92.
7. Jarvis, Edward, Remarks quoted in "Proceedings," *American Journal of Insanity*, 1857, page 81.
8. Tomes, Nancy, op. cit., pages 85-87.
9. It should be pointed out, however, that the Pennsylvania Hospital was intended from the outset to provide care for the mentally ill. The first words of Franklin's petition made it clear that the hospital was intended for the great "Number of Lunaticks," or "Persons distemper'd in Mind," or those "deprived of their rational Faculties," whose numbers "hath greatly encreased in this Province." It was the poor insane who were going at large, and were a "Terror to their Neighbours," or others who were "continually wasting their Substance, to the great Injury of themselves and Families, ... " that Franklin and his fellow petitioners had uppermost in their minds. *Petition for a small Hospital for Lunaticks*, January 23, 1750, *The Papers of Benjamin Franklin*, Vol. 5, July 1753—March 1755, Yale University Press, page 285.
10. Deutsch, op. cit., page 98.
11. Pliny Earle letter to Kirkbride, August 18, 1858. Earle was the superintendent at Northampton State Hospital, Northampton, Mass.
12. Ray, Isaac, quoted by Nancy Tomes, op. cit., page 87.
13. Tomes, Nancy, op. cit., pages 85-87.

III

THOMAS KIRKBRIDE

Thomas Story Kirkbride was born on July 31, 1809 into an old and distinguished Bucks County Quaker family. He was the first of seven children of John and Elizabeth Story Kirkbride. The stone house in which Thomas was born had been built by his father on the family's 150-acre farm near the town of Morrisville. John Kirkbride was not only a prosperous farmer who raised livestock and who cultivated fruit trees, but he also operated a small plaster mill on his estate as well as a ferry across the Delaware River to Trenton.[1]

Thomas's great-great-grandfather, Joseph Kirkbride, had come to America in 1682 as a member of William Penn's original Pennsylvania settlement. Joseph had arrived in the new world as a runaway apprentice but he went on to become a prominent merchant and leader in the Bucks County Society of Friends. When Joseph died, he owned 13,000 acres of land adjoining the Delaware river.

Throughout Thomas's life he adhered to many of the teachings of the Quakers. He wore simple clothing, avoided public display and kept a certain detachment from the world.[2] When, however, the Philadelphia Friends split into Hicksite and Orthodox over the teachings of Elias Hicks, he, as well as his parents, joined the less radical Orthodox group. Orthodox Friends held that involvement in the secular world was proper, while Hicks preached that it was not.[3]

The young Kirkbride had a "naturally delicate constitution" and was, therefore, unsuited to follow in his father's footsteps. John Kirkbride decided, moreover, that if his eldest son "ever manifested any taste for medicine, he would do all he could to advance the subject." Since the Society of Friends regarded medicine as an appropriate profession for its members and his father did all that he could to advance the idea, at a very early age Thomas "began to regard medicine as his path in life."[4]

After attending neighborhood Friends schools in Bucks County, he spent four years at the Reverend Jared D. Fyler's "Classical Institution," a well known school at Trenton, New Jersey across the river from the family farm. In those days it was easier to take a boat across the river than to go even a shorter distance by the poor roads in the county. From Fyler, Thomas acquired a classical education. This classical background was followed by a year in mathematics (especially Algebra) with Professor John Gummere, at the Burlington Boarding School in Burlington, New Jersey. This institution's fame was widespread. Many West Indies planters, for example, sent their sons there. Thus, Thomas also acquired a broad social as well as a formal education.[5]

Deciding to pursue his chosen field of medicine, he commenced study with Nicholas Belleville, a Trenton physician. Belleville had come from France with LaFayette during the American Revolution. He had an excellent personal and professional reputation. Benjamin Rush and Phillip Syng Physick were numbered among his medical friends. Belleville also played an active role in the local medical societies around Trenton and in the Medical Society of New Jersey and thus was able to provide Thomas with the latest advances in medical practice.

Thomas received a thorough grounding in the basics of bedside medicine from Belleville. The Frenchman taught his students to scrutinize the physical clues in an effort to determine the body's internal condition—blood, feces, perspiration, pulse, temperature, respiration, skin color and urine all were checked. The student had to learn the significance of the different states of these indicators: the importance of the color of the blood, the amount of sediment in the urine, the strength of the pulse and the sound of the lungs. In a medical era before the clinical thermometer, stethoscope, and X-ray, such measures were the physician's only diagnostic tools.[6]

When the patient had a high fever or respiratory difficulties, which to Thomas's mentor represented excessive bodily "excitement," he readily employed a "depleting" regimen. Kirkbride wrote in his student notebook that Belleville had bled and purged one male patient with a violent headache and fever three times within one twenty-four-hour period. The patient recovered. Although his family appreciated his treatment, the young man did not. Kirkbride noted, moreover, that if he had died the family certainly would have complained that the doctor had "bled him to death."[7]

A former student described Belleville's methods as "curious and minute in investigation—keen in observing—careful and deliberate in deciding."[8] Although he prescribed an active treatment when he recognized a specific disease, Belleville advised his students, "If you do not know, nature can do a great deal better than you can guess."[9]

Following his study with a private practitioner, Thomas Kirkbride enrolled in the University of Pennsylvania Medical School in Philadelphia. While most doctors of the day had no more than a secondary education (some not even that), the ambitious Kirkbride knew that greater success would come to those physicians who possessed more training. At medical school, he was required to attend three years of lectures to graduate. The courses, however, were the same ones each year and involved little clinical work.

In school Kirkbride continued to practice the basic principles of therapeutics that he had learned from Belleville; however, he learned to apply them in a different fashion. American doctors were beginning "to consider their countrymen as less prone to diseases caused by excess energy or excitement, and more susceptible to ones caused by too little energy, or debility." It was believed "that the influence of a civilized, sedentary life had made Americans less robust." Consequently, they did not need heroic treatment to restore health, but rather a gentle, strengthening regimen to build up their depleted systems. ... Kirkbride was taught to avoid harsh drugs such as mercury, to use emetics or purges that acted violently on the body sparingly, to trust more in the body's own healing powers, and to interfere only cautiously in its internal processes."[10]

After graduating in March of 1832, he fully anticipated an appointment to the one available residency at the Pennsylvania Hospital. When he discovered that a fellow student also was applying for the position, he decided to withdraw and wait a year in favor of his friend. That summer, however, he was offered and accepted a position as the Resident Physician at the Friends'Asylum for the Insane, at Frankford. He spent one year at Frankford, taking an active interest in everything relating to the care of the patients and the management of the Institution. He received a flattering testimonial from the Board of Managers when he left. They requested that the young doctor return and take charge of the Institution.[11]

He declined their offer, having determined to become a surgeon, and accepted a residency at the Pennsylvania Hospital. There, with a fellow resident, William W. Gerhard, he carefully noted for the next two years all of the cases under his treatment. The two doctors later published these observations, which were among the first hospital clinical reports published in this country.[12]

In 1835 Thomas Kirkbride commenced private practice in Philadelphia, applying himself particularly to surgery. Although comparatively young for a surgeon, he was frequently called on to aid some of his older brethren in the performance of surgery and thus gradually acquired a reputation and clientele of his own among both the artisans and wealthy of the city.[13] During this time, he also served as physician to various public institutions such as the House of Refuge and the Institution for the Blind.

In the fall of 1840, he was asked by the Board of Managers of the Pennsylvania Hospital to give up his prospects of being elected Surgeon to that Institution, an appointment which he had every reason to believe he would receive, and to accept instead the post of physician-in-chief and superintendent of their new Hospital for the Insane, then nearly completed, on the west side of the Schuylkill River.

He gave up his long-cherished plans with great reluctance, but having done so, entered his new position with enthusiasm. He took up residence in the old mansion on the hospital grounds and began the work of finishing and furnishing the hospital. He was to remain there for 43 years.

The Pennsylvania Hospital for the Insane was, however, only a base for Thomas Kirkbride. From this position he was to become the leading exponent on the moral treatment and care of the insane in America, as well as a national authority on hospital construction. He was one of the thirteen founders of the Association of Medical Superintendents of American Institutions for the Insane, and its President from 1862 to 1870. To this association he attributed "the real progress that was made in the provision for the treatment of insanity" between the years of 1845 and 1880.[14] Among the tenets that this group developed were:

>That insanity is a disorder of the brain, to which everyone is liable.

>That properly and promptly treated, it is as curable as most other serious diseases.

>That in most cases, it is better and more successfully treated in well-organized institutions, than at home.

>As little restraint as possible should be used, and then only for the best interests of the patient. When required, moreover, it should be under the direction of the chief medical officer.

>The insane should never be kept in almshouses nor in penal institutions, and separate facilities for the recent or chronic insane are not recommended.

>That the superintendent, a medical officer, should have complete charge of medical, moral and dietetic treatment of the patients, and the unrestricted power of appointment and discharge of all persons employed in their care.

>That the best hospital—best built, best arranged, and best managed—is always the least expensive in the end, no matter for what class of the insane it is intended.

Rules number five and seven were to become nearly as important in nineteenth-century American care of the mentally ill as moral treatment was; by the turn of the century they also were as controversial. But in the decades following mid-century, asylums adhering to the Kirkbride design were built all across the country; at least thirty, including in 1851 the Pennsylvania State Lunatic Hospital at Harrisburg. Albert Deutsch claimed that Dr. Kirkbride's word on hospital construction "was accepted as law in America" for over a generation.[15]

No item of detail was too small for inclusion in Kirkbride's design of a hospital. At the same time, his plans included some major innovations in building concepts, especially in the heating and ventilation of large structures. All these were documented in his *On the construction, organization, and general arrangements of Hospitals for the insane.*

First published in 1847, he revised and enlarged it in 1854. This monumental work covered not only building design (always to be constructed linearly in two eight-ward wings, each emanating from a central building); but also site selection and preparation, drainage and water supply, heating and ventilation, layout of the surrounding "pleasure grounds," appointments of patient's rooms, location of the kitchen, height of the ceilings, number of pigs in the piggery, and the daily duties of each employee—all dictated, not from any arbitrary, aesthetic point of view, but rather from the sole consideration of an item's impact on the treatment of the insane.

Great then as Thomas Kirkbride's concern was for the make- up of a good mental hospital, it was never his main concern; his patients were. Having introduced the idea of evening amusements for the patients, for example, he made it a point to attend all of them without fail, even excusing himself from important guests to do so. His weekly hospital officers' teas, moreover, always included a liberal number of patients from each of the wards, even the most disturbed or agitated from the eighth ward.[16] In presiding at this meal, it was evident that, "while apparently engrossed in making those about him happy, his thoughts were also busied with the interests of many, reached only by his eye and not his voice."[17]

Thomas Kirkbride was one of the early advocates of the use of patient labor as a form of therapy. He recognized, however, the possibilities for its abuse, and that the rightful, the only, issue was its potential to heal the sick in mind. He wrote: " ... it is hardly possible to exaggerate the importance of occupation of some kind for every class [of patient], but also, that harm quite as easily as good, may follow employment, in unwise forms." ... "Moderate, wisely regulated labor is really serviceable to many of the insane, but hard work, so carried on as to be profitable to any institution, is very rarely of benefit to the patients."[18]

Kirkbride recognized, too, that the "public inclination to

regard mental diseases as mysterious afflictions, entirely remote in origin and nature from all other diseases"[19] had to
be changed. From an early date he began using his medical
reports, with their wide array of statistics, to combat ignor-
ance and superstition. Filled with supporting data, they were
still written in a language aimed at the layman. In one he
wrote: "It should never be forgotten that every individual who
has a brain is liable to insanity, precisely as every one who
has lungs is liable to pneumonia, or as every one with a
stomach runs the risk at some period of being a martyr to dyspepsia ... "

As a convincing testimonal to his belief in mental illness
as a disease just as any other, and in moral treatment as the
best means of its cure, Thomas married Eliza Butler, a former patient, in 1863. Eliza bore him four children all of whom
went on to distinguished careers. Today this probably would
be a questionable action for a psychiatrist to take. In 1863,
however, his associates looked on this more as a witness to
the power of the asylum movement rather than as an embarrassment.[20]

A significant part of Kirkbride's book, *On the construction,
organization and general arrangements of hospitals for the
insane*, was devoted to the hospital staff: its size, how it was
to be selected, the detailed duties of each position, the opti-
mum pay, and—long before the idea of training schools for
nurses or staff—how the attendants were to be prepared for
their work.

Although he was, according to one biographer, "gentle as
a woman," he was "firm as adamant."[21] His tranquility and
his tenacity both were ascribed to his Quaker inheritance and
training. Even the gate-keeper at the hospital once remarked,
"Dr. Kirkbride is a most mild and gentle man, and yet he is
not the sort of man one likes to be reproved by." He was so
well known in Philadelphia, that a prominent British psychiatrist used to tell the story that a street car conductor that
he approached could not tell him where the Pennsylvania
Hospital for the Insane was, but readily directed him to "Kirkbride's."[22]

Thomas S. Kirkbride died on December 16, 1883. In the
annual *Report of the Pennsylvania Hospital For The Insane*

the following year, the hospital managers said that he possessed: "untiring diligence, unceasing labor, and the greatest conscientiousness"; that his "labor was lavished" on his hospital and his patients; and that his "rest was grudging and sparingly if ever taken."[23] To describe the spirit of the man, their affection for him and their support of his ideas, they quoted in this report the Pharaoh's commission to Joseph:

> For as much as God hath showed thee all this, there is none so discreet and wise as thou art, thou shalt be over my house, and according to thy word shall all my people be ruled.

Genesis 41: 39-40

END NOTES

1. Tomes, Nancy, *A Generous Confidence, Thomas Story Kirkbride and the art of asylum-keeping, 1840-1883,* Cambridge University Press, 1984, page 46.
2. "Thomas Story Kirkbride," article in the *Annual Report of the Pennsylvania Hospital for the Insane, 1883,* page 148.
3. After the First World War, the Hicksites and the Orthodox branches began to work together and in 1955 the two groups merged into one Yearly Meeting. Yarnall, Elizabeth B., *Addison Hutton, Quaker Architect, 1834-1916,* The Art Alliance Press, Philadelphia, 1974. page 75.
4. Bond, Earl D., Dr. Kirkbride, J. B. Lippincott Co., Philadelphia, 1947, page 14.
5. "Thomas Story Kirkbride," article in the *Annual Report of the Pennsylvania Hospital for the Insane,* 1883, page 27. Bond, op. cit., pages 9-11.
6. Tomes, Nancy, op. cit., pages 55-56.
7. Kirkbride, Thomas S., "Notes on the Practice of Dr. N. Belleville," 1830, pages 5-6.
8. Rodgers, Fred B. "Dr. Nicholas Belleville, Aristocratic Physician," article in the *Journal of the Medical Society of New Jersey,* 1958, pages 74-76.
9. Kirkbride, Thomas S., "Notes on the Practice of Dr. N. Belleville," 1830, pages 5, 12, & 22.
10. Tomes, Nancy, op. cit., page 59.
11. "Thomas Story Kirkbride," article in the Annual Report of the Pennsylvania Hospital for the Insane, 1883, page 148.
12. Ibid., page 28.
13. Lack of anesthetic and the risk of infection limited the types of surgery that could be done in the early nineteenth century. Surgical practices of the day consisted largely of setting fractures, the removal of bladder stones and minor bone and joint surgery. Nancy Tomes, op. cit. page 59.
14. "Thomas Story Kirkbride," article in the *Annual Report of the Pennsylvania Hospital for the Insane, 1883,* pages 102-103.
15. Deutsch, op. cit., page 208.
16. The wards in a Kirkbride hospital were arranged so that the least excited patients stayed in the first ward next to the central building. Proceeding outward then, ward by ward, were housed progressively the more and more excitable

patients. Thus the most difficult to manage residents were kept in the eighth, the farthest removed, ward.

17. "Thomas Story Kirkbride," article in the *Annual Report of the Pennsylvania Hospital for the Insane, 1883*, page 66. The personal reminiscences in this article apparently were written by Eliza Butler Kirkbride.
18. Ibid., pages 62-63.
19. Deutsch, Albert, *The Mentally Ill in America*, Columbia University Press, New York, 1937, page 207.
20. Tomes, Nancy, op. cit., pages 232-233.
21. Bond, Earl D., "Thomas Story Kirkbride," article in the *Dictionary of American Biography, Vol. V*, Charles Scribner's Sons, New York, 1932.
22. "Thomas Story Kirkbride," article in the *Annual Report of the Pennsylvania Hospital for the Insane, 1883*, pages 127-129.
23. Ibid., page 56.

IV

PENNSYLVANIA SURVEY AND MEMORIAL

In the literature of the nineteenth century we begin to find the insane being portrayed more often as benign individuals than as maniacal ones. Charles Dickens, for example, in his semi-autobiographical David Copperfield draws the picture of the amiable idiot, Mr. Dicks. Wise in his madness, the friendly Dicks's favorite pastime is to fly kites, while his most "sane" activity is a "memorial" to the Lord High Chancellor—one that he regularly spends hours revising. As if to strengthen the connection with Dorothea Dix, Dickens has Mr. Macawber, who is unable to remember Dicks's name correctly, believe that he is called "Dix," because his name is Dixon.[1]

The word "memorial" is seldom used in this sense today. In the nineteenth century, however, it was frequently used as meaning "to petition an authority for the correction of a wrong." Memorials—the way a commoner directly and formally addressed a state authority—often were written to legislative bodies and to the Governors of the United States as well as to the English Lord High Chancellor. The most famous one to the Pennsylvania State Legislature was one written in 1845 by Dorothea Dix, a Boston teacher, writer and advocate on behalf of the insane.

* * * *

For nearly two years, during 1842 and 1843, before the completion of the railroad west of Harrisburg, when travel to parts of the State beyond the Appalachian Plateau was primitive, Dorothea Dix had visited systematically each of the fifty-eight counties in Pennsylvania.[2] With a will that must have been the envy of many a man, she sought out and went through every jail and poorhouse in the state, cataloguing the good and the bad that she had found.

No keeper—though some tried by guile and others directly—was able to deny her entry. Her bearing, tall and straight with a face of strong but delicate, patrician features; her raven-black hair, combed back and then knotted; her determination, firm and unyielding—these warranted to all her right to be there.

Dorothea Dix found that the Washington county alms-house contained seventy paupers, seven of whom were insane. A considerable number of the paupers were also "idiotic," while others were "epileptic" and "imbecilic." Dix wrote of her visit: "In a large yard, common to all the inmates of the establishment, was a small building, consisting of a single room, perhaps twelve by fourteen feet. It being a hot day, two windows were opened. I looked in, as requested, and saw first, a young woman apparently demented, standing upon a sack of straw. At first, I thought there was no other occupant; but a little to the right, ... I discovered a woman of middle age, seated on some straw in a packing box—in a state of entire nudity. On the opposite side of the room, stood a similar box, which at first, I supposed to be empty; but the sound of voices roused a female. She lay coiled up. I cannot imagine how she could have contracted herself into so small a space. Some straw, too, was in this box, and excepting that, she had neither clothing nor covering of any sort of description. ... and this was where, in 1839, it was officially announced, 'that the insane of this county are so well provided for, that a state hospital would be useless."

In the poorhouse at Gettysburg, there were eleven "crazy and idiotic" patients chained in damp unventilated basement "crazy rooms" eight by eight by eight feet high. Some had been there for years with nothing to sit or lie down on. In the Adams county jail she found one insane man—"or one whose mental faculties had been defective from birth"—"loaded with chains; a ring about the ankle, connected by a sort of hinge, to a long, stout iron bar, reaching above the hips, and to this the iron wristlets were attached."

At the jail in Allegheny County children and adults, men and women, sane and insane all shared common facilities.

She wrote: "If it had been the deliberate purpose of the citizens of Allegheny County to establish a school for the inculcation of vice, and obliteration of every virtue, I cannot conceive that any means they could have devised, would more certainly have secured these results, than those I found in full operation last August."

Dorothea Dix described the Perry County poorhouse, near Landisburg, as "a respectable establishment having some good buildings, and a productive farm." Nonetheless "the rooms or cells for the insane were in a small wooden building; above ground, ... but very defectively ventilated, and badly constructed." She found the insane sitting on damp ground, in slight apparel, and exposed, of course, to colds and rheumatic attacks ... She went on to write: "I have reason to apprehend they experience much suffering."

Although the conditions Miss Dix found in Dauphin County, both at the poorhouse and the jail, were better than those she uncovered elsewhere (The Harrisburg *Telegraph* made much of her findings), the insane inmates still were kept chained at all times. She described the chains as "light as is consistent with strength, but yet are a source of great discomfort and evident mortification to the wearers."

The result of her travels by buggy, canal boat, and wagon was a 55-page memorial to the Pennsylvania legislature. A detailed study, county by county, of the conditions throughout the state, it opened:

> I come to represent to you the condition of a numerous and unhappy class of sufferers, who fill the cells and dungeons of the poor-houses, and the prisons of your state. I refer to the pauper and indigent insane, epileptics and idiots of Pennsylvania. I come to urge their claims upon the commonwealth for protection and support, such protection and support as is only to be found in a well conducted Lunatic Asylum.
>
> I must ask you, as I have done, to examine with patient care the condition of this suffering, dependent multitude, which are gathered to your alms-houses and your prisons, and scattered under adverse circumstances in indigent families; weigh the iron

chains, and shackles, and balls, and ring- bolts, and bars, and manacles; breathe the foul atmosphere of those cells and dens, which too slowly poison the springs of life; examine the furniture of these dreary abodes, some for a bed have the luxury of a truss of straw . . . Examine their apparel. The air of heaven is their only vesture . . .

Do your starled perceptions refuse to admit these truths? They exist still; the proof and the condition alike; neither have passed away ... Gentlemen, it is just, not generous action, I ask at your hands.[3]

* * * *

Dorothea Dix did not appeal simply to the humanity of her request. "You are not solicited to commence a work of doubtful value," she wrote. " ... thousands, through the skillful care received in hospitals for the insane, have been restored to society and to usefulness, to reason and to happiness." And to drive her message home, she continued: " ... all alike may suffer, the rich and the poor, the learned and the uneducated, the young, the mature, and the aged; from this malady none are sure of exemption ... Through the bond of our common humanity, we may become as they now are."[4]

She also quoted liberally from members of the medical profession urging "that all experience goes to prove, that in its earliest stages it [insanity] is generally curable, and that every week it is left without treatment goes to diminish the prospect of restoration." She went on to appeal to the legislators' pocketbooks, mentioning again "the economy" of early treatment—that "if this was done, a large proportion of them would in a few months, be restored to society, instead of continuing ... a charge to their friends or the public, during the remainder of their lives."[5]

Convincing the legislators of the "value" of such an effort was important. Pennsylvania's and the nation's banking systems and general state finances were only beginning to be restored from the disarray of the panic of 1837. Government as well as individuals had been using scrip and loans to speculate in land and to finance internal improvements such as canals and railroads to an extent that the state of Pennsylvania was still in debt eight years after the panic.

When he became governor of Pennsylvania in 1839, David Porter had placed the state on an austerity program. He eliminated all spending for improvements, vetoed bills permitting banks to continue issuing specie money, and raised taxes to enable the state to pay off its fifteen million dollar indebtedness. After two Porter terms the state's finances were beginning to return to normal, but with some legislators the need for economy was still an important one.[6]

* * * *

Dorothea Dix's Memorial was read in the Pennsylvania House of Representatives on February 3, 1845. When the Clerk was finished with the reading (all 33,000 words of it), the document was "laid on the table" for consideration. James Burnside, a representative from Center and Clearfield counties, moved that 2000 copies of it be printed in English and 500 in German for distribution, so that it could be better and more widely studied and it was "so ordered."[7]

On February 21, the Memorial was referred to a "select committee," on the motion of Burnside. On March 8, the committee, of which Burnside had been a member, reported out a bill, No. 493, entitled "An Act to establish an asylum for the insane poor of this commonwealth to be called the Pennsylvania State Lunatic Hospital and Union Asylum for the Insane."[8]

On March 29 the House resolved itself (on Burnside's motion) into a Committee of the Whole to consider the bill. The only changes of significance that carried were to reduce the state's contribution from twenty-five to fifteen thousand dollars and to direct that the commissioners were required to "appoint a committee of five in every city and county in this commonwealth, to solicit and receive private subscriptions for this laudable and benevolent object."

Jeremiah Burrell of Westmoreland County did attempt to amend the bill to have five men from his home county appointed as commissioners and to specify that they purchase a tract near Greensburg, but Representative Burnside got the motion defeated 52 to 27.

The Senate took up House bill 493 on March 31 and referred it to the Committee on Finance. The committee reported the bill out (with unspecified amendments) on April 4. Senator William Bigler of Clearfield County (Governor of Pennsylvania from 1852 to 1855) was one of the primary supporters of the Senate version of the bill.[9] As Speaker of the Senate a few years later, Bigler was noted as an outspoken critic of "logrolling" (the practice of attaching to popular legislation unrelated and undesirable items that otherwise would be unlikely to pass).

Joseph Quay, the Senator from Lycoming, attempted to postpone implementation of the bill's provisions by an amendment that required that the act would become law only after a referendum at the next general election. Quay's motion was defeated 20 to 9 and the bill was passed and sent back to the House on April 11. On April 14 it was sent to Governor Shunk. That same afternoon he reported back to the House and the Senate that he had signed the bill.[10]

While Dorothea Dix may have faced indifference, even hostility, at some places during her travels throughout Pennsylvania, her reception in Harrisburg had been most generous. On receiving their copy of her memorial, the Senate described her as "a lady of Boston, distinguished for her intelligence, moral courage and philanthropy." Then they passed the following resolution: "as an evidence of the high sense, which the Senate of Pennsylvania entertains of her benevolent labors in the cause of humanity, it is ordered that 1000 copies of said memorial be printed."

Copies of the Dix memorial were popular. Several days after their printing, the President of the Senate angrily reported that the State Printer was selling copies of it and demanded an investigation, as it had been printed "by order and for the use of the legislature."[11]

* * * *

The "Lady of Boston" was not only tapping a well of deep sentiment in favor of establishing a state facility for the care of the insane; hers was also far from the first voice raised in their defense. Near the end of his last "Annual Message to the Senate and House of Representatives in January, 1845, Governor Porter had said:

> Although the system of imprisonment adopted by Pennsylvania some years ago, ... has been justly regarded as the most admirable to be found among all nations, yet there is one department which remains to be provided for, that of establishing, ... a department for the charge of the insane inmates. There have been, almost every year, since I have been Governor of the commonwealth, some unfortunate persons confined in the penitentiary, ... who either were partially insane when committed, or became so afterwards. As the law now stands, there is no remedy for these cases, but to pardon them, or confine them in the same manner as other criminals are confined. Both these modes are oftentimes wrong, and I respectfully urge it upon your consideration to make some provision for redressing the evil in future.[12]
>
> Now that Pennsylvania's economic ills ("a subject of the deepest solicitude," Governor Porter called them) were "disposed of" he urged the legislature to turn to issues of public beneficence, among them the care of its indigent insane.[13] Pennsylvania was ready to fulfill Charles Dickens's comment that in America "the State is a parent to its people; has a parental care and watch over all poor children, ... sick persons and captives" and it was ready to extend his list of its beneficiaries to include the mentally ill.[14]

30

END NOTES

1. The thought that Dickens, a reformer in his own right, may have been alluding to Dorothea Dix and her efforts for the insane, while convincing is largely circumstantial. While the author met and breakfasted at the home of her close friend, William Ellery Channing, in Boston, there is no record that Dickens met Dix during his American tour. We do know, however, that he visited at least one mental institution while in this country. *David Copperfield* was written in 1849-1850, by which time Miss Dix had memorialized several state legislatures on behalf of the insane.

2. Twenty-one of the counties contained poorhouses for the indigent and the insane and thirty-seven "sustained their paupers by annual distribution in families, who receive them at the lowest rate for which they are bidden." Those who had committed a criminal act were chained in prison, usually basement dungeons.

3. Dix, Dorothea L., *Memorial to the Honorable, the Senate and the House of Representatives of the Commonwealth of Pennsylvania*, February 3, 1845, pages 3-4.

4. Dix, Dorothea L., op. cit., pages 4-5.

5. Dix, Dorothea L., op. cit., page 10.

6. Governor Porter claimed that "not a single dollar has been appropriated or paid under my administration, towards the commencement of any new work ... however meritorious in itself ... " Porter, David R., "Annual Message to the Senate and House of Representatives of the Commonwealth of Pennsylvania," January 8, 1845.

7. All Pennsylvania bills and government documents in 1845 were still being printed in both German and English. As a result of the Dix Memorial, it was moved "that the Committee on Retrenchment and Reform be instructed to inquire into the expediency of reporting a bill for the discontinuance of the printing of the Journals of the two branches of the legislature, the Executive Documents and the Laws in the German language." The motion carried 75 to 7.

8. Burnside continued in later years to take an active interest in the hospital, visiting it often as a member of legislative inspection teams.

9. Curwen, John, "Provision For the Insane in Hospitals Specially Constructed for the Insane," article in *The Pennsylvania Medical Journal*, Vol. II, No. 4, September 1898, page 190. William Bigler, publisher of the *Clearfield Democrat*, along with his brother, John, was also a successful lumber producer. John was to become Governor of California at the same time that William was the Governor of Pennsylvania.

10. The Pennsylvania House of Representatives Journal—1845, Vol. I, pages 285-568 and the Pennsylvania Senate Journal—1845, pages 554-677.

11. Pennsylvania Senate Journal—1845, pages 554-677.

12. Porter, David R., "Annual Message to the Senate and House of Representatives of the Commonwealth of Pennsylvania," January 8, 1845.

13. Ibid.

14. Dickens, Charles, letter to John Forster, March 15, 1842.

V

DOROTHEA LYNDE DIX

Samuel Eliot Morrison has described the early decades of the nineteenth century as ones of "reformers, revivalists, and Utopians." It was a time of "isms"—from "Bloomerism" (a new female costume) to Millerism (a theory of the Second Coming of Christ). While Emerson remarked that "a certain tenderness grew on the people," during this time, he also wrote that "the key to the period appeared to be that the mind had become aware of itself. ... The young men were born with knives in their brain."[1]

Men such as Thomas H. Gallaudet, who established the first American school for the deaf, marched out at the head of all manner of reform movements. Philadelphia became a hotbed for crusaders of all sorts: Abolitionists, feminists, prison reformers, temperance advocates and trade unionists. A new evangelism, that rebelled against such Calvinist ideas as man's depravity and predestination, preached that individuals could take action not only to save their souls but also to change society.[2] Women such as Lucretia Mott and Elizabeth C. Stanton, who founded the movement for women's suffrage, also apparently "were born with knives in their brain."

The most remarkable of these men and women, however, was a shy, sickly New England girl by the name of Dorothea Lynde Dix. While she possessed every bit as much steel as the best of the others, there was a quality of womanliness and gentleness, even timidity, about her that most of the others lacked. She was first a schoolteacher, then a writer and finally the most famous philanthropist of her day.

There has been much speculation, but little is known of her youth. She once dismissed that part of her life with the remark: "I never knew childhood." She refused ever after all requests to speak on the subject. The written record first finds her living in Boston with her grandmother and teaching school at age 14. Tradition has it, on the other hand, that she spent an unhappy childhood caring for her younger brothers and keeping house for an indolent mother and father.

We do know that her father, Joseph Dix, married an older woman against the wishes of his parents. For this he was forced to leave Harvard, as married undergraduates were not permitted in that day. The couple moved to what was then the wild, uninhabited Massachusetts frontier—"unploughed Maine," as Emerson called it. There Joseph apparently was responsible for managing his father's extensive property holdings. It was there, too, that Dorothea Dix was born on April 4, 1802. It appears that her father spent most of his time as an itinerant Methodist lay preacher. He published numerous small religious books, including one attractive children's Bible. All evidence indicates that Joseph was a poor provider for his family and it was probably because of this that, by the time she was a teenager, Dorothea was living with her grandmother, Dorothy Lynde Dix, in the Dix mansion in Boston.

Dorothea's grandmother was well advanced in life, a widow nearing 70, when her granddaughter came to live with her. The elderly woman "was a typical example of the New England Puritan gentlewoman of the period—dignified, precise, inflexibly conscientious, unimaginative, and without trace of emotional glow or charm." It was the age, moreover, of training the young "to habits of rigid industry, of exacting iron diligence over the school lessons, and of inculcating the dogmas of the catechism." This severe sense of duty, then, was the only aspect of love or even affection that Dorothea ever received. Although the child owed her grandmother a debt of lasting obligation for her education and training in habits of unremitting diligence, it was a time of suffering and loneliness for her in a grim and joyless home.[3]

There were few acceptable jobs in Boston for an intelligent, sensitive young woman other than teaching. Dorothea Dix, therefore, opened and then taught in several of her own schools for girls.[4] One of the first of these was established in the Dix mansion. "The arrangements of the school," wrote one pupil, "were very primitive,—no desks for the girls, only a long table through the middle of the room, at which we sat for meals, and at which it was very inconvenient to write. The studies embraced a rather limited range of subjects. Spelling, arithmetic, and composition were rigorously and accurately taught, as well as geography and history. ... The main stress, however, was laid on the formation of moral and religious character."[5] Dorothea confided in a letter to a friend that:

> To me the avocation of a teacher has something elevating and exciting. While surrounded by the young, one may always be doing good. How delightful to feel that even the humblest efforts to advance the feeble in their path of toil will be like seed sown in good ground. I love to watch the progress of a young being just emerging from infancy, when thoughts first spring into existence and infant fancy is excited by every passing occurrence.[6]

From the very beginning, too, she was drawn to the disadvantaged. She believed with the Rev. Mr. Thom that "What we as Christians are, may be judged from what we suffer the poor around us to be."[7] Soon after opening her "Dame School," as it was called, she became interested in providing similar facilities for poor children, for whom there was little offered at that time. Knowing that her grandmother would be obstinate over the matter, she wrote her a letter rather than confront her. "Had I the saint-like eloquence of our minister, I would employ it in explaining all the motives and dwelling on all the good, good to the poor, the miserable, the idle, and the ignorant, which would follow your giving me permission to use the barn chamber for a school-room for charitable and religious purposes. ... Do, my dear grandmother, yield to my request, and witness next summer the reward of your benevolent and Christian compliance." Her grandmother finally consented to let her use the room over the stable for this purpose.

During the summer months of these years the young teacher also served as a private tutor to the children of William Ellery Channing, the Unitarian minister. She apparently learned as much from Channing as his children did from her. His fine intellect and noble character made a deep, lasting impression upon her. These months spent in the Channing home also brought her in contact with many of the New England intellectuals of the day. It was through Channing that she met Ralph Waldo Emerson, Julia Ward Howe and John Greenleaf Whittier. Here too, she was introduced to the great ideas of the day. Of this period of Dorothea Dix's life, the daughter of Channing, Mary C. Eustis, wrote to a friend:

> She was tall and dignified, but stooped somewhat, was very shy in her manners, and colored extremely when addressed. This may surprise you who knew her only in later life, when she was completely self-possessed and reliant. ... She was strict and inflexible in her discipline, which we her pupils disliked extremely at the time, but for which I have been grateful as I have grown older and found how much I was indebted to that iron will from which it was hopeless to appeal. ... Fixed as fate we considered her. ... I think she was a very accomplished teacher, active and diligent herself, very fond of natural history and botany. She enjoyed long rambles, always calling our attention to what was of interest in the world around us.
>
> We all became much attached to her, and she was our dear and valued friend, and a most welcome guest in all our homes. She was a very religious woman, without a particle of sectarianism or bigotry. ... She delighted to drop in unexpectedly, and then suddenly receiving a letter from a poor soldier at Fort Adams, would start off at a moment's notice to right his wrong and persuade the government to improve the arrangements for the comfort of the men.[8]

One of her regular correspondents and occasional visitors in Boston during this period was her cousin, Edward Bangs. They became engaged for a time but did not marry. The reasons were never stated by either party. She also had a social life of sorts at this time. She was reticent about mingling with people in large gatherings, but did go to occasional parties. Of one such occasion, an informal reception in honor of Lafayette, she wrote: "I half dread going but I may never enjoy the opportunity again so shall summon all my courage and confidence to meet the emergency of the case."[9]

During this period she not only taught school but also wrote.

It was her habit to rise each morning at four (five in the winter), read her Bible for an hour and then after breakfast commence working. She seldom was in bed before midnight. Her first book, *Conversations on Common Things,* required great amounts of research and grasping for language but was finally finished in 1824. In the book's preface, she described its purpose as "the improvement of children, and their advancement in the pathway of learning." The book was written in the form of a dialogue between a mother and her daughter. Among the many "common things" that Dorothea Dix explained for young girls who should, but might not, know of, were ones such as: alligators, almonds, asbestos, bank notes, brandy, cigars, coffee, elephants, fresco, ginseng, paper making and naphtha.

The *United States Literary Gazette,* called it a "compendium of information covering nearly three hundred topics more or less interesting." The reviewer went on to state "we are gratified with finding an American writer who duly estimates the importance of giving to American children knowledge ... instead of filling their minds with vague, and therefore useless, notions of subjects not accommodated to their age."[10]

Other written efforts followed: A book of hymns for children, a book of devotional passages and poems, *Meditations for Private Hours,* and another small book of devotional studies entitled *Evening Hours.* In a letter to Ann Heath in 1826 she wrote: "Our time is divided between books and needle-work, walking and riding when favorable, ... Cowper, Montgomery, Wordsworth, and Percival daily contribute to our social intercourse. We have read Swinburne's travels in the Sicilies and Spain, Hasselquist's journey through Egypt and Palestine, and are now engaged in Robertson's *Scotland.*"[11]

Her rigorous schedule eventually began to tell on her frail physique. Her voice grew husky and she suffered from chest pains. Tuberculosis was the diagnosis. Commencing in 1826 she stopped teaching and left the severe New England climate each winter and spent time in Philadelphia and Alexandria, Virginia. Her summers then were spent with the Channings at Portsmouth, Rhode Island. There she continued to walk, write, and visit with friends. To help her health mend, in 1830 the Channings invited her to spend time on the island of St. Croix. There she was able to study the unusual tropical flora and fauna. There too, she formed her first strong opinons of slavery. "Disguise thyself as thou wilt, still, Slavery, still thou art a bitter draught, and human nature will not wear thy chains without cursing the ground for the enslaver's sake."[12]

When she returned from St. Croix, she flung herself with her old intensity once again into her work of teaching and writing. In 1841 she was approached by John Nichols, then in the Harvard Divinity School, for a recommendation of an individual to teach Sunday School to the women in the East Cambridge jail. Young Nichols had tried to hold services with them, but became convinced that it would take a mature, sympathetic woman to reach them. When she proposed teaching them herself, he protested, concerned for her health. "I shall be there next Sunday," was her answer, and thus she was launched on her life work.

There were about twenty women in the jail; drunkards, thieves, prostitutes and vagrants. After the service, Dorothea was shocked to find several insane women among the hardened criminals. When she discovered that their only crime was their affliction, and when the jailor dismissed the fact that their quarters were even more uncomfortable than those of the criminals by saying that "lunatics did not feel the cold as others," she determined to act on their behalf.[13]

She enlisted the support of Samuel Gridley Howe, who wrote an article for the *Daily Advertiser*, in which he reported on the conditions that he had seen. When the public reaction was to protest that his report was untrue, she got Charles Sumner to attest in a public letter to the "horrid" conditions in the jail. She then presented her case to the Cambridge Court. The quarters for the insane were renovated and heat was provided. Although Dorothea was encouraged, she began to wonder about the conditions in other prisons and almshouses. Visits to jails and poorhouses in nearby towns convinced her that the situation in Cambridge was not isolated. Thus she embarked on her first survey of an entire state—that of Massachusetts.[14]

Adopting from the very first the methods she was to use throughout her life, she spent the next two years conducting a survey of all the jails and almshouses across the state — from Berkshire in the west to Cape Cod in the east. After completing her survey, in January 1843 she reduced her accumulation of misery and outrage to a written report, a memorial to the state of Massachusetts. None of the horrible details were omitted. "You would not treat your lowest dumb animals with such disregard to decency!" she wrote. And then closed it with an impassioned plea:

> Men of Massachusetts, I beg, I implore, I demand, pity and protection for these of my suffering, outraged sex. Fathers, husbands, brothers, I would supplicate you for this boon—but what do I say? ... put away the cold, calculating spirit of selfishness and self-seeking, lay off the armor of local strife and political opposition; ... consecrate [these halls] with one heart and one mind to the works of righteousness and just judgment. ... Gentlemen, I commit you to this sacred cause.[15]

The shock of her memorial was followed by cries of disbelief. "Incredible! Incredible!" and "Sensational slanderous lies!" were typical of the editorial response when her report was made public. What Dorothea Dix had done was to make clear that it was the system, and not the acts of isolated individuals that was responsible; therefore, it took the support and effort of men such as William E. Channing, Horace Mann and Luther V. Bell of the McLean Asylum to convince, with letters and with speeches, that her catalogue of horror was true.[16]

Rhode Island was her next state, followed by Pennsylvania and New Jersey. The hospital at Trenton and the one at Harrisburg were the first ones, however, actually to be built in response to her memorials—both completed at about the same time—Dorothea Dix called them her "first born." In all there were more than 30 such institutions built throughout the world, that were a result of her efforts.

* * * *

During the Civil War she volunteered her services to the

Surgeon General in Washington. She was appointed "Super-intendent of Women Nurses." Her duties included selecting nurses from among the thousands of women who were volunteering and then assigning them to appropriate military hospitals as well as managing the distribution of the enormous stores of clothing, bandages and food that were being donated and procured for the sick and wounded.[17]

When, after the war, Edwin Stanton, Secretary of War, asked her what she wanted in exchange for her years of free service, she responded that she wanted only "A stand of The Flags of my Country." These he sent to her in acknowledgment of "her benevolent and diligent labors and devoted efforts ... for the Care, Succor, and Relief of the Sick and Wounded Soldiers of the United States on the battlefield, in camps and hospitals." During the remainder of her life, they stood in her quarters at the Trenton State Hospital. After her death, they were bequeathed to Harvard College.

* * * *

Today, at a distance of over one hundred years, reading the written material left from the period, it is hard to identify exactly what Dorothea Dix's role was and why during her lifetime it was considered to be so significant. Was she first to identify the needs of the insane? No! Others were often there ahead of her—Horace Mann earlier had identified the same problems in Massachusetts that she did; Joseph Konigmacher got two bills passed in Pennsylvania before she came to the state. Was she the first to propose that "the insane are wards of the state?" No! It was Mann who, years before her first memorial, did so in the Massachusetts legislature.[18] Was she a philanthropist, as she was often called? No! At least not in the sense of doling out vast amounts of her personal wealth—although she was "well situated," she was not wealthy.[19] Was she a lobbyist, catalyzing legislative opinion? Perhaps, but that term in no way accounts for the high esteem she enjoyed. Everywhere doors were open to her: in state capitals throughout the United States as well as at the White House; in England and Scotland; in Turkey and Japan.

The deference, the respect, the affection which was accorded her are unknown in political circles today. She had no constituency, could deliver no votes; yet legislators and governors treated her as if she controlled millions. She gave no speeches, never inflamed passions with rhetoric; she simply demanded privately and then usually got what she wanted. Why? How?

The answer probably lies hidden in an understanding of the nineteenth-century heart and mind, the relationship that existed between men and women in a completely male oriented society. Dr. Francis Lieber, the German publicist who helped with her campaign in South Carolina, once wrote her that "you as a woman have a great advantage over us, for with firmness, courage and the strength of a male mind you unite the advantages of a woman."[20] Women were still pedestal-bound in men's minds; beheld as objects of honor and purity. Dorothea Dix, while at the same time remaining remarkably feminine, apparently out-maled men in her knowledge, her preparation of material and her attention to detail, her sense of right, her regard for duty, her selflessness, her single-minded resolve; so that they were over-awed. "Fixed as fate she was" and men bowed to do her bidding.

She did not originate the practice of treating the insane humanely but she did "drive that idea into the consciousness of the American public and shape their sentiments until they were able to perceive for themselves that it was their duty to provide this humane care ... ."[21] The power that she exerted, even among her enemies (in this case the Democratic legislators of North Carolina) is evidenced in a letter she wrote in 1848:

> This morning after breakfast several gentlemen called, all Whigs, talked of the hospital, and said the most discouraging things possible. I sent for the leading Democrats [who were opposed to the plan]; went to my room and brought my Memorial, ... "Gentlemen," I said, "here is the document I have prepared for your assembly. I desire you, sir, to present it," handing it to John W. Ellis, a Democrat popular with his party, "and you, gentlemen," I said, turning to the astonished delegation, "you, I expect, will sus-

40

tain the motion this gentleman will make to print the same.''

    They took leave ... The memorial was presented; the motion to print twelve extra copies for each member was offered and passed without one dissenting vote.[22]

It was her good fortune or, perhaps, great skill to always find a man of courage and indomitable humanity, one well situated in the seats of power, who was eager to engineer her bills through the various state legislatures. In Pennsylvania it was Konigmacher; in Massachusetts S. G. Howe. As Dr. Howe wrote: "When I look back upon the time when you stood hesitating and doubting upon the brink of the enterprise you have so bravely and nobly accomplished, I cannot but be impressed with the lesson of courage and hope which you have taught even to the strongest men. ... You are pleased to overrate the importance of my efforts. I can only reply that if I *touch off* the piece, it will be you who *furnish the ammunition.*"[23]

Although the insane were her life's work, she had other charities that she advanced; orphanages, a seamen's home, and libraries. It was she who got the government to give three hundred dollars for a library and then induced Mr. Corcoran to give a bit of land in the district and $25,000 for the buildings. Dorothea Dix accomplished many great things. No item, moreover, of the unfortunate was too small to escape her notice. Her friend John Greenleaf Whittier wrote the following poem to adorn the fountain that she donated for thirsty animals in Custom House Square in Boston:

    Stranger and traveler!
    Drink freely and bestow
    A kindly thought on her
       who bade this fountain blow;
    Yet hath for it no claim
       Save as the minister
    Of blessing in God's name.

Ill and bedridden, she spent the last years of her life in her rooms at Trenton State Hospital. At the end she told her doctors: "Don't give me anything. None of those anodynes to dull senses or relieve pain. I want to feel it all. And, please tell me when the time is near. I want to know."

Although the marble marker in the cemetery at Cambridge simply bears the words "Dorothea L. Dix," one friend, Dr. Charles H. Nichols, wrote, after her death in 1887, the most eloquent statement of her life: "Thus has died and been laid to rest in the most quiet, unostentatious way the most useful and distinguished woman America has yet produced."[24]

END NOTES

1. Morrison, Samuel Eliot & Commager, Henry Steele, *A Concise History of the American Republic*, Oxford University Press, 1977, pages 218-220.
2. Ibid.
3. Tiffany, Francis, *Dorothea Lynde Dix*, Houghton, Mifflin and Company, Boston, 1890, pages 8-9.
4. Girls were not permitted to attend public schools in Boston before 1790, and until 1822 they were admitted only during the summer months, when there were not enough boys to fill them. Marshall, Helen E., *Dorothea Dix*, Russell & Russell, New York, 1937, page 19.
5. Tiffany, Francis, op. cit., page 37.
6. Dix, Dorothea, letter to Ann Heath, undated.
7. John H. Thom (1808-1894) was a Unitarian preacher in Liverpool. He married the daughter of Dorothea Dix's friends the Rathbones.
8. Tiffany, Francis, op. cit., page 34.
9. Dix, Dorothea, 1825 letter to Ann Heath.
10. Quoted in Helen E. Marshall, op. cit., page 33.
11. Quoted in Helen E. Marshall, op. cit., pages 35-36.
12. Dix, Dorothea, 1831 letter to Mrs. Samuel Torrey.
13. Marshall, Helen E., op. cit. page 61.
14. Tiffany, Francis, op. cit., page 85.
15. Dix, Dorothea, *Memorial to the Legislature of Massachusetts*, January 1843.
16. Horace Mann, who several years before had attempted unsuccessfully to bring the plight of the insane before the Massachusetts public, wrote: "I have felt, in reading your Memorial, as I used to feel when formerly I endeavored to do something for the welfare of the same class,—as though all personal enjoyments were criminal until they were relieved." Tiffany, Francis, op. cit. pages 87-88.
17. Tiffany, Francis, op. cit. pages 336-337.
18. It should be pointed out, however, that Mann's call for state responsibility did not necessarily imply that the state should build the hospital itself as did Dorothea Dix. Fostering the construction of adequate private facilities would have sufficed.
19. When her grandmother died, Dorothea Dix received a portion of her estate. With the income from this and the earnings from her books she was able to live modestly for the rest of her life. One biographer at the turn of the century estimated her income at about $3,000 a year.
20. Wilson, Dorothy Clarke, *Stranger and Traveler*, Little, Brown and Company, Boston, 1975, page 170.
21. Haggard, Howard, 1931 radio talk, quoted in Bond, Earl D., *Kirkbride and His Mental Hospital*, page 90.
22. Tiffany, Francis, op. cit., page 135.
23. Ibid., page 89.
24. Ibid., page 375.

VI

FOUNDING OF THE PENNSYLVANIA STATE LUNATIC HOSPITAL

The problems of the poor and the mentally ill that Dorothea Dix had "memorialized" were easy to hide when the country was rural and thus they had been ignored or avoided by most citizens. But by 1845, with greater numbers of people beginning to move to urban areas, which were becoming increasingly industrialized, the effects of poverty, as aggravated by periods of unemployment, became more visible. The nation's evolving political system and the "democratization" of the lower classes, who were beginning to have a greater say in their lives, moreover, contributed to the growing consensus that government should provide services that theretofore had been handled by private means.[1] Thus we see calls for the beginnings of public control over banking, the state's development of canals and railroads and the providing of social services such as hospitals, poorhouses and prisons. An expanding network of regional newspapers, moreover, facilitated the communication of such needs. Editors trying to expand circulation or with political axes to sharpen, delighted in running sensational articles that would help to sell more papers.[2]

The opening pages of Dorothea Dix's memorial to the Pennsylvania legislature readily acknowledged that: "successively in the years of 1838 amd 1840, earnest efforts were made by benevolent citzens of the state, to procure for the pauper and indigent insane, the benefits of curative treatment and hospital protection. The gentlemen who engaged in this object, I have learned, spared neither time nor labor to accomplish what was justly deemed so important a work." She went on to describe how Thomas Cope and Joseph Konigmacher had gotten bills introduced and passed in the 1838 and 1841 legislatures.[3] The first was vetoed by Governor Porter because of the state's "financial embarrassment." The second he signed into law but the hospital was never built.

Pennsylvania legislators, along with the governor were understandably wary of spending bills. They might agree with the need for some philanthropic project but often would shrink from providing outright financial support. Sometimes they would elect to foster development by chartering corporations to which they might give preferred land grants or even "seed" money. In other instances they might "buy in" on the initial development effort and leave considerations of continued maintenance to future legislatures. On occasion the legislature even mandated that the directors [specified in an act] should take out a loan and that: "if such loan cannot be made for the whole amount of the sum necessary, ... [it] shall immediately be added to the county tax to be paid by the county treasurer to the directors."[4]

The Legislative Session of 1841 was an especially busy one, writing philanthropic acts to establish poorhouses in several counties, to provide pensions to Revolutionary War veterans, and to establish an "Asylum for the Insane of this Commonwealth." For the several poorhouses, the legislators elected to pass the costs back to the counties. For the asylum, provided for in Act 34, which was signed by Governor David R. Porter on March 31, 1841, they furnished $50,000 "seed" money to buy the land and construct the building but nothing for its continued maintenance.

The Act did not completely overlook the issue—it did specify that the "authorities having care and charge of the poor in the counties, districts and townships of this Commonwealth, shall send to the asylum such insane paupers under their charge ... and they [the authorities] shall be severally chargeable with the expenses of the care and maintenance of such paupers. The act also directed the hospital trustees to apply "to the maintenance of insane persons in or to the general use of the asylum any grant of land, any donation or bequest of money or other personal property" that they received. But this money would not have been enough to run a large hospital. In all probability the legislature expected the trustees to be private fund raisers—a practice commonly used in supporting private hospitals and poorhouses of the day.

The association of Thomas Pym Cope with the 1841 effort

to build the first state-run asylum tends to support this idea. Born to a plasterer in Lancaster, Pennsylvania, Cope walked to Philadelphia while still a boy. There he became a lowly merchant's apprentice but, by the time he was a young man, he had made a fortune sending ships to Europe and the Orient. Eventually he became one of the leading philanphropic citizens of Philadelphia, involved in a wide variety of civic and charitable projects.[5] Among all his many successes, however, the establishment of an asylum for the insane of Pennsylvania would not be one.

Joseph Konigmacher, a freshman state legislator from Ephrata, had introduced Act 34 into the legislature and then, with Cope's support, pushed it through to passage. The project's overseers bought land outside of Philadelphia, secured the renowned architect William Strickland to design the structure, and laid the building's foundation.[6] Then the group ran into political and financial difficulties. Cope blamed failure of the effort on political interference; that the assignment of "the carrying out of it to party men, more intent on making jobs for themselves and [their] political friends" had killed its chances. In his diary he went on to write: "a lot was contracted for at an extravagant price and another agreement made with an unprincipled demagogue [to furnish the materials for the building] who afterwards ran away to escape punishment ... and the whole thing was abandoned."[7]

Some of the defects in Konigmacher's bill of 1841 were corrected by the one of 1845—the third one of the Pennsylvania legislature, the one that resulted from Dorothea Dix's efforts. The most glaring flaw in the earlier bill—the politicization of the effort—was solved by designating the specific commissioners in the new act. They were Luther Reily, James Lesley, Jacob Haldeman, Joseph Konigmacher, Charles B. Trego, and Hugh Campbell. Reily and Campbell were physicians, Konigmacher and Trego state legislators, the others farmers and businessmen.

* * * *

These men first met in July of 1845 in the Harrisburg offices of Jacob Haldeman on Front Street and later moved to those of James Lesley.[8] It was the group's usual practice to meet for short sessions of an hour or two. But on the days when they met (usually once or twice a week) it was their habit to meet three times in a single day—morning around 10:00 o'Clock, afternoon around 3:00 o'Clock and in the evening at 7:00 o'Clock.

Dorothea Dix was there lending her support. Harrisburg's *Patriot* and *Union* newspaper reported that "it gives us pleasure also to state that Miss Dix, ... is here and lending her aid, counsel and energy in the matter." It took the commissioners several meetings "to organize." Finally on the morning of July 8, Luther Reily was elected President and James Lesley was appointed Secretary. That same afternoon the commissioners "jointly executed an official bond for fifteen thousand dollars," conditioned on "the faithful and proper application of the funds placed in their hands [the state pledged $50,000] and performance of their duties."

Luther Reily had come to Harrisburg from Meyerstown in what is now Lebanon County. He studied medicine in the city with Martin Luther. The young apprentice marched off in the War of 1812 as a private but was soon promoted as a medical officer. He opened a practice in Harrisburg on his return from the war. He was an affable man and a sympathetic physician and soon became the most popular doctor in town. Reily was so well liked that he was elected a member of the Twenty-fifth Congress. He much preferred the professional life, however, and declined to return to a legislative position. After several years of practice, he took his brother-in-law, Edward L. Orth, in as an understudy. Although Orth "eventually won the confidence and love of his patients," as a junior to Reily, he "met many a rebuff" from prospective patients due to the hold the older physician maintained on the town's residents.[9]

The meetings of the hospital's commissioners seem to have been well run. They were brief, usually addressing no more than one or two issues, and Reily frequently established ad hoc committees to resolve specific questions. James Lesley soon emerged as the group's writer. On July 9, they appointed the five-man committees called for by the Act of 1845 for each of the state's 67 counties. At this meeting they also approved Leslie's draft of the circular to be sent to each of the county committees. It read:

> In pursuance of the duty imposed upon us ... we hereby appoint you a committee for the purposes ... of the subscription paper hereto annexed. We earnestly solicit your prompt and efficient action for this important and benevolent object. Let us speedily redeem our beloved state from the opprobrium which now rests upon her, for immuring in dungeons, ... a portion of our fellow-citizens, deserving our kindest regard and sympathy.
>
> Let it no longer be the reproach of Pennsylvanians that whilst they have munificently provided for the advancement of the welfare of the sane part of their population, they refuse to give of their abundance a small pittance for the comfort of those whom the Almighty in his providence has deprived of reason— thus disqualifying them from providing for themselves.
>
> It would be well to draw the attention of your citizens to this subject by publications in your newspapers, and by calling public meetings and having suitable addresses delivered.
>
> You are requested to report at the earliest day practicable ... the amount that may be subscribed in your county.

Not only were each of the counties expected to raise money, private funds were also requested.[10] One of these was a request of Thomas P. Cope by Miss Dix for the very considerable sum of $10,000. He declined. There were many demands for his money and he was not "inclined to be a pack horse to politicians." She must have described the request as a reasonable one in comparison to the need, for he noted in his diary that: "She can prefer no just claim on me to meet her 'modest' tax on my means, for considering the heavy indebtedness of the State, I could not encourage her application at this time. My experience teaches me that the Institution ... would be placed in the hands of partizans selected as rewards for political sycophancy."[11]

In early October the commissioners dedicated three days to looking over farms available in the vicinity of Harrisburg. Two days later they authorized Charles B. Trego "to enter into articles of agreement" for the purchase of the Ridgway farm north of the city. On the same day, October 6, they authorized the president "to issue proposals for the stone for the basement ... and for preparing clay, moulding and burning bricks for the building." They also authorized him "to make arrangements with the Canal Commissioners that will secure the conveyance on the State Canals and Railroads, of all the material required ... free of toll."

Ridgway was out of town and Trego was unable to find him before mid-November. When he did, Ridgway reported that he had sold the farm to another buyer. The commissioners moved with little hesitation to buy a nearby tract known as the Sales' Farm. This major action having been concluded, they traveled to Philadelphia a few days later for a visit to The Pennsylvania Hospital. The superintendent, Thomas Kirkbride, gave them an extended tour of the building and the grounds. From him they got "much valuable information with regard to the plan, arrangement, and internal ecomony of a well constructed building." On the evening of their return they adopted a resolution that the state asylum would be a hospital of "Kirkbride-design."

By the year's end the commissioners were beginning to feel, however, that there were deficiencies in the original enabling legislation, so Trego was directed to draft a report to the legislature suggesting a supplementary Act. Their proposal passed the House in the 1846 Session but was not taken up in the Senate. The commissioners declined to proceed further under the original act and did not meet again for two years, until February 1848.

When they reconvened (probably in desperation over the inaction) they decided to "memorialize" the legislature for the passage of their supplement to the original act of 1845. On Feb 15 the secretary (now Trego) was requested to draft and prepare 200 copies of the memorial. Three days later, in what must be a model for legislative efficiency, Trego reported that the memorial had been prepared, printed and laid on the desks of the members of the legislature. Moreover, he mentioned that it had been presented in the House of Representatives that very day and had been referred to a Select Committee, who, at a meeting held in the afternoon, had unanimously agreed to report a bill out to the House. The supplemental legislation was approved on April 11, 1848.

At their next meeting, on April 25, 1848, Reily introduced the new, additional commissioners who had been appointed by the supplemental legislation: Aaron Bombaugh, John A. Weir and James Fox. They apparently were added to provide expertise that the original commissioners lacked—Weir and Bombaugh were bankers and Fox was a member of the Dauphin County Bar.[12] The copy of the supplement also contained an important revision of the restrictive statement that they were to "build, finish, furnish and complete the asylum for the sum of $50,000." It now read that the money was to be the state's "contribution" toward whatever was required. The words "Union Asylum" were also removed from the name of the proposed hospital. The new name was simply "Pennsylvania State Lunatic Hospital."

On May 10, 1848 Samuel Holman of Harrisburg was appointed architect and general superintendent for erecting the building. President Reily was authorized to invite proposals according to Holman's specifications for excavating the ground for the cellars, for delivery of the stone for the rough work and for bricks or the clay to fire them on site. At the same meeting two months later at which they opened the proposals, they decided to drop Holman and "to adopt the plan and specification furnished by Mr. John Haviland and also to accept his proposals for building the State Lunatic Hospital for the sum of $100,000."

The switch appears to have been based on Haviland's reputation and experience rather than any specific dissatisfaction with Holman. Holman was used later to build some of the outbuildings (the wash house and the carriage house) on the grounds at Harrisburg. It may have been the invisible hand, too, of Haviland's fellow Quaker and Philadelphian, Thomas Kirkbride. Not involved publicly with the commissioners, the force of his entry on the scene two years later as a trustee suggests that he may have been involved behind the scenes much earlier.[13]

Haviland, an English trained architect, who had opened his Philadelphia practice in 1816, had several major structures in the city to his credit by 1848, including the Walnut Street Theater, and the Franklin Institute, as well as several churches. He was, however, better known for the Penitentiaries at Pittsburgh and the Eastern State Penitentiary at Philadelphia. "The principal elements that went into the design of the Eastern State Penitentiary had all been used before, but Haviland was the first to give every prisoner a separate cell, with its own exercise yard, arranged along corridors radiating from a central core—a scheme that offered maximum surveillance with a minimum of supervisory personnel."[14] This building represented the culmination of a generation of experiments in penal reform and as one of the most famous American structures of the day became the embodiment of the "Pennsylvania Plan" for prisons, a plan which was studied worldwide.

* * * *

Construction of the Pennsylvania State Lunatic Hospital was started sometime between July 1848 (when the commissioners went out to the farm and "agreed upon the location for the building, marking the corners by stakes") and October 18, when they paid Haviland $2,500 for the work completed to that date.[15] He had submitted bills for excavation, bricks, lumber and the stonemason's work in the amount of $2,750. (The excavation was for the foundation, as the building had no true cellar.) The commissioners also had to pay the farm tenant $30 for the corn destroyed when the work was started.[16]

The work began well enough, with Haviland estimating that the building would be completed by November 1850 at a cost of $50,000. In December of 1850 they paid the final installment to him, bringing the total to $55,800. By then it was obvious, though, that the hospital would not be finished by the January 1851 contract date, so the commissioners threatened him with legal action if it was not completed by April

10.[17]

John Haviland, considered by many to be a brilliant designer, was apparently not equally expert as a builder. Completion was not the only problem between him and the commissioners. In March of 1851 they unanimously agreed that Haviland's "present provision for heating the Hospital building is altogether insufficient." Reily and Konigmacher met with the architect and got him to relinquish the portion of his contract for heating so that they could pursue other options.[18]

The commissioners also had trouble with one of their own. Jacob Haldeman had pledged $1,000 toward the purchase of the farm.[19] He claimed that his pledge had been based on a selling price of $10,000. As the price they paid was $8,000, he insisted that his "subscription" should be eight hundred dollars—he stated that he had a letter from Dorothea Dix to prove it. He did not produce it. Eventually they settled out of court. He gave them $1,175 which included the interest due during their two year long squabble. The idea of a "subscription" suggests, however, that the commissioner's appointments—the jobs were unsalaried—may have been "bought" ones.[20]

* * * *

In the afternoon of February 14, 1851, a new group of men met at Coverly's Hotel in Harrisburg. They were the "Trustees" for the Pennsylvania State Lunatic Hospital. It was this group that would see that the hospital was run properly once the building was finished. Several of the building commissioners (Reily, Campbell, Konigmacher, and Bombaugh) had been named Trustees by Governor Johnston. The Governor also had appointed several new individuals—most notable among them Thomas Story Kirkbride.

The trustees got to work immediately. At their first meeting Reily was also made Chairman of the new group. Thomas Kirkbride was named secretary pro tem and John Wier became their treasurer. The trustees set the date of June 2, 1851, for the reception of patients and established the superintendent's annual salary at $1,500. At this meeting they also read the letters of recommendations of the candidates for Superintendent. The board then voted and from the four applicants, John Curwen, a Kirkbride protege at the Pennsylvania Hospital for the Insane, was elected.[21]

Dix's and Konigmacher's dream of a great state hospital for the mentally ill in Pennsylvania was nearing reality.

When John Haviland climbed the stairs to the unfinished third story or up into the dome of the Pennsylvania State Lunatic Hospital to inspect the completed work, he could look out across the Pennsylvania canal at the foot of the hill (the same canal that Charles Dickens and Dorothea Dix had traveled west on), past the railroad, and even beyond the Susquehanna River, well down the Cumberland Valley—nearly, it seemed, to the church spires of Carlisle.[22]

A hundred years earlier this whole area had been largely forested—with touches of marshland near the river. Now it was virtually all cultivated farmland. Rising on the architect's left, however, and continuing in front up the river through the narrows at Dauphin, the black smoke and grey ash of a dozen restless locomotives brushed the scene menacingly. The tall stacks of factories in the city of Harrisburg and along the west shore of the Susquehanna also pierced the blue sky like the trunks of giant fire-blackened hemlocks. The signs of change were all around him.

END NOTES

1. "Under the Constitution of 1838 with its several amendments, the government of Pennsylvania was thoroughly democratized. Virtually every important position at the State level was brought within reach of the voters." Coleman, John F., *The Disruption of The Pennsylvania Democracy, 1848-1860*, The Pennsylvania Historical and Museum Commission, Harrisburg, 1975, page 8.

2. It is interesting to note that in 1850 nearly two- thirds of Pennsylvania daily newspapers were classified as political journals and were receiving financial support from political parties. Coleman, John F., op. cit., page 11.

3. Dix, Dorothea L., *Memorial To the Honorable, the Senate and the House of Representatives of the Commonwealth of Pennsylvania*, page 4. Thomas Cope had led the public pamphleteering and association work in Philadelphia and Konigmacher the legislative work in the House of Representatives in Harrisburg.

4. Act 67 of March 1841: "To provide for the erection of a House for the Employment and Support of the Poor of the county of Bedford."

5. Cope, while still a young man, became a member of the Philadelphia City Council. One committee on which he served was charged with introducing public water into Philadelphia. He was also a supporter of Haverford College, a contributor of money to the hospitals and poorhouses of the city and helped set the stage for the acquisition of Fairmount Park. (Harrison, Eliza Cope, *Philadelphia Merchant, The Diary of Thomas P. Cope, 1800-1851*, Gateway Editions, South Bend, Ind., 1978, page vii.) Cope was also a friend of Thomas Scattergood, the founder of the Friends Hospital at Frankford, Pa.

6. Strickland was a pupil of Benjamin Henry Latrobe. His greatest contribution as an architect was as a planner of institutional buildings in the Greek Revival style. Among them were the Second Bank of the United States, the Philadelphia Exchange and the Tennessee State Capitol. He also designed and built the Friends Asylum at Frankford in 1816. Gilchrist, Agnes Addison, *William Strickland*, Da Capo Press, New York, 1969, "Documentary Supplement, pages 2-3.

7. Cope, Thomas P., op. cit. The foundation for the building was laid on land west of the Schuylkill River outside of Philadelphia.

8. Haldeman, an iron maker, was the founder of New Cumberland, Pa. A street in the town still bears his name.

9. Laverty, George L., *History of Medicine in Dauphin County Pennsylvania*, The Telegraph Press, Harrisburg, Pa., 1967, page 49-50. Reily Street in Harrisburg, where he owned a large riverfront property, is, of course, named for Dr. Reily.

10. The only funds that the Commissioners accounted for (according to their minutes) was for the money, $70,000, received directly from the State Treasurer. These privately solicited funds must have been used, therefore, for other than the purchase of the land or the construction of the building.

11. Cope, Thomas P., op. cit.

12. Bombaugh, a staunch Abolitionist like Weir, was also to become one of the first trustees of the hospital.

13. The dropping of the words "Union Asylum" from the name specified in the original act of the legislature probably also was due to a Kirkbride recommendation. He was known to object to the term "asylum" because it gave the impression that the insane needed "a place of refuge or security, as though they had committed some crime, ... " (Tomes, Nancy, op. cit., page xiii.)

14. Tatum, George B., "John Haviland", article in the *Macmillan Encyclopedia of Architects*, The Free Press, New York, 1982, pages 333-334.

15. Governor Johnston did not lay the cornerstone, however, until the following spring—on April 7, 1849.

16. The tenant farmer had asked for $60. Bombaugh (a former farmer) and Weir were appointed to review his claim. They measured the acreage involved and recommended approval of his request. In a meeting of all the commissioners it was halved, however, to $30.

17. The architect finally turned the building over to the commissioners on June 19, 1851.

18. The heating was eventually installed by Birkinbine and Trotter, a Philadelphia company. Their contract for $12,200 was "to install the heating apparatus, laundry and steam pipes." In his first annual report, Curwen went into detail to describe it. The steam was heated in two 40-foot- long boilers, then carried through eight-inch cast-iron pipes through an archway to the main building. There it branched into "hot air chambers" situated under each of the building's wings and thence into radiators of three-quarter-inch wrought-iron pipe. The system contained a total of sixteen thousand feet of pipe.

19. Reily had pledged $500 and the other commissioners had each pledged either $100 or $200.

20. During the long dispute, the final payment due on the farm was delayed. When Dorothea Dix heard of this, she sent Weir her personal check for $1,000 to ensure that the loan would not be in default. Her money was returned to her after Haldeman made settlement.

21. The other candidates, all physicians, were: Benjamin Malone of Bucks County, William S. Bishop of Harrisburg and D. T. Brown of New York.

22. The stairs had also been a point of contention between Haviland and the hospital commissioners. They claimed that he had located them other than as indicated in his drawing and insisted that they be moved back.

Dorothy Lynde Dix, 1802-1887

1863 Harpers drawing of Camp Curtin with the Pennsylvania State Lunatic Hospital in the background.

Interior of Kirkbride Building, male side, about 1900.

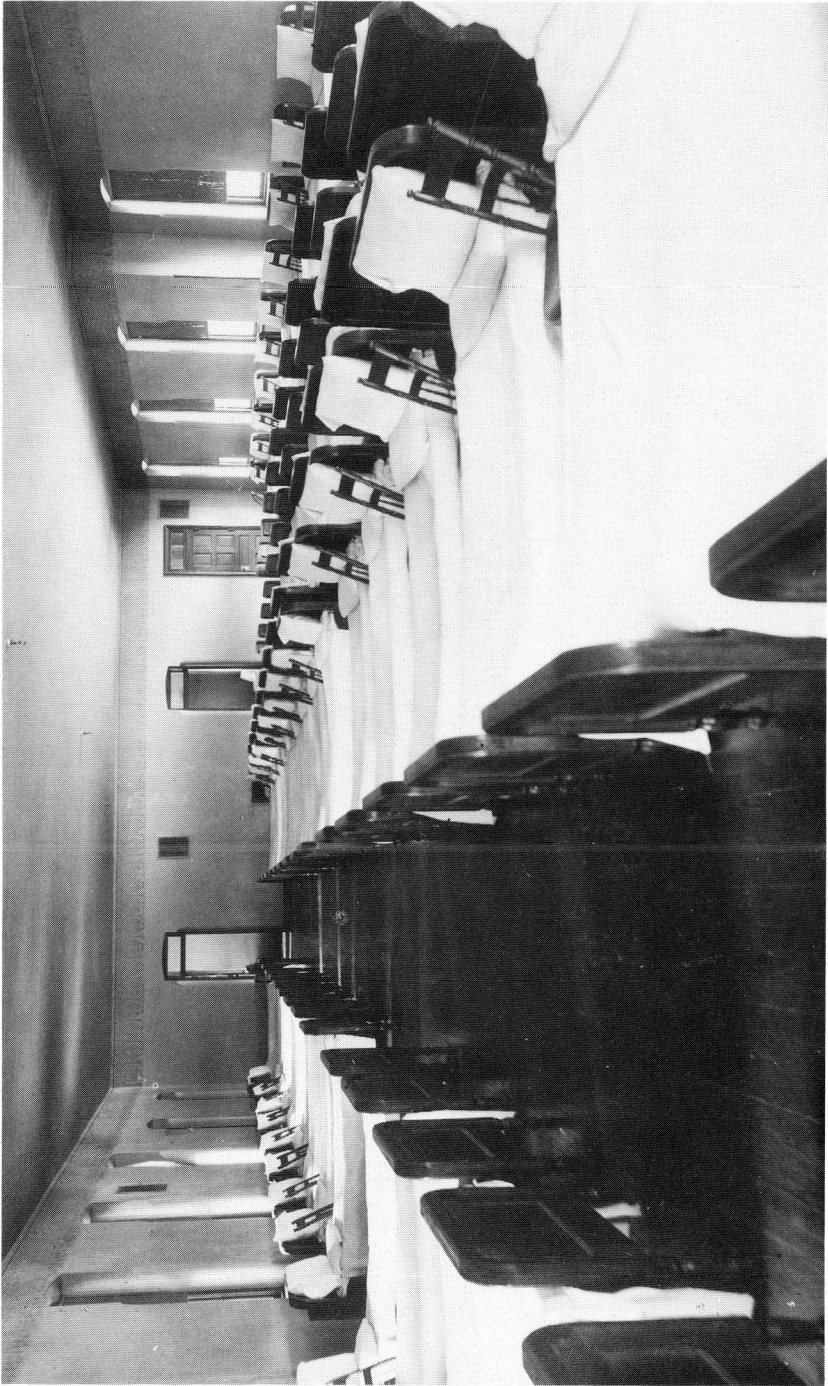

Interior of Female Nine showing close living arrangements, about 1890.

"Dr. John" Curwen
First Hospital
Superintendent
1851-1881

Jerome Z. Gerhard
Superintendent
1881-1891

Pennsylvania State Lunatic Hospital Band, 1885.

View of hospital from the Laundry Tower, about 1900.

Male and female attendants, about 1900.

Female 9 and 10 building with Laundry Tower and Machine Shop on the right.

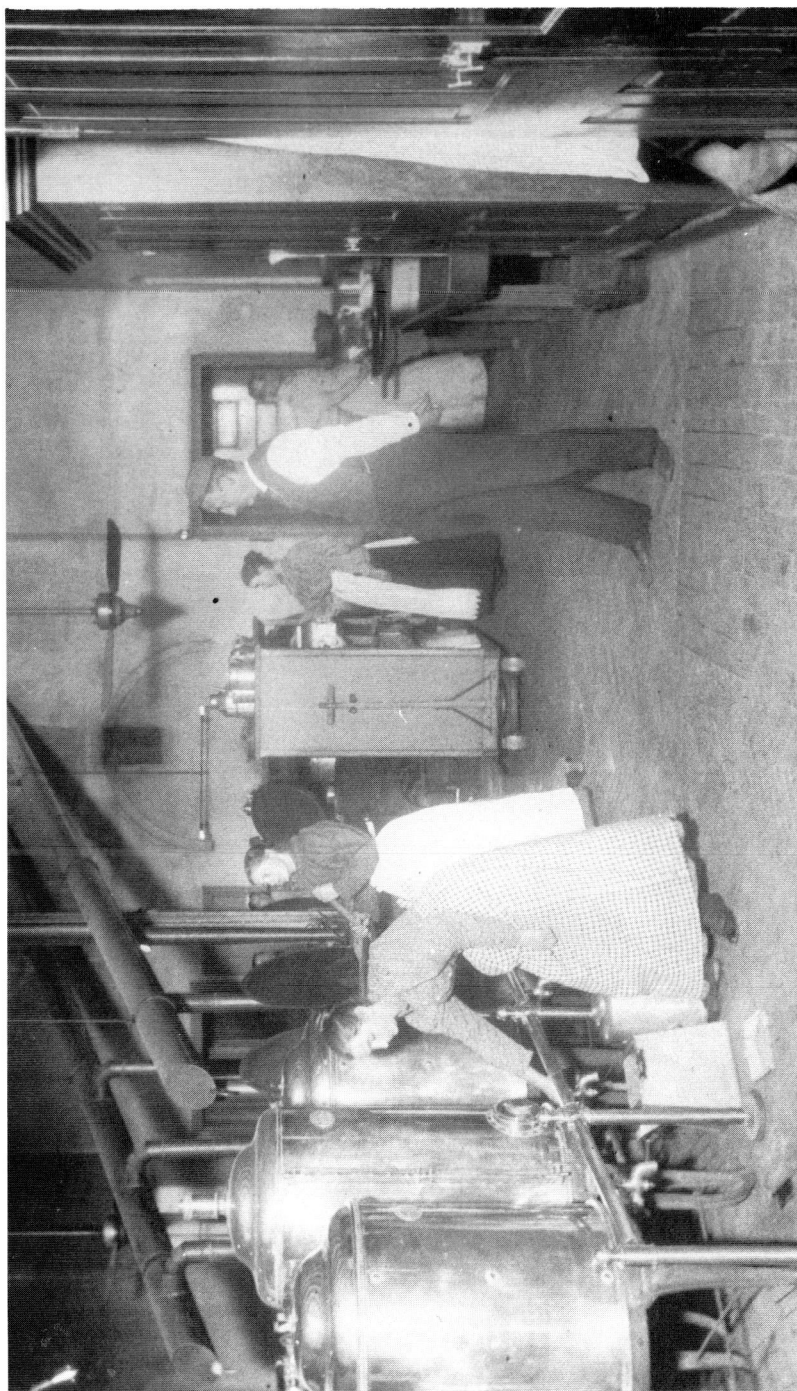

Kitchen in old building with cart being readied to transport food to one of the hospital buildings, 1890's.

Ice House and pond, first snow of the season, October 30, 1925.

VII

JOHN CURWEN

The Curwens came to America from Little Broughton, Cumberland County, England, as immigrants of means. Soon after his arrival in 1785 the elder John Curwen bought a large farming estate outside of Philadelphia. Unlike most new Americans, however, he purchased the farm outright with money from an inheritance. There he established his wife and their growing family. The farm, which he renamed Walnut Hill, was to remain in the Curwen family for five generations, until the twentieth century.[1]

The first John Curwen was involved, in addition to farming, in the building of the Lancaster Turnpike through Chester County.[2] For these efforts he was appointed Turnpike Superintendent in 1795, a post he held for 15 years. In November 1787 he was commissioned a Justice of the Peace. As a result of this position he was privileged to write "esquire" after his signature, an evidence of the growing importance of the Curwen name.[3]

John and Mary Curwen had four children. One, Joseph, took up a mercantile career. He represented Stephen Girard and other Philadelphia merchants such as Thomas Biddle in London, on the Continent and in South America for nearly thirty years. To another son, George, fell the responsibility of farming Walnut Hill. This he did for some years.

George was kindly, warm, introspective and of a literary bent. He was as much interested in writing poetry as in farming. As did several of the Curwens he speculated in land in Ohio and western Pennsylvania, losing heavily. He died at age 57, "a gentleman of fine talents," according to church records, and left Walnut Hill to his wife, Elinor. Although George had attempted to sell the farm to settle his debts, she had no intention of abandoning it and continued there for 32 years after her husband's death. She sold off some parcels and rented the remaining land to contract farmers.[4]

George and Elinor had four children: John, George, Maskell

and Mary. John, the eldest of the four Curwen children, was born at Walnut Hill in 1812. He received a secondary education, as did his brothers, in the Newburgh Academy in Newburgh, N. J. There he was given the basic classical education from the Rev. Mr. Phinney. Phinney prepared him well enough that he entered Yale as a member of the sophomore class.[5]

"Doctor John," as the family took to calling him in later years, and his brother Maskell both entered professional careers—medicine and law—and were only too happy to let their brother George continue to run the farm for his mother. The three Curwen boys all seem to have been attractive to the young women. Their diaries tell of dinner parties at home to which they frequently brought female companions.[6]

* * * *

In 1838 New Haven was an isolated town of some 13,000 inhabitants—a kind of "backwoods Athens." The Farmington Canal was then the main route for traffic in and out of town, although stagecoaches did operate regularly from the old "coach tavern" in the center of town. Life at Yale College was equally primitive. The faculty numbered only 31 (all strong and stern but kindly men) and the total attendance in all departments was but 560 students.[7]

Students arose at 5:30 each morning and at six went to prayers in the chapel, which was lighted by whale-oil lamps. Then they marched across the still dark campus to the recitation rooms. In the words of John Curwen's Yale friend, the author Donald G. Mitchell: "These were beastly places in those times, foul with whale-oil smoke and heated with Professor Olmstead's patented two-cylindered stoves, far up into the tune of the eighties of Fahrenheit. I have an uneasy sensation of nausea even now as I recall the simmer of the iron pot upon the stove, the steam of wet garments, the ancient fish-oil smell, the rustling of the papers as the tutor smoothed out his check list and probed with thumb and forefinger into his box of names."[8]

The students studied primarily Latin, Greek, philosophy,

and mathematics. This basic material, however, was supplemented by occasional instruction in chemistry, pharmacy, mineralogy, geology, rhetoric, oratory, and astronomy. The young Philadelphian graduated from Yale in 1841 and went on to the University of Pennsylvania, where he got his medical degree in 1844.

Doctor John continued his medical studies with a cousin, William Harris, who had a practice in Philadelphia. He then won (after an unsuccessful try at a residency at the Pennsylvania Hospital) an appointment as the assistant physician at the Wills Eye Hospital in Philadelphia. Finally in 1846 John Curwen joined Thomas S. Kirkbride in the Mental and Nervous Department of the Pennsylvania Hospital. He remained there for five years, eventually becoming Kirkbride's assistant. This in effect made him not only the Superintendent's protege but also the second in command at the hospital.

It was Curwen's duty, among others, to make the rounds each morning with Kirkbride, assisting the senior physician in administering the patient's medical and moral treatment. Although he was responsible for knowing each patient's condition intimately, as an assistant John seldom was permitted to make treatment decisions on his own. He did observe, however, Kirkbride's manner with the patients—those he encouraged by invitations to the afternoon teas; those he disciplined by removing from a more favored ward to the dreaded eighth one.

He had been seeking a Superintendent's position unsuccessfully for some time and was about ready to go into private practice when the offer at Harrisburg was made.[9] Curwen accepted the appointment, as he told Dorothea Dix, so that he would be able to marry, not because he particularly wanted the position. Its location struck him as being far removed from the amenities to which he was accustomed.

The new superintendent appears to have been a rather crisp, business-like individual, although in later years he did wear sporty large mutton-chop sideburns that hung beneath his lower jaw. When Governor Johnston invited him to the Governor's Mansion in 1851 to discuss the hospital's proposed by-laws, Curwen apparently was anxious to conduct his business and leave. He wrote afterwards that Johnston spent "some useless breath" in discussing a recent storm. Dr. John apparently had little appreciation or interest in even the simplest of social or political maneuvering. In one letter to his former chief at the Pennsylvania Hospital for the Insane, he wrote:

> I learned this afternoon one cause of the feelings on the part of certain members of the Board toward me; that I have not made it a point to call on them at their own houses when I was in Harrisburg, which I think is a rather lame reason but as their vanity has been touched, I will endeavor hereafter to apply to the wound the application needed.[10]

His correspondence, too, shows only occasional flashes of humor. In one letter he states that Commissioner Bombaugh, who previously had wanted the wash house located near the ravine and away from the main building "because of the odor," later decided that the noisy residents should be housed near the wash house, prompting Curwen to write rather dryly: "The smell from the wash house in this case is forgotten."[11]

John Curwen seems, moreover, to have been a very cautious, careful physician. He instituted the practice of having three persons certify to a patient's condition before he would admit them to the Pennsylvania Lunatic Hospital. And on difficult or perplexing cases he would ask other physicians for advice. His favorite, often stated, expression, according to one newspaper report, was: "I cannot afford to take chances."[12]

He was, however, a man of conviction as well as of resolve. When his first steward, Will Slaymaker, did not work out, he fired him without hesitation. When, as a newly appointed commissioner for the construction of a new state hospital at Wernersville, he first saw the site, he exclaimed, "You are not thinking of putting a hospital here in this hole?" When it turned out they were, and for political reasons, he resigned immediately.[13] The site, he discovered, had been selected before the bill was submitted to the legislature, an action designed to favor several officials of the Reading Railroad.

Curwen continued to write to Thomas Kirkbride for some

twenty years after he accepted the position at Harrisburg. During the first years at his new post, Curwen relied heavily on his former boss for advice. During this period he wrote to Kirkbride several times each week (sometimes long, three or four page letters) and he regularly traveled to Philadelphia to visit the more experienced doctor. The two would sometimes meet for lunch, even breakfast, and John Curwen seems to have had no compunctions, moreover, in telling Kirkbride that he would be in Philadelphia on a certain day and wanted to see him for a couple of hours. He consulted, however, with the senior physician primarily on hospital management issues; only occasionally on patient matters.

The Curwen letters are filled with requests for information such as: "where to procure the proper locks for the doors or screening material for the windows?" or on "ways to improve the bars on the windows to prevent escapes through them," or with questions such as "by whom your baker's oven was set up?" On one occasion he even asked Kirkbride to go into Philadelphia and buy canvas suits for the male patients at Harrisburg who were in the habit of regularly removing all their clothing.[14]

When the commissioners authorized him to draw up the specifications of a contract, so that a building Holman was to construct would be "put up exactly according to his directions," Curwen wrote to Kirkbride: "I will be very much obliged for any suggestions you may have to make about the matter as they may be of material value to me."[15]

He also felt free to solicit the Philadelphian's influence on the hospital's trustees or commissioners when he believed that the weight of Kirkbride's reputation was needed. When Commissioner Bombaugh decided that adding rooms at the ends of the present building for the noisy and violent patients would make the building too long, Curwen wrote to Philadelphia: "I have again need of your assistance in a matter which both of us in common I believe ... thought definitely settled but which has been again agitated."[16]

He continued many of the practices at Harrisburg that he had learned at the Pennsylvania Hospital. He regularly advised each patient's family how their relative was doing. And he seems to have had the welfare of his patients uppermost in his mind. Even when he came under fire for administrative problems at the hospital, there was never any claim against his reputation as a doctor.[17]

* * * *

In August 1849, John married Martha Elmer, one of the young women he had brought to dinner at Walnut Hill.[18] They had a son Charles, who did not live to maturity and one daughter, Mary, who married the successful Harrisburg businessman, David Fleming. Fleming was the owner of the Harrisburg Foundry and Machine Works.

Martha Elmer Curwen died in May, 1873. John then married Anna Wyeth of Harrisburg, the granddaughter of John Wyeth, book seller, printer, postmaster, and publisher of the *Oracle of Dauphin,* the county's first newspaper.[19] Anna Wyeth had a taste for literary work, as did her grandfather. She was also a fine amateur botanist. She contributed articles to leading magazines and periodicals of the day and her botanical collection was described as one of the finest in the state. Annie, as she was invariably called, was a woman of "grace, simplicity and kindness."[20] She died of Bright's disease in 1899 after an illness of fourteen years.

It was Anna Curwen who once thwarted an inmate who was planning to "elope" from the hospital. She was cutting bread for Sunday tea, while her husband was at Chapel with the other patients, when the man appeared before her in his slippers. "By pointing out that he would not get very far in his slippers, she dissuaded him from going through with his planned escape."[21]

Although the Curwens lived on the grounds of the hospital during the thirty years the doctor was in central Pennsylvania, they were active in Harrisburg city life. He was a founding elder of the Covenant Presbyterian Church, to which he contributed much of the land for the first church building.[22] (Anna was the daughter of the Reverend Charles Wyeth, a pastor of the church.) A memorial Curwen window still exists in the now closed sanctuary. For well into the twentieth century the Pennsylvania State Lunatic Hospital and the Covenant Presbyterian Church enjoyed a close relationship.

* * * *

The only protege of Kirkbride's ever to manage a large public mental hospital, John Curwen accepted a similar post at the state hospital at Warren, Pennsylvania in 1881. He was the author of numerous papers and books on insanity. He served for many years as the Secretary and eventually as the President of the American Medico-Psychological Association (formerly the Association of Medical Superintendents of American Institutions for the Insane; now the American Psychiatric Association) and he was a recognized nineteenth-century authority on the treatment of mental disorders. He also served as a member of the Pennsylvania commissions that built the hospitals at Danville, Dixmont and Warren.

Late in life "Doctor John" assumed responsibility for settling not only his mother's affairs but also those of his brother George, who was destroyed financially by the crash of 1873. He borrowed $31,000 to save Walnut Hill, and for some time paid the interest on the loan from his own pocket.

After he retired in 1900, John Curwen returned to Harrisburg to live with his daughter, Mary Fleming. It was there that he died suddenly on July 2, 1901. In excellent health until the last day of his life, he got up in the morning feeling fine and collapsed later that day of the "extreme heat and partial paralysis."(23) The *Harrisburg Patriot* claimed that "the city loved him for his kindly ways and uprightness." He was buried in the Curwen family plot of the Old Baptist Church near Bryn Mawr, Pennsylvania.

END NOTES

1. Davis, Patricia Talbot, *A Family Tapestry, Five Generations of the Curwens of Walnut Hill*, Livingston Publishing Co., Wynnewood, Pa., 1972, page 3. "Walnut Hill" occupied land that was a part of present day Villano.
2. In one celebrated court case the elder John Curwin [sic] was upheld for having "entered upon the enclosed land and thrown down Robert McClenachan's fences," without due process or any recompense for damages, in order to construct the highway. When William Penn and his successors had granted land, it was on the basis that, in order to build roads, they retained the right to six acres for every 100. (Article "Philadelphia and Lancaster Turnpike," *The Pennsylvania Magazine of History and Biography*, Vol. XLII, 1918, page 248- 252.
3. Davis, Patricia Talbot, *A Family Tapestry, Five Generations of the Curwens of Walnut Hill*, Livingston Publishing Co., Wynnewood, Pa., 1972, page 17.
4. Ibid., pages 66-67.
5. Ibid., page 62.
6. Ibid., page 69.
7. Dunn, Waldo H., *The Life of Donald G. Mitchell, Ik Marvel*, Charles Scribner's Sons, New York, 1922, page 43.
8. Mitchell, Donald G., Preface to the *Semi-Centennial Historical and Biographical Record of the Class of 1841 in Yale College.*
9. Tomes, Nancy, *A generous confidence, Thomas Story Kirkbride and the art of asylum-keeping, 1840-1883*, Cambridge University Press, New York, 1984, pages 170-171.
10. John Curwen letter to Thomas Kirkbride, January 15, 1852.
11. John Curwen letter to Thomas Kirkbride, April 5, 1851.
12. The *Harrisburg Patriot*, September 2, 1899.
13. The *Harrisburg Patriot*, September 2, 1899.
14. Canvas suits were placed as restraints on patients who were prone to destroying their clothing.
15. John Curwen letter to Thomas Kirkbride, April 30, 1851.
16. John Curwen letter to Thomas Kirkbride, April 5, 1851.
17. In 1899 the *Harrisburg Patriot* stated: "There is not a smirch on his reputation." *Harrisburg Patriot*, September 2, 1899, page 1.
18. This date is not consistent with the comment he reportedly made to Dorothea Dix about marriage.
19. Her uncle, Francis Wyeth, distinguished himself as a hospital commissioner from Pennsylvania during the Civil War and her cousin John Wyeth was a senior partner of Wyeth Brothers pharmaceutical company in Philadelphia.
20. Hartz, Fred & Hoshino, Arthur Y., *Warren State Hospital*, Warren, Pennsylvania, 1981, page 83.
21. Davis, Patricia Talbot, op. cit., page 72.
22. He was still an elder of and a major contributor to the Harrisburg church when Anna was buried from it in 1899. *The Harrisburg Telegraph*, September 6, 1899.
23. Patricia Davis claims that Curwen's death was due to a chill he caught, after insisting on wearing his winter underwear in an alumni parade at Yale on a hot day in late June. Davis, Patricia Talbot, op. cit., page 73.

VIII

EARLY YEARS

If the hand of Thomas Story Kirkbride worked invisibly in installing John Curwen as the first superintendent of the Pennsylvania State Lunatic Hospital, it worked openly and indelibly in establishing the rules for running the new institution. At the trustee's second meeting in March, 1851 at the Front Street home of Luther Reily, Kirkbride presented an extensive "draft" of his proposed "By-Laws" for the hospital—eight chapters of detailed instructions, including job descriptions for each of the major staff positions.

Rule one of the third chapter of the by-laws, which was entitled "Of the Superintendent," made it clear how and by whom the hospital would be managed. It opened:

> The Superintendent shall be the Chief Executive Officer of the Hospital. He shall appoint and exercise entire control over all subordinate officers and assistants in the institution and shall have entire direction of the duties of the same.

While John Curwen was the appointed superintendent, this was to be a Kirkbride-run hospital—one in which moral treatment was supreme. Rule number four of this same chapter directed that the superintendent "shall visit all the patients daily, or learn their condition." The chapter, moreover, which dealt with the assistant physician, directed him to accompany the superintendent on his morning rounds as well as to visit the patients each evening. The assistant also was to "make himself intimately acquainted with their disorder, exert over them all the moral influence in his power, and direct their exercise and amusements."

John Curwen did object to his mentor about several of the rules. Of the one concerning employment of a chaplain, he wrote Kirkbride: "I have no confidence that we will be able to obtain the regular services of the clergy in this place."[1] And he complained in general over the "union of the by- laws and the instructions."[2] They stayed, however, the way Kirkbride drafted them—comprehensive and detailed.

Governor William Johnston also requested removal later in March, when Curwen took the by-laws to him for review, of the rule that related "to all communications verbal or written passing through the Superindendent" ... Curwen told him rather curtly simply to "erase the obnoxious clause." The Governor "drew his pen through it" and the hospital's by-laws were ready to go to the printer.[3]

* * * *

That spring and summer of 1851, John Curwen was busy overseeing the completion of the building and in readying it for the admission of patients. He moved to Harrisburg in early April and soon was involved in problems of completing the interior. "The workmen cannot finish the plastering until the river falls because they ran out of sand and can't bring it in until the river diminishes." And there was much work to be done, even after John Haviland completed and turned the building over to the trustees.

The superintendent complained to the trustees, for example, that the water closets used "ten times the amount of water that an ordinary water closet does." He was authorized to fix them. He and Joseph Konigmacher, who headed the trustees' committee on furnishings, also had to buy bedding, furniture, clothing for the patients, dishes and kitchen utensils—much of it in Philadelphia. After one such trip Curwen wrote: "My eyes are a little inflamed ... by the sparks from the locomotive which kept flying in my eyes every few minutes" (a train ride in the days prior to ventilating systems meant open windows.) He needed to hire a gardener, too, but it was months before the board gave him permission to do so. He claimed that "their heads are so full of other matters that it is next to impossible to confine them to one subject until a definite answer has been reached."

The placement of the wash house and the stable also were

critical items about which he and the trustees debated. The most interesting, however, was the decision over where to locate the entrance road to the hospital. The architect, with the commissioners' approval, proposed placing it in the low-lying meadow in front of the building. From this position there was an impressive view of the hospital, but having been on site frequently that spring, Curwen knew that the meadow (actually part of Wetzel's Swamp) was flooded during heavy rains. When he had tried to inspect the site, he had been "obliged to climb along the fence for some distance" to keep out of the water.[4] Eventually he reported, they agreed to place it "just as I wanted it."

The new superintendent also had some personal items of concern. He complained to Hugh Campbell, one of the several physicians on the board of trustees, about his salary. Curwen expected the "prerequisites to include board, furnished apartments, a domestic and the use or keeping of a horse and carriage." This, he claimed, was "the same in details as given superintendents elsewhere." Campbell dismissed him with a "there was nothing said about anything but board."[5] There is no written record of how the issue was settled, but undoubtedly Curwen got, at least, some of the "prerequisites" that he wanted.

* * * *

On October 1, 1851, John Curwen wrote in his *Journal:* "This was the day fixed upon for the acceptance of patients but none came. A watchman and watchwoman, four male attendants and one female are now here."[6]

The first patient finally appeared at the doors of the Pennsylvania State Lunatic Hospital on October 6, 1851. She was Elizabeth B- of Londonderry Township. The 42 year old wife of a carpenter, she was suffering from dyspepsia and melancholy. This probably was brought on by the death of two of her three children the previous July from scarlet fever. Following the loss of her children, she "was taken" in the words of Curwen, "with the idea that she can never die." Inexplicably, she had attempted to strangle herself but in the superintendent's judgment she had "no propensity to suicide" by the time she came to the hospital.

When she was admitted, her husband, Joseph, had agreed to pay $3.00 weekly for her board, to pay for her clothing, which was provided by the hospital, and for any damages she might cause to hospital furniture or property. The standard contract form that John Curwen had prepared, with the approval of the Board of Trustees, required that three persons (one of whom must be a physician) certify "that they believe the patient to be insane." For Elizabeth, her husband, Benjamin Meisse, a Middletown, Pennsylvania doctor, and a C. Caslow signed the form.[7]

In the months following her admittance, she improved gradually and appeared "quite comfortable" in her new surroundings. At times of visits from her husband, however, she became very much troubled and distressed. John Curwen's first patient then was a "textbook" moral treatment case. She had come for cure during the early stages of her illness; she was away from her home environment (which apparently contributed to her anxiety); and she had been placed in a modern, family-type facility located in a rural setting.

On January 8, 1852, Joseph came and took his wife home against the advice of John Curwen.

When Joseph first drove their wagon up the winding, gravel roadway to the hospital, the couple confronted a large, impressive building, second only to the State Capitol two miles away in the city. The center building of the Pennsylvania State Lunatic Hospital was four stories high, surmounted by a dome. There was a long flight of twenty steps leading up to the entrance, which was covered by a large Tuscan portico. On either side of the center building, the wings, each of three stories, extended outward in sections (or projections, as the architect called them) and were arranged so that the second section receded twenty feet behind the first and the third twenty feet behind the second. In this way each projection was open at both ends. This "rendered them light and cheerful, and insured a free natural ventilation at all times."[8]

From the top of the front steps, the Susquehanna River was in full view, including the new Pennsylvania railroad bridge at Rockville. The village of Dauphin reposed just beyond the bridge at the foot of the mountain. Along the northern line of the landscape, stretching the whole length of the horizon, were the Blue Mountains. The "passage of the cars on the railroad and the boats on the canal formed an agreeable and diversifying feature."[9]

By late October, 1851, there were 12 patients in the Pennsylvania State Lunatic Hospital—six males and six females. They were a cross-section of Pennsylvanians. John O- of Philadelphia, a 24-year-old single man, had been at sea for several years in charge of vessels belonging to his father. His insanity commenced about three years before his admittance. He was under the "delusion" that a certain girl was following him wherever he went and that she was the cause of "all his troubles." Five days after John O- arrived at the hospital, the superintendent wrote in his patient log: " ... strongly suspect that his insanity was brought on by masturbation and that he continues the habit though not yet able to obtain any decisive evidence of the fact."

The "solitary vice," as he called it, was a subject to which John Curwen returned on several occasions during the next few years. In 1857 he gave it as the cause of insanity for 28 males and one female patient and claimed that it was "more productive of insanity than would appear by reference to the tables given." He went on to explain: "It may safely be affirmed, without fear of contradiction, that nothing undermines the nervous system more insidiously, but more certainly; and it is also painfully true, that in no class of cases is the prospect of restoration so unfavorable."[10]

Farmers or the wives of farmers made up nearly half of the patient population during the first years that the hospital was open. Jane D- of Clearfield County was one of these. She was 30 years old and the mother of nine children. Jane's "derangement" was attributed to the death of her mother during Jane's confinement with her last child. She was "impressed with the idea that her heart was dead and consequently she has no life in her." Jane was admitted on October 22, 1853 and escaped from her ward by slipping under the window guards on December 5.[11] She "eloped" again on February 7, 1853 and somehow made her way as far as Lewistown. In

March of the the following year, she, too, was discharged when her husband came for her. A year later John Curwen heard from her husband that she had been perfectly well since her return home.

* * * *

At five each morning the hospital steward, William Slay-maker, would ring the wake-up bell. The assistants and the attendants were expected to rise immediately and start work for the day within the half hour. (The steward was also responsible for seeing "that they retired in proper season at night.") The attendants would waken the patients, see that they were washed and their hair combed and that they were properly dressed for the day. The bedding was to be aired and the floors swept. The assistants helped with these chores as well as in setting the tables in the two dining rooms (the men and women ate in separate rooms in the center building). The matron, meanwhile, was busy in the kitchen and the dining rooms overseeing the preparations for breakfast.

The steward and the matron were the most important non-medical individuals in the hospital. The steward not only took care of all the buying (including furniture, implements and even farm stock) and the accounts (including patient charges) but also saw to the opening and closing of the house each day, its security, as well as its cleanliness, warmth and ventilation. It was he, moreover, who was "to receive visitors, give them suitable information and accompany them to such parts of the building and grounds as are open for examination." Curwen had trouble filling this position with the right man. He eventually hired Will Slaymaker on a probationary basis, later promoted him as the steward, but was forced to dismiss him less than a year later.

The matron, Mary Ann Wilt, was in charge of all the domestic concerns of the institution, including seeing "that the bedding and the clothing of the patients were always kept clean and in good order." She had oversight and direction of the domestics and superintended the cooking and distribution of the food. She also was responsible "to see that the supply [of food] was abundant, varied, well cooked and neatly served in all the dining rooms." Wilt stayed at Harrisburg for over 15 years. She was hired in the fall of 1851 on a probationary basis and it was not until the following April that Curwen approached the trustees to make her permanent and to start paying her. She, of course, received board and had a room on the first floor of the center building as did the steward.

The Curwens' more spacious quarters were on the second floor of the main structure, while the domestics lived in basement rooms under the wings. The attendants had rooms near the patients' wards for which they were responsible. Speaking tubes and bells were used to communicate between the wards and the kitchen so that the attendants never had to leave their charges.

* * * *

The new superintendent's duties extended well beyond those of a medical practitioner. He was not only responsible for each patient's care and welfare, he was also the hospital's personnel director, its building manager, its public face—in short, its alter ego.

No responsibility was so heavy that the head of the hospital was not expected to shoulder it; no chore was so trivial that he could permit it to slip between his fingers. One of his earliest tasks concerned the hospital's inability to find a regular supply of butter and eggs for the kitchen. That first October, John Curwen spent days driving all over Dauphin County searching for a farmer willing to furnish them. Finally late in the month, near Hummelstown, he found a farmer, John Hummel, who was willing to supply them. The butter was dear at 18 cents but at least for the next year, his patients would have butter for their bread as well as eggs for their breakfast. The baker, too, he felt would be pleased. The road tolls of 37.5 cents between Harrisburg and Hummelstown would have to be added each week to the cost of the butter and eggs but at last this job was done.

On October 14 Curwen reported: "Election day. Started the fires under the steam boilers; apparatus works well with only a few leaks."[12] Although Birkinbine's "apparatus" did its job that first winter, he had difficulties getting and keeping a fireman to operate it. On November 5 the superintendent wrote in his journal that the "fireman entered on his duties." Two weeks later he "discharged the fireman as he was unwilling to perform the duties assigned him." It was not until December 2 that a "new fireman entered on his duties." In the interim, John Curwen saw to the house's heat, which was maintained "generally at a summer's temperature."[13]

Much of the heat that was generated, however, escaped through the windows that Haviland had installed. In early November, Curwen again wrote to Thomas Kirkbride:

> A northwester is roaring around, making the windows rattle and throwing in an abundance of cool air through every crack and crevice and you may know that any abundance of them are to be found about this house. The windows are so fitted that in many of them an opening through which your finger may be pushed is found. ... I could occupy a sheet with accounts of such things, doors shrunk so as to blow open with the wind, the room doors in the wards hardly allowing the bolt to catch.[14]

In what must have been a novel idea for the day, the superintendent recommended to the trustees that the windows be "double sashed" to cut down on the heat loss, although there is no record that this was ever done. On December 1, he reported another storm of "fearful violence." "You may have heard the wind blow but if you want to hear it *war*, this is the place," he wrote to Kirkbride.[15] On this occasion, he admitted to being thankful for Haviland's work, which did not sustain any damage.

That first December in Harrisburg John Curwen was busy thinking about how to put together his first annual report, which was due in January 1852. He suggested to Kirkbride arranging it thus: "first an account of the admissions, then some remarks on insanity and early treatment and then a short sketch of the efforts to establish the Hospital with a general account of the buildings, dealing entirely in generalities and descending to as few particulars as possible." He apparently had learned his lessons well while at the Pennsylvania Hospital for the Insane in Philadelphia. The final report, the longest narrative report the doctor was to write, followed the plan he had described. It did, however, also include an extensive, detailed description of the buildings and the grounds.

While the trustees would second-guess their superintendent and usually had the last word (when he had wanted the plaster painted as a moral treatment issue, they had insisted that it be white-washed to save money), John Curwen was largely on his own. In a December 1851 letter it seems that perhaps at times he was a little unsure of himself and would have appreciated some advice and counsel, or at least occasional access to the trustees. In it he wrote:

> Our visiting trustees do not trouble themselves much about us; Dr. Reily and Dr. Rutherford visited us three times in six weeks and now Dr. Reily says their time is up and it is the time of the other two; none of them have been near us for a fortnight nor has our treasurer visited us officially since the opening of the institution. When the trustees did visit us they only wanted to see such parts of the house as contained patients and were always in a hurry to be off. I do not like such a way of doing things but it does not become me to say anything ... [16]

* * * *

The superintendent, on the other hand, was expected to make periodic trips each year to report to the governor and then to the State Capitol to present and then to defend his annual appropriations requests. Although he seldom got everything he asked for, the presence of influential friends during the early years ensured that his requests were considered favorably.

Joseph Konigmacher, of Ephrata, was one of these friends. Konigmacher, an influential state figure between the years of 1837 and 1855, first came to prominence as a member of the Reform Convention, which was responsible for revising the Pennsylvania Constitution in 1837-1838. He was elected a state legislator in 1838 and a state senator 10 years later. It was he who authored the three Acts to establish a state mental hospital in Pennsylvania. Later, as a member of the Senate Appropriations Committee, for a number of years he helped push through Curwen's annual appropriation requests for the Pennsylvania State Lunatic Hospital.[17] If anyone associated with the the hospital's establishment deserves to be known as the "Forgotten Samaritan," it is Joseph Konigmacher.

Konigmacher was, in spite of his personal wealth, always strongly identified and popular with the working class. Even his name, which meant awning maker, helped to endear him with the Pennsylvania Germans he represented. A short, heavy set man, he was of a kind, amiable disposition. At one time he owned great amounts of property in Ephrata, including a farm, a hotel and a tannery and was President of the Reading and Columbia Railroad. He died broke, however, in 1861 in Michaels's hotel in Lancaster.[18]

Michaels' hotel, at 17 North Queen Street, was little more than a rooming house. John Michaels, the proprietor, also lived upstairs. The former state lawmaker made out his will the day before he died. It is not clear whether he knew the full extent of his liabilities, but when Konigmacher's estate was settled they exceeded his assets and his heirs were left with nothing. His wife had died the year before and their son became a ward of her brother.

After the departure of Konigmacher, things became a little more difficult. In an 1861 letter John Curwen mentioned that "I had a talk with the Chairman of the Committee of Ways and Means and then made a statement to the Committee about our appropriation and the next morning the Chairman told me they had agreed to report $20,000. Today I see by the North American they have reported $15,000. There must be a mistake somewhere in the matter."[19]

* * * *

In his first annual report, John Curwen, made a point of stressing the advantages of early treatment and the success of an uninterrupted course of treatment until restoration is effected. "An impression is very generally prevalent in certain classes of the community that a few weeks' hospital treatment is sufficient to effect a decided change or restoration, ... and disappointment and dissatisfaction are expressed by friends if this result be not perceived; ... very few cases entirely recover in less than from three to six months."

He also felt that it was necessary to try to dispel the idea of supernatural origins for insanity. (There were already two patients in the hospital, one whose condition he recorded as "Religious excitement" and the other as "Millerism.")[20] Choosing his words very carefully the doctor wrote: "There have been those who believed, and many still continue to entertain the belief, that insanity is to be attributed to supernatural agency; that it is either a direct punishment from the Almighty, by visitation of God, for sins committed, or that it is through the agency of the Prince of Darkness. That such *might be,* the fact is not denied, but it is much more in accordance with true religion and sound philosophy to refer it to natural causes, which are known to be effective in its production."

He went on to describe insanity as "being a deranged manifestation of the mental and moral faculties, caused by disorder in the organs by means of which those faculties act." Thus he continued, "it is obvious that the earlier remedial measures are applied, the sooner, in all probability, will those derangements be corrected and removed." When he read these words, Thomas Kirkbride must have been gratified with the choice of John Curwen as the superintendent of the first state lunatic hospital in Pennsylvania.

* * * *

Although the superintendent was convinced that the supernatural had nothing to do with the onset of insanity, his many references to storms and to the wind in and around the hospital do bring to mind that many people in the nineteenth century (and some even today) believed that the weather, just as "luna," the moon, directly affected an individual's mood and behavior. Attacks of depression and melancholia or of manias and general excitement were often attributed to natural events. It is doubtful that Curwen placed credence in the idea, nevertheless, references to the elements (unconscious concerns, perhaps) crop up regularly in his correspondence and his journal.

His first annual report also acknowledged that he had been wrong on one point. "To the clergy who have officiated in the chapel," he wrote, "we are under obligations for the very satisfactory manner in which these exercises were conducted." The chapel, which was on the third floor of the main building, contained a stained glass window in the center of which was a copy of the coat of arms of the State of Pennsylvania. The window was a gift of Martha Elmer Curwen. The superintendent also reported that, although they were not able to get crops into the ground, they did get the garden and fields plowed for the next spring's planting.

During that first year of operation, there were numerous gifts to the Pennsylvania State Hospital for the Insane. In addition to Mrs. Curwen's stained glass window for the chapel, Dorothea Dix got a member of the Society of Friends to donate a "large and very handsome Bible." In the next few years the hospital received gifts of every description from individuals in all walks of life. Simon Cameron and Judge John C. Kunkel of Harrisburg sent seeds for the garden; the Presbyterian Board of Publications forwarded a large collection of books for the library; William Calder, Jr. sent a horse and some chickens; there were flying squirrels from Gettysburg ("for the amusement of the patients"); a kaleidoscope, an African monkey, a large steam horn, deer for the "Pleasure Grounds," and a very beautiful copy of one of Landseer's finest engravings, "The Free Kirk."

A number of editors of Pennsylvania newspapers also began the practice of providing a regular supply of their issues, "thus contributing to the entertainment and restoration of the patients." The first of these was the *Democratic Union* of Harrisburg. By the end of the decade, however, there were more than 55 from all over the state, many with unusual, even exotic names such as: the *People's Advocate* from York, the *Mining Register* of Pottsville, the *Valley Spirit,* from Chambersburg, the *Perry County Freeman*, the *Venango Spectator*, the *Warren Ledger*, the *Lewistown Gazette*, the *Muncy Luminary*, the *American Volunteer* from Carlisle and the *Genius of Liberty* from Uniontown.

* * * *

The patients at the Pennsylvania State Lunatic Hospital came from every class and occupation. There were blacksmiths, carpenters, coopers, dyers, farmers, laborers, lawyers, lumbermen, millers, ministers, shoemakers, teachers, even an umbrella maker. Most of the women were listed as "wives of" or "daughters of" men in one of the above occupational categories, although there were a few teachers, domestics and seamstresses listed.

The causes of insanity for over half of those that were admitted was given as "unknown." For to whom Curwen was able to ascribe some cause, "so far as they could be traced," he listed the following: domestic trouble, grief, disappointment, over-exertion, failure in business, fright, injury of the head, loss of money, ill treatment, intemperance, childbirth, opium eating, spiritual rapping, anxiety, Millerism, excessive study and novel reading. After unknown, domestic trouble headed the list of the reasons given for his patients' insanity. Among the men separately, "intemperance" was cited most often and among the women "disordered menstruation." Most of these reasons were taken at the time of admittance from the patient or a family member and are, of course, unreliable though interesting.

Curwen frankly acknowledged that "great difficulty is experienced in arriving at even an approximation to the true history, in a great majority of cases," and that the hospital needed to do a better job of gathering pre-admittance patient histories. Sometimes, weeks after a patient's admittance, he would write letters to family members soliciting information about "the onset" of an individual's delusions. For these reasons, he explained to the legislature, "further caution is necessary in placing a proper estimate on the cause con-

86

sidered influential in bringing on the attack of derangement. The cause assigned may be only the immediate exciting cause, in which case the long train of events, in progress before this, fails to receive a proper consideration; and also, moral and physical causes may both, as in a large number of cases is the fact, contribute their portion, and only one of them will be stated as the cause."[21]

It was natural for family members to seek the comfort of a single traumatic event on which to place the blame, especially one that was outside of the home. An unrequited love, a loss of business, a visit to an "anatomical museum" or one to a pornography shop, or being in Ford's Theater the night Lincoln was shot; all were the sort of causes which were sufficient in the eyes of many laymen to bring on the destruction of a previously normal mind.[22]

Curwen's statistics also made a great deal out of the "place of nativity" of the patients. He felt that those "who are natives of other countries" were subject to "a different class of causes." He went on to explain that "the disappointment of their hopes, so fondly cherished and often so rudely crushed, the entire change of climate and mode of life, the difficulty of obtaining employment and support for their families, with the too frequent resort to intoxicating drinks, all contribute their share to bring on that condition of the system which ends in insanity."[23]

One area that especially concerned him was the number of young children that he had to treat. His very first year at Harrisburg there were two, a boy of six and a half years and a girl of thirteen. The following year there was a little girl, three years and four months old. Curwen seems to have believed that forced, excessive study was the primary cause for this situation. In 1858 he took the education system to task for their "neglect of hygienic measures, which are as applicable to mind as to the body." He went on to explain:

> The great tendency of the period is to over- exertion and stimulation in every department—the haste to be accounted learned, as well as the haste to be rich, and the moral of the fable of the hare and the tortoise, is more frequently neglected than heeded.

As a general thing children are sent to school too young, and if they manifest any evidence of smartness, they are encouraged and urged forward to a degree their powers are unable to bear ... Under ten years of age very little mental effort should be required of children, and they should be allowed a large amount of exercise, bodily health and strength being more necessary and desirable than any learning ... The good old rule of what is worth doing, is worth well doing, is too much over-looked, and instead of laying deep and strong the foundations, and impressing on the mind carefully and thoroughly the fundamental principles, they are passed over hurriedly and slightly, and ever after the super-structure is found weak and defective, where it should be firm and steady.

But while the mind has been kept hour after hour thus engaged, now on one study, then on another, the body has been suffering the penalty of the close confinement; the limbs and the back ache, the head feels heavy and dull, and an indescribable feeling of uneasiness and restlessness comes over the whole frame ... Leaving out of account all physiological laws which are thus ruthlessly violated, it must be evident to every reflective mind, that a repetition of such a state of things must inevitably result in injury either to the body or the mind, and probably to both.

Regular bodily exercise should be as much a part of every system of education; ... and this exercise should be at such intervals in the day, that all the evil effects before mentioned may be obviated.[24]

Several of the children at Harrisburg were epileptic. There was little, however, that Curwen could do other than to place such patients in a quiet environment and on a regulated diet, hoping to reduce their excitement and thus the frequency and severity of their convulsive attacks. Of the young boy, Curwen wrote: "I am very much interested in him but have not quite made up my mind what to do with him." He described him as "a quick, bright boy with a bright intelligent countenance" and asked Thomas Kirkbride to look at him during his next trip to Harrisburg. Of the young girl, he mentioned that her epileptic convulsions had ceased six months ago following "a severe attack of bilious fever."[25]

There were other cases, too, for which the superintendent was not able to offer much help. In 1853 a widow was admitted, who had "a peculiar bronzed appearance of the skin" and who frequently asked her doctor to explain the reason for "her becoming so much like a mulatto." Curwen was unable to assign any cause to the woman's condition, but after her death in 1856 he heard of the cases described by Thomas Addison, of London. The symptoms of his patient at Harrisburg corresponded in all essential respects with those described by the London doctor.[26] The cause of Addison's Disease is still unknown today.

Curwen's diagnoses of his patients' illnesses fell into a few relatively simple categories: Mania, (acute, chronic and epileptic), monomania, melancholia and dementia. Patients afflicted by melancholia and acute mania appear to have constituted the greater number of his admissions. These two groups, moreover, seem to be the primary ones for which moral treatment was intended. Melancholy patients were listless, complained of bodily problems and always seemed to be struggling with periods of depression. It was anticipated that removing these individuals from their work or home situation and placing them in an attractive, clean rural environment with kindly attendants would help many achieve "restoration."

Those patients suffering from acute mania (the garrulous, the gesticulating, the violent), on the other hand, could be segregated into the seventh or eighth wards. There, closely watched, but without restraints in most cases, they were free to work out their delusions, while their "alienated minds" gradually healed under the care of their "alienist" physician. It was, of course, such patients who most frequently were subjected to depleting regimens, such as purges. Curwen seems, however, to have used bloodletting or restraints very seldom.

More of the melancholy patients were women than men. "One singular circumstance respecting our female patients," the superintendent wrote, "is that four of them are melancholy; one when she came had two lives and could not die; the next her heart was dead; the third can never die and the fourth dies quite a number of times in the day."[27]

By 1853 Curwen was beginning to report patient "restorations." That year there were 27 out of the 269 under treatment. One of them was a female patient Mary B-. He wrote to Thomas Kirkbride that "she had turned poetess since she left the Hospital ... She has written some quite lovely pieces." Unlike many other superintendents, he always stated his data on restorations in whole numbers and never reduced them to percentages. There were also 17 deaths as well as 7 "elopements" that year. Among those that walked away were four of the men who had been sent to Harrisburg from the Eastern State Penitentiary. Curwen reported that "the influence direct and reflex exerted by them, was without any qualification bad."[28]

* * * *

Finances were a continual problem. In January, 1855, the trustees told the governor: "The present condition of the hospital, financially, as your Excellency and the Legislature must perceive, requires immediate attention. Two hundred and fourteen miserable human beings requiring their daily bread, anxious creditors demanding their just dues, with an empty treasury! The only possible means of supply, until the Legislature shall extend relief, will be a floating list of claims due the hospital by the counties of Cambria, Bucks, Philadelphia, Greene, Bradford, Tioga, Crawford, Luzerne, Northumberland, etc., some of long standing, which the trustees have found most difficult to collect. This neglect on the part of the county authorities to defray the actual cost of their insane poor, in the State Hospital, is inexcusable; and it is thought right and just the fact should be known, that it may be remedied."

The trustees contended that their problems stemmed from having adopted a credit system, which necessitated that they estimate their income. These estimates, of course, were unreliable. They claimed a cash system would permit them to save money for the state by yielding lower prices for the merchandise that they bought. Having insufficient funds to do this, they continued to buy goods on credit. The state had appropriated twenty-five thousand dollars for the hospital in January, 1854, all of which had been expended, and the trustees reported "we commence the new year with a debt of twelve thousand eight hundred dollars." The following year the situation was no better. To shame those who owed the hospital money, they listed in their 1855 annual report the 58 governmental units that were in arrears. Leading the list was the City of Philadelphia with $1,419.30. The cash problem was so bad that, in the annual reports for several years, the accounts showed an "amount due to the treasurer," John A. Weir, for money he personally had advanced the hospital to pay some of its bills.

There were also natural disasters. On the afternoon of June 16, 1855, a tornado passed over the hospital. Although it was confined to a very narrow limit, its violence and the damage it caused were severe. The carriage house roof was blown off and one wall blown in so that it was necessary to take the building down. The north museum roof was bodily lifted off and the tin scattered in different directions over the grounds. The slate and spouting, moreover, on the main building, especially that over the portico, was badly damaged. Many of the largest trees nearby and about a quarter of the fencing around the grounds was "prostrated."[29]

And among the setbacks, Curwen had to report the following year that "the long continued dry weather of the summer and fall disappointed our expectations ... from our farming operation. ... the failure having been principally in our great staple for winter use, potatoes. Moreover, he stated, "the continued rain during the early part of the autumn of the previous year rendered the ground ... so wet as to interfere with its proper cultification, and consequently we had no wheat this year."[30].

There were also man-made problems. Shortly before 11 o'clock on the night of May 12, 1859, the barn was discovered to be on fire. According to the superintendent, "It was half gone before the first persons could reach it." He went on to state that "there was no reasonable doubt that it was the work of a man who had at one time been an inmate of the hospital." The ex-patient, Martin Henry W., had returned to the hospital, from which he had previously walked away, and asked John Curwen to give him a "release." When his request was refused, Martin became abusive, broke up furniture, and threatened to kill the doctor. Taken to the Dauphin County jail for his behavior, Martin was later found innocent by reason of insanity and sent to the poor farm. He walked away from the farm within hours of his arrival and returned to the hospital grounds to get even. The barn and the sheds and the fencing destroyed by the fire, which were covered by insurance, were quickly rebuilt.

Progress on improving and expanding the Pennsylvania State Lunatic Hospital continued, however, in spite of all these difficulties. Construction, to the patients, must have seemed to be almost a part of hospital life. In 1856 the water works was erected in the hollow to the southeast of the hospital buildings. The dam was capable of holding about 400,000 gallons of water. The water was driven through six- inch pipes to the washhouse and the center building by a 10 horse-power steam engine and pump. In the main building the water was pumped to two 29,000-gallon tanks on the top floor. A branch line was laid to the garden, so as "to furnish an abundant supply to the gardens in case of need." And four fire plugs also were installed across the grounds in front of the center building.[31]

There were also other accomplishments to report. The Harrisburg *Morning Herald* of September 27, 1855 mentioned the fine cattle and swine from the hospital that were in the stalls at the state fair held in the city that year. Patchwork spreads and hearth rugs made by the women at the Pennsylvania State Lunatic Hospital also were on display. The fair was important enough that President Franklin Pierce, "accompanied by his suite," spent several days visiting the many agricultural, mechanical and floral exhibits. There he watched plowing contests, looked over displays of sewing machines, saws, pianos and French needlework. There were also preserves and pickles, a "self-acting" gate and an adjustable invalid's bedstead for him to see.

The President, whose wife, Jane, suffered from severe bouts

of melancholia, took one afternoon off from inspecting the "handsome display of stock cattle" at the Harrisburg fair and visited the hospital. He was shown through the building by the superintendent and "expressed satisfaction with the arrangements of the establishment."[32]

END NOTES

1. John Curwen, letter to Thomas Kirkbride, March 20, 1851.
2. John Curwen, letter to Thomas Kirkbride, February 27, 1851.
3. John Curwen, letter to Thomas Kirkbride, March 24, 1851.
4. Ibid.
5. John Curwen, letter to Thomas Kirkbride, March 20, 1851. In addition to Kirkbride, Reily and Campbell the original board of trustees included another physician, John K. Mitchell. Originally from Virginia, he had become a prominent Philadelphia physician by the time he was appointed to the board. He was the Professor of the Practice of Medicine at Jefferson Medical College and was also a close friend of Kirkbride's. Mitchell's son, S. Weir Mitchell (1829-1914), a notable neurologist, later became one of the outspoken opponents, however, of asylum medicine as practiced by Kirkbride and Curwen.
6. The primary duty of the watchman and the watchwoman was to walk the house at night and watch for fires. The stairs at the end of each of the wards were made of iron as a safety measure.
7. In 1869 Ebenezer Haskell, Thomas Kirkbride's nemesis, successfully lobbied the Pennsylvania State Legislature for a law requiring that two doctors certify to a patient's insanity.
8. Curwen, John, "Superintendent's Report," *First Annual Report of the Board of Trustees of the State Lunatic Hospital*, page 10.
9. Ibid., page 11.
10. Curwen, John, "Superintendent's Report," *Annual Report of the Trustees of the State Lunatic Hospital*, 1856, A. Boyd Hamilton, Harrisburg, 1857, page 14.
11. The upper sash of each window throughout the building was made of cast iron and was stationary in its frame. The lower sash was wooden and moveable, but was covered with a wrought-iron guard on the outside. In adherence to good "Kirkbride-design" the screening was on the inside of the windows to reduce the patient's access to glass. The use of iron sashes was a typical moral treatment measure. It meant that patients did not have to be chained and that the windows were not covered with exterior iron gratings, which gave a prison-like appearance.
12. Curwen, John, *Journal.*
13. John Curwen, letter to Thomas Kirkbride, December 1, 1851. This apparently was a perennial problem. In December, 1852, he again reported: "My engineer went off on Wednesday and left things in such a state that I was obliged to act as an engineer myself during the day."
14. John Curwen, letter to Thomas Kirkbride, November 3, 1851.
15. John Curwen, letter to Thomas Kirkbride, December 1, 1851.
16. Ibid.
17. Spohn, Clarence E., editor, *Journal of The Historical Society of the Cocalico Valley*, Vol. XIV, 1989, pages 32-33.
18. Harris, Alex, *A Biographical History of Lancaster County*, Elias Barr & Co., Lancaster, Pa., 1872, page 346.
19. John Curwen, letter to Thomas Kirkbride, March 4, 1861. The *North American* was a Philadelphia newspaper.

20. Millerites, or the followers of William Miller, a Protestant revivalist, believed that the Second Coming of Christ would occur on October 22, 1844. Many of them disposed of all their property and gathered on an upstate New York hillside to await the event. Disillusioned by the date's uneventful passing, most of Miller's 100,000 followers left the movement. For years, however, patients at institutions around the country occasionally would identify the cause of their dementia as "Millerism."

21. Curwen, John, "Superintendent's Report", *Report of the Board of Trustees of the State Lunatic Hospital of the State of Pennsylvania, 1854*, pages 13.

22. Tomes, Nancy, op. cit., pages 94-95.

23. Curwen, John, "Superintendent's Report", *Report of the Board of Trustees of the State Lunatic Hospital of the State of Pennsylvania, 1854*, pags 13.

24. Curwen, John, "Superintendent's Report, *Report of the Board of Trustees of the State Lunatic Hospital of the State of Pennsylvania, 1858*, pages 15-16.

25. Curwen, John, "Superintendent's Report," *First Annual Report of the Board of Trustees of the State Lunatic Hospital of the State of Pennsylvania*, page 6.

26. Thomas Addison first described these symptoms in a paper he read before a London medical society in 1849. In 1855 he expanded his ideas in a book *On the Constitutional and Local Effects of Disease of the Suprarenal Capsules*. It would appear, based on this evidence, that Curwen was well read or at least well informed on current medical practices.

27. John Curwen, letter to Thomas Kirkbride, December 1, 1851.

28. The practice of assigning convicted criminals, who were judged to be insane, to the nearest state mental hospital (with the expectation that they would be secured as well as treated) continued until the twentieth century. Many including those sent to the Harrisburg facility simply walked away (often to the relief of the superintendent). Today separate, secure facilities have been designated for the criminally insane.

29. Curwen, John, "Superintendent's Report," *Annual Report of the Board of Trustees of the State Lunatic Hospital of the State of Pennsylvania for 1855*, A. Boyd Hamilton, State Printer, 1856, page 18.

30. Curwen, John, "Superintendent's Report," *Annual Report of the Trustees of the State Lunatic Hospital, 1857*, A. Boyd Hamilton, Harrisburg, 1858.

31. Curwen, John, "Superintendent's Report," *Annual Report of the Trustees of the State Lunatic Hospital, 1856*, A. Boyd Hamilton, Harrisburg, 1857.

32. *The Morning Herald*, September 29, 1855. The Pierces had lost three sons, the last in a train accident in which the parents were unhurt. Jane Pierce interpreted this as a sign that God intended that her husband be free of family concerns so as to be able to carry out his responsibilities as President. She seldom ventured out of her rooms in the White House and spent her time writing notes to her dead Bennie. Her aunt served as the President's first lady.

IX

CIVIL WAR
&
THE SECOND DECADE

During the final years of the 1850s the grounds and the road system in the rear of the hospital were developed. The individual roads were graded and then, in some cases, macadamized.[1] And early in the spring of 1859, "the grounds immediately in front of the hospital were carefully prepared, and then laid down in grass; and by care and attention during the summer, a beautiful lawn was secured." This lawn, from which a view of the canal, the railroad and the Susquehanna River was possible, contained a large basin for a fountain, the "small sheet of water imparting a freshness and picturesqueness" to the overall scene.[2]

In 1859 John Curwen also reported that a "fine deer park" with trees, a great number of bushes and a fine stream of running water had been enclosed with high fences "secure from all intrusion."[3] And Christmas each year was a "festal day" at the hospital. For a number of Christmases the National Guard Brass Band volunteered their services for a serenade which "enlivened and animated all by their cheerful music." The south reading room was decorated with a Christmas tree and "other devices" and then thrown open to the patients to partake of refreshments provided for them by the hospital's many friends in Harrisburg.[4]

The end of the Pennsylvania State Lunatic Hospital's first decade also saw the coming of the Civil War to Harrisburg. While the "High-Water Mark" of the Confederacy is usually considered to be at Gettysburg, great war activity occurred in Harrisburg throughout the years of the conflict. Located centrally on the rail lines headed both east and west as well as south to Washington and down the Cumberland valley, Harrisburg became one of the great Civil War centers where troops were marshalled for the Army of the Potomac.

Each call of President Lincoln for fresh troops brought a similar call from Pennsylvania's Governor Curtin for volunteers from the state. In the fields between the Susquehanna River and the Pennsylvania Canal, on the high ground across from the meadow through which the trustees had wanted to place the access road to the hospital, Camp Curtin was established in April 1861. Through this camp, the most important of the central Pennsylvania military sites, passed hundreds of thousands of volunteers.[5] The first and often only military training these raw recruits received, before heading south to engage the Confederate Army of Robert E. Lee, was at Camp Curtin. And, after each major battle, the casualties that survived front-line hospital care streamed north back to Harrisburg.[6] The camp was also a mustering-out installation, from which six-month, nine-month, and one-year volunteers were given their final pay and sent home.

Life in the camp was primitive. Many men were without shelter. Dust was everywhere from the tramping of marching soldiers. "I think it is four to six inches deep," one recruit wrote home.[7] Food preparation was limited. Laundry and bathing facilities were practically nonexistent. After they were driven from the Susquehanna River, where they bathed naked in view of the residents on Front Street, the men took to the Pennsylvania Canal, much to the chagrin of local citizens who came to visit the Pennsylvania State Lunatic Hospital.[8]

In addition to caring for an increasing number of its own resident patients, the hospital quickly became an extension of the camp. "Every appliance of the hospital" was "freely placed at their disposal," John Curwen reported. And during the spring and summer of 1861, "thousands of pounds of beef and ham were cooked and hundreds of gallons of coffee were made." Bandages and other articles for the sick also were prepared whenever they were requested by camp authorities, and none were denied the privilege of the laundry.

It became the custom for whole platoons of men to appear at the hospital doors. In one letter the superintendent wrote: "a Lieutenant came with 43 men, marched up in order, were shown through the house, and then asked if they could bathe here. I told them yes and took them in parties of six to a bathroom.''[9] Curwen, who was a firm supporter of the Union cause, later said: "it has been a source of sincere gratification to have been able to have contributed to the comfort and gratification of those who had been summoned to the defence of their country."[10]

The hospital's support, moreover, extended well beyond the hospital grounds at Harrisburg. In a letter to Thomas Kirkbride, the superintendent mentioned that, "under the urgent call of the Governor for medical men to go to Gainesville to attend to the wounded, I have allowed Dr. Schultz to go with the party which will leave here at 1 A.M. tonight."[11] Schultz, one of Curwen's assistant physicians, must have departed tired as he had just returned from taking two patients to Crawford County. Undoubtedly too, the assistant physicians, S. S. Schultz and J. A. Miller, were among the local doctors who, from time to time, were called on to examine the incoming recruits. These examining physicians were unpopular with the men, who felt they were being subjected to unheard-of indignities. "We were stripped," one soldier wrote home, "and brought out simply into an open tent in view of the whole company and we were felt and fingered all over, ... I would have given five dollars to have gotten clear."[12]

Schultz became so active in war duties that by 1863 he left Curwen and was placed in charge of the Cotton Mill hospital.[13] Located in downtown Harrisburg, the mill had been idle for about a year due to the lack of Southern cotton. Its large, warm rooms were ideal for housing the sick and wounded. One patient remembers that "we were very comfortable" there.[14] The mill, the pride of Harrisburg, had been built in 1851 by Charles T. James, United States Senator from Rhode Island, at a cost of $200,000. Power was furnished by a "non-condensing 130 horse power steam engine." James, an advocate of steam power and of manufacturing closer to the source of cotton, constructed the mill in Harrisburg to prove his theories. About two hundred employees worked twelve-hour days before the war, when the mill was producing fine fabrics.

*   *   *   *

Although the Pennsylvania State Lunatic Hospital's facilities and staff were strained by war aid, service to regular patients seemed to go on without serious interruption. There were magic lantern exhibitions (the slides were mainly of scenery and buildings from around the world)[15] and readings from the classics as well as lectures by the assistant physicians and local authorities three evenings each week. The outside speakers talked on a wide variety of subjects; ones such as Buddhism, Cuba, Infusoria, the Holy Land and on the "Future Race of America." Most of these were given by ministers,[16] but one on "the condition and prospects of Syria" was given by a Mr. G. M. Wortabet of "Beyrout."

The hospital also continued to receive a large sampling of newspapers, including even the *Morning Star*, from Dover, New Hampshire and, through the efforts of Miss Dix, from the Philadelphia Fund, numerous books and a new Mason & Hamlin cabinet organ for the Chapel. Over the years this fund, of which Dorothea Dix was the trustee, donated to the hospital cash and articles in the amount of more than five thousand dollars. Among the items was a carriage and horses for the exclusive use of the patients, a dioptic lantern and a polyorama, a melodeon for use in the wards by "convalescent musical patients" and several flutes and violins.[17]

There were visits by the Harmonic Society (a Harrisburg choral group), the Continental Old Folks and the Pupils of the Pennsylvania Institution for the Blind (both apparently singing groups) and by Sanford's Opera Troupe. During the summer and early fall months, moreover, there were concerts by many of the Regimental Bands from Camp Curtin.[18] The museums, reading rooms and the bowling saloon also were "profitable places of resort at those periods when outdoor exercise could not be taken, and much benefit was derived from them." By 1861, Curwen was able to report that the "careful and systematic improvements" being made each year to the hospital's "pleasure grounds" had greatly added to their beauty. The building program also picked up again after the Civil War. In 1866 there were additions to the wash house, along with the installation of a new Shaker Washing Machine and a new Harrison steam boiler which was reputed to be economical in fuel usage.[19]

The farm, the garden and the grapery, which was planted in 1860, were beginning within a few years to "yield abundantly" and to provide "ample returns for the labor bestowed." Not only were they "valuable auxiliaries in the treatment [of patients] by the occupation they afford at different seasons," but they furnished an abundant supply of excellent fruit and vegetables for the residents throughout the year. They also provided income to the hospital through local sales. For the year 1861 receipts totaled $7,478.95 against those of $3,889.97 for expenses.[20]

Potatoes, which were the hospital's year-round staple, were grown in ground that the local farmers had scoffed at. John Curwen was so proud—"We are in capital humor just now at the success of our potato crop," he wrote one fall—that for a number of years he sent the gardener to the Lancaster Fair to show them. He was also able to obtain money from the sale of articles of needlework made by the female patients. With this money and the premiums awarded for their fancy needlework at the Dauphin County Agricultural Fair and also the Pennsylvania State Agricultural Fair, he was able to buy a "fine electrical machine" with which to illustrate most of the facts of that branch of science.

*   *   *   *

In the eighteen-sixties Curwen and Weir, still the hospital's treasurer, seem to have gotten the financial situation somewhat stabilized. Each year, from 1861 to 1865, they received between $40,000 and $45,000 for the board of patients, both private and public supported ones, and an appropriation from the legislature of about $10,000. The legislature, moreover, had responded to the trustees' appeals for help by passing a law in 1859 which authorized the hospital to bring suits in Dauphin County for the recovery of debts due from any of the state's counties or townships for patients who had been moved to Harrisburg from the county poorhouses. This helped materially to close the debt gap. In most cases just the prospect of a suit "had a beneficial effect."[21]

With all these sources of income and that derived from the sale of farm and garden items, the treasurer was able to balance the books, occasionally carrying forward a small amount to the following year—in 1863, the amount was $171.56. By 1867 the state's financial contribution had risen to $15,000 and the amount received from patients to $56,664.71. Expenses kept pace though, and the surplus was a mere $5.17. There is no indication that the hospital received any federal money for goods or services furnished to the soldiers at Camp Curtin, as did private establishments, but presumably this hospital effort was covered by the legislature's annual appropriation. It appears unlikely, moreover, from a review of the accounts, that the beef and pork that the staff prepared for the military was actually from the pantry at the Pennsylvania State Lunatic Hospital.

Just as several miles away the Susquehanna River moved slowly but inexorably, John Curwen reported in 1865 that "the current of Hospital life flows in such an equable stream, and so little disturbed by the various incidents of daily occurrence, that, to a looker on, the slight ripples on the surface only serve to indicate the healthy agitation produced by favoring prosperous gales." He went on to write that "we note only those occurrences which change the usual routine of each day, and by their action increase our joy or sorrow, our anxieties or disappointments, our hopes or fears: so the changes in ordinary Hospital life, during successive years, are so slight, as to afford little matter of interest to those who are not part of that life."[22]

There were problems, however, in spite of the superintendent's claim of an "equable stream." In addition to the Assistant Physican, Schultz, who left in 1863, J. A. Miller resigned the following year. He was replaced by Richard Koch, who only remained one year and one of the two Koch replacements left the year following his appointment, while the other man only stayed two. None of Curwen's assistants seemed to remain more than a few years, although he always lauded them in his annual reports. Most of these younger physicians reportedly resigned to "go into private practice." Whether they were simply using the hospital as a training ground or had difficulty working under the superintendent was never indicated.[23]

Even more vexatious was the problem of retaining attendants. John Curwen frequently reported that he had difficulty finding as well as retaining attendants, especially male ones. He claimed that the hospital took "the best we can find and seek to make them better." His standards, of course, were difficult to attain, even for the best of men. He expected them:

> to commence early in the morning and see that each patient under their care is properly prepared for breakfast; to serve that breakfast and be sure that each one obtains what is needful and sufficient; to put the ward in proper order; and have every part cleanly and as it should be; ... to soothe the fretful, to calm the excited and noisy; to comfort the timid and complaining; to restrain those inclined to mischief; ... to bear calmly and without provocation or resentment the reproaches and taunts which may incessantly pour into their ears; to give to each one that degree of attention which will satisfy them and not excite the jealousy of others; ... to call for the exercise of patience, forebearance and good nature, with a great deal of that gift which we call tact and management.[24]

The problem, however, that exacerbated all the others, was the growing number of patients. This led the trustees in 1867 to report to Governor John W. Geary that "the crowded state of the hospital has caused much anxiety," and that "should an epidemic break out in it, a fearful loss of life might be the result." They went on to state that "there is, therefore, an urgent demand for an additional hospital. In the Commonwealth there is about one insane person for every 800 citizens," and that "a fair computation of the number of insane in Pennsylvania would be 3,000." The trustees reported, moreover, that The Pennsylvania Hospital for the Insane, at Philadelphia, would not accommodate more than 450, The Friends' Asylum, about 60, and that at Dixmont (the only other State facility at that time) 200. With the 306 patients at Harrisburg, this left about 2,000 state insane outside of hospital reach.[25]

The following year the crowding of his facility was so bad that Curwen reported that they had removed the bathrooms and were using the infirmaries in the wards to increase the sleeping rooms to be able to accommodate 200 of each sex. That year he also introduced for the first time his concern over ventilation in the hospital wards:

> Anyone who has slept in a close room, or been obliged to remain several hours, in the day or evening, where a large number of persons have breathed over and over again the same air, will feel a sense of dullness and discomfort, and often positive pain, which he will at once attribute to the right cause— the impurity of the air he has been compelled to breathe.[26]

After two pages of continued discussion on the subject of the need for fresh air he recommended that "a system of forced ventilation, by means of fans driven by steam power," be installed. The next year they were.

Overcrowding was a problem at all of the country's institutions for the insane. The superintendents became so concerned over the situation that they got the Association of Medical Superintendents of American Institutions for the Insane to adopt unanimously three resolutions in 1872 identifying the "extraordinary dangers" and the "subversion of good order" which was occurring and then concluded that "the greatest good will result to the largest number, and at the earliest day," by adopting "such measures as will effectually prevent more patients being admitted ... than can be treated with greatest efficiency." There was little chance, of course, that any state legislature would accept such a course of action.

The greatest fear of all, however, was of fire. Several institutions for the insane and many almshouses, including the one in Lancaster, suffered disastrous fires, some with loss of patient lives. There were several fires at the Pennsylvania State Lunatic Hospital during John Curwen's years in Harrisburg. Fortunately none were in the center building. At midnight one Christmas evening the building containing the bake house, wash house, ironing room and drying room was discovered on fire. As was usual, "before anything could be done the building was completely destroyed." It was believed by the staff that vagrants "who had not obtained all that they desired" had set the fire. Unfortunately, one of the hospital's firemen was found dead in front of the boiler in the cellar of the burned building.[27]

And the following year "the whole house was greatly startled by an alarm of fire." It was customary to throw the chips and shavings from the carpenter shop down into the boiler room to be used along with the coal to fire the boiler by which the steam was generated. This drove the engines for the fans installed for ventilating the main building. The chips were hosed down while they were lying on the floor to prevent them igniting. The man on duty one spring night became uncomfortably warm and opened the doors leading to the fans. He left the room for a short period and by the time he returned the chips had caught fire and "the fans were drawing in the smoke and driving it into every room of the house." It was necessary to vacate the entire building. Fortunately there were no casualties, although some patients wandered off. They were all located, however, and returned by the next morning.[28]

*　*　*　*

By the late eighteen-sixties all of the original trustees, including Thomas Kirkbride, were gone. Among the new ones appointed by the governor was John L. Atlee of Lancaster. Atlee was a member of a distinguished family of physicians, one that traced its medical service back to the eighteenth century (and also would bring it forward into the mid-twentieth century). It was through Atlee that the problem of frequent changes in assistant physicians at the Pennsylvania State Lunatic Hospital was to be solved. In February 1870 an Atlee protege, Jerome Z. Gerhard, was appointed as an assistant physician. Later he became the First Assistant, a position he held for eleven years. Eventually he would replace John Curwen as superintendent.[29]

There were other, far more portentous changes for the Pennsylvania State Lunatic Hospital and its superintendent, however, than the appointment of a new First Assistant. They were the establishment in 1871 of the Board of Public Charities and the appointment of Hiram Corson, of Plymouth Meeting, to the hospital's Board of Trustees.

Although John Curwen never seems to have had such a case, many superintendents, including Thomas Kirkbride, became embroiled in spates of newspaper condemnation and even public suits by complaining "inmates." (Curwen once proudly exclaimed in a letter that he only ever had one habeus corpus case.)[30] Both the newspapers and noncompliant individuals would paint sensational pictures of asylum life. Ebenezer Haskell, Kirkbride's most prominent patient adversary, introduced Philadelphia newspaper readers to the dreaded seventh ward, where the never-ending "yelling and howling" of the patients unnerved him. There and in the second ward, to which he later was promoted, he reported the attendants choked patients and subjected them to the "douche" (a cold bucket of water thrown in the face) to quiet them. He wrote, moreover, of such devices as the "stomach pump"—rubber tubes which were used to force feed reluctant patients—or those trying to starve themselves to death.[31]

It was in part because of such public and media outcries, but also due to the need to standardize data reporting and to eliminate competition over appropriations between individual hospitals, that the Board of Public Charities was established in 1870.[32] By this action, the legislature hoped to gain control over expenditures for the growing number of public supported charities in Pennsylvania. Many of the older asylum superintendents, including John Curwen, saw the board's establishment as an attack on their authority within their institutions. (After several meetings with the board, Curwen reported: "I found their charity towards me was limited.")[33] It also was viewed by the advocates of "moral" treatment as an attack on the system's basic concepts—both the physical Kirkbride-design facility and the technique's methods of patient care.

The Pennsylvania Board of Public Charities, however, was responsible for much more than the several state institutions for the insane. The commission was established because of the "bad condition of the county poor-houses and jails, and of the abuses of the inmates of these and other public and private institutions." It was largely then the continued "keeping of the insane poor in jails and filthy apartments in county alms-houses, with no proper care or medical attendance" (in spite of the original law and Dorothea Dix's intent) that precipitated the board's establishment, not perceived abuses in the state-run institutions.[34]

The Board's first report in 1871 actually lauded the Pennsylvania State Lunatic Hospital and its superintendent:

> The Board have made several visits to this institution, and have been highly gratified with the earnest and intelligent administration of its interests, under the wise superintendence of the physician-in-chief, Dr. John Curwen, who has occupied this position since Febraury 13, 1851.

The report, moreover, supported Curwen's demand for a large appropriation by stating that "the hospital has been much crowded" and that great good had been "done with the limited accommodations at command." The inspectors also agreed that there was "great necessity for the introduction of forced ventilation by fans, that the air may be kept pure at all times and the health of the inmates maintained, or promoted where it is impaired." Their report even went so far as to agree with the moral treatment premise that to do the greater amount of good "recent cases shall have preference over those of long standing."[35]

This report, however, gave only one page to Curwen and the hospital. Thus the Board of Public Charities served to act as a wall between the asylum superintendent and his source of funds. John Curwen could no longer place the emphasis exactly as he wanted to support his claims for appropriations. More important, it was the Board that now decided on the amount and made the presentation to the legislature for all public charities, not the hospital superintendent. While the superintendents may have seen this as an obstruction, the legislature surely must have seen it as a relief.

Curwen and his successors continued to prepare reports, but from 1871 on they were addressed to the Board of Public Charities, not the governor or the legislature.[36] In his reports he would still go to great lengths to repeat the arguments for early treatment—that the "conviction has gradually been gaining in the minds of a large portion of the community ... " but that many obstinately adhere to the antiquated notions, and think that the mental disorder can be removed by letting it take care of itself." And he would also commend Jerome Gerhard for his "great zeal, earnestness and fidelity" and report that during the superintendent's absence in the spring his new assistant had managed the affairs of the hospital with entire satisfaction, but now all of his comments were directed to the three-man "Lunacy Committee" of the Board of Public Charities.

There were achievements, however, for John Curwen to relate to whoever would read his annual reports. In 1871 he seemed pleased and relieved to be able to state that:

> By the advance of chemical science, we have been placed in possession of certain remedies, which have enabled us to give more speedy and complete relief to many great sufferers. By the use of bromide of potassium we are now able to control, in great measure, that most fearful of maladies, epileptic mania, and render those afflicted with it more comfortable and less a terror to others ...[37]

He went on to explain that "the most distressing feature in all mental disorders is the great sleeplessness with which the greater number are troubled, and the consequent restlessness. Now that chemistry has given us hydrate of chloral, and physiological research has demonstrated the immense advantage of hypodermic injections of some of the soporific medicines, we feel almost sure that we can give sleep to the most distressed and excited. ... "[38]

But that same year, buried in Weir's miscellaneous expenses for postage, magic lantern slides, bay rum, six wheelbarrows, and for coffins was one of $66.00 for a "restraining apparatus."

END NOTES

1. The process of macadamization was named after the Scotchman, John Loudon MacAdam, who invented it in 1815. The processes involved constructing the road surface of layers of crushed stone. Each layer is then rolled until the stone particles are tightly packed together; the final surface being bound with asphalt, tar, or stone dust and water. The first macadamized road in America was the Lancaster Turnpike from Philadelphia.

2. Curwen, John, *Annual Report of the State Lunatic Hospital of Pennsylvania*, 1859, Theo. F. Scheffer, Harrisburg, 1860, page 13.

3. Curwen, John, *Annual Report of the State Lunatic Hospital of Pennsylvania*, 1858, A. Boyd Hamilton, Printer, 75 Market Street, 1859, page 17.

4. Curwen, John, *Annual Report of the State Lunatic Hospital of Pennsylvania*, 1854, A. Boyd Hamilton, Printer, 75 Market Street, 1855, page 16.

5. The typical number of men in Camp Curtin at any one time was about 5,000, although the number did reach as high as 15,000 on one occasion. Miller, William J., *The Training of an Army*, White Mane Publishing Company, Inc., 1990, page 107.

6. Ibid., pages 126-155.

7. Ibid., page 108.

8. *The Patriot and Union*, July 20, 1861.

9. Curwen, John, letter to Thomas Kirkbride, December 10, 1861.

10. Curwen, John, *Annual Report of the State Lunatic Hospital of Pennsylvania*, 1861, Theo. F. Scheffer, 1862, page 14.

11. Curwen, John, letter to Thomas Kirkbride, August 30, 1862. Kirkbride, a pacifist, took no strong stand on the war. This did not seem, however, to strain the two doctors good relationship.

12. North, Samuel, letter to his brother, in *History of the 126th Pennsylvania*, Ted Alexander, editor, Beidel Printing House, Shippensburg, Pa. page 109.

13. *Patriot and Union*, February 26, 1863. Schultz eventually became the Superintendent at the Danville State Hospital.

14. Miller, William J., op. cit., page 131.

15. John Curwen especially liked to have "pleasant pictures" hung on the otherwise bare walls of the hospital. He believed that they gently stimulated the minds of his patients and regularly requested donations of them for the institution.

16. Curwen, John, *Annual Report of the State Lunatic Hospital of Pennsylvania*, 1861, Theo. F. Scheffer, 1862, page 17 and Curwen, John, *Annual Report of the State Lunatic Hospital of Pennsylvania*, 1862, Theo. F. Scheffer, 1863, page 15.

17. Curwen, John, *Annual Report of the State Lunatic Hospital of Pennsylvania*, 1853 A. Boyd Hamilton, Printer, 75 Market Street, 1854.

18. Among the Regimental bands that visited the hospital during 1861-1862 were the Eleventh, Forty-fifth, Forty-sixth, Forty-seventh, Forty-eighth, Fifty-first, Fifty-second, Fifty-fourth and Fifty-sixth Pennsylvania Volunteers as well as the Milton Silver Cornet Band and the Second Ohio Regimental Band.

19. Curwen, John, *Annual Report of the State Lunatic Hospital of Pennsylvania*, 1861, Theo. F. Scheffer, 1862, page 17 and Curwen, John, *Annual Report of the State Lunatic Hospital of Pennsylvania*, 1862, Theo. F. Scheffer, 1863, page 15.

20. Ibid.

21. Curwen, John, *Annual Report of the State Lunatic Hospital of Pennsylvania*, 1862, Theo. F. Scheffer, 1863, page 6.

22. Curwen, John, *Annual Report of the State Lunatic Hospital of Pennsylvania*, 1865, Theo. F. Scheffer, 1865, page 2.

23. Curwen seems to have treated his first assistants reasonably well. Several of them he sent to Europe to visit hospitals for the insane. Among these was William R. DeWitt, a Harrisburg native, who was a Curwen assistant from 1852 to 1859. In 1855 the superintendent sent DeWitt to England, France, Belgium and Germany to study the methods being used in those countries. DeWitt

resigned in 1859 to accept a position as the surgeon in the U.S. Hospital at Honolulu. He later served as the assistant surgeon at Georgetown College hospital and as a surgeon-in-chief in the Union Army. After the war, he returned to Harrisburg, where he practiced until his retirement. He died in May 1891.

24. Curwen, John, *Annual Report of the State Lunatic Hospital of Pennsylvania*, 1872, George Bergner, Harrisburg, 1872, pages 9-10.
25. "Report of the Trustees," *Annual Report of the State Lunatic Hospital of Pennsylvania*, 1867, Theo. F. Scheffer, 1867, page 5.
26. Curwen, John, *Annual Report of the State Lunatic Hospital of Pennsylvania*, 1868, Theo. F. Scheffer, 1869, page 11.
27. Curwen, John, *Annual Report of the State Lunatic Hospital of Pennsylvania*, 1873, George Bergner, 1873.
28. Curwen, John, *Annual Report of the State Lunatic Hospital of Pennsylvania*, 1874, Theo. F. Scheffer, 1874, page 11.
29. John Light Atlee was born in Lancaster in 1799. He graduated from the University of Pennsylvania in 1820 and opened an office in Lancaster. He helped to found the Lancaster County Medical Society in 1843 and the Pennsylvania State Medical Society in 1848. He was also one of the organizers of the American Medical Association in Philadelphia and became its president in 1882. He was a professor of anatomy at Franklin and Marshall College. *Biographical Annals of Lancaster County*, J. H. Beers & Co., Lancaster, Pa., 1903, page 166.
30. Curwen, John, letter to Thomas Kirkbride, November 24, 1870.
31. Haskell lobbied the Pennsylvania legislature for the 1869 law requiring two doctors' certificates of insanity. Tomes, Nancy, op. cit., pages 256-257.
32. Among the many standard forms that the Board of Public Charities designed were one for: Patients Admission Books and Registers, Certificates for Admitting Physicians, Court and Judicial Officer forms, and those for recording discharges, removals and deaths.
33. Curwen, John, letter to Thomas Kirkbride, May 27, 1874. The letter continued: "I think the word charity will not convey the true intentions of the actions of that board."
34. Commissioner's report, "Work of the Board of Public Charities," April 25, 1881, *Pennsylvania Legislative Documents*, Vol. 4, document No. 23, 1880-81, page 1. It should be pointed out, too, that the insane in both county and state facilities were the responsibility of a subcommittee of five members (including three professionals) of the Board. The board's responsibilities included poorhouses, orphanages and a variety of training schools. These responsibilities, moreover, were not restricted to state institutions but also included private ones.
35. "Annual report of the Board of Public Charities," February 23, 1871, *Pennsylvania Legislative Documents*, document No. 33, page 1041.
36. The cost of printing the hospital's annual reports was not a trivial one. Although John Weir listed it under miscellaneous expenses, at $457.50 it was in 1871 the second largest such expense.
37. Curwen, John, *Annual Report of the State Lunatic Hospital of Pennsylvania*, 1871, George Bergner, 1871.
38. Ibid.

X

DECLINE OF MORAL TREATMENT

There is no further record of what kind of a "restraining apparatus" John Curwen bought for $66.00, but, at that price and description, the device must have been more than a jacket or canvas suit. It probably was something on the order of a "Utica crib." After he made his first inspection of the hospital in 1877, the new trustee, Hiram Corson, wrote that "beside the torturing appliances, pleasantly called 'restraining measures,' there were cells in which they [the patients] could be shut up for slight breaches of rules, ..."[1] Whether these devices were used humanely as "restraining" or inhumanely as "torturing" ones depended largely on the individual attendants. Although Curwen expected them to use restraints only as a last resort, we do know that attendants were dismissed from time to time because of reported abuse of the patients.

Hiram Corson had gotten himself appointed as a trustee of the Pennsylvania State Lunatic Hospital in 1877 as a result of a series of newspaper articles he had written about the "bad management of the insane in the Montgomery County Almshouse." The series had attracted the attention of Governor Hartranft. Corson came to Harrisburg, moreover, determined to correct "the bad management of the insane" that he believed also existed there.[2]

A country doctor,[3] a staunch abolitionist,[4] an avid reformer, he was determined on several things connected with the insane: that the poor deserved equal treatment with the rich, that there was a woeful lack of "employment for the poor inmates" and that the superintendents of public and private mental hospitals were "tyrants" over their patients as well as bad managers of their facilities.[5]

There was a philosophic difference between Curwen and Corson regarding using patients for labor. While Corson, and especially many state legislators, felt that they should be worked to the maximum extent possible (not only for their mental well-being, but also to help pay for their room and board), John Curwen claimed with some validity that:

> The processes of the human mind are so recondite and mysterious, ... that it is impossible to calculate what may be the effect of any given means employed; and for this reason, it is desirable and necessary to vary all the occupations, amusements, and recreations in such a way that some spring may be touched. ... The constant repetition or steady use of any one thing may tire and lose its effect and this is why the means should be provided for introducing as great a variety as ingenuity can devise.[6]

More than any other practice, however, that Hiram Corson deplored, was that women, whom he believed were as capable physicians as men, were not used to treat female patients. All these issues then were to become important ones, not only at Harrisburg, but also as ones over which the battle to continue or to replace moral management would be waged nation wide. Nancy Tomes has gone so far as to claim that the attack on Curwen was intended as an indirect assault on Kirkbride, whose position "was unassailable."[7]

* * * *

Hospital superintendents at both public and private facilities learned early that their continued success (measured largely by their ability to raise money and to "cure" patients) depended on their skill in convincing their constituents—public and legislative—on the value of their service. Publicity thus quickly became one of the more important by-products of patient care, and statistics became the most important tool in effective publicity.

As early as 1842 some hospitals were beginning to emphasize "cure" rates in their annual reports. To achieve higher restoration rates, techniques such as separating the patients into "recent" and "old" cases and eliminating deaths from cure calculations were adopted. Ultimately restored rates were inflated by computing them from among only those who were discharged. And among the discharged as "recovered" were often the same patient—some as many as six and seven times within a single year. These reporting methods then were the pillars in what Deutsch calls "the structure of mathematical curability."[8]

There were a number of critics of these techniques among the superintendents, but many succumbed to its blandishments.[9] One, Dr. William McClay Awl, of the Ohio State Lunatic Hospital at Columbus, eventually reported a cure rate of 100 percent. This earned him the sobriquet of "Dr. Cure-Awl."[10] The "cult of curability," as Deutsch calls it, also was closely tied up with the notion that the earlier a case was discovered and "treated" the more likely "restoration" would be. Most physicians, who ascribed to moral treatment methods, held this belief, including Kirkbride and Curwen. Their annual reports regularly included comments designed to encourage the early admission of patients into their care.[11]

Although both doctors were cautious in their claims of "cures," John Curwen was not above expressing pride in the fact that he had been "instrumental in effecting the change in those that were restored to the community and to their families and especially to *productivity*."[12]

The Harrisburg superintendent seemed, moreover, to enjoy telling the story of the tortoise and the hare, as it appeared several times in his annual reports. He would explain at length how a careful, deliberate, moderate life style was the best defense against mental illness, just as it was for stomach ailments. Abuse in all forms was to be avoided. The brain was simply another organ that could become diseased through overexertion. The winner in the race of life would go to those who used their physical resources wisely. For John Curwen then the tortoise and the hare became a metaphor for moral treatment, at least as he understood it and practiced it. The tortoise was a symbol not only for a successful life but also for the hospital.

Statistical reporting, too, was a manifestation of a power struggle within the profession. Credibility as a physician and as an administrator not only got greater appropriations for a hospital, but also enhanced a superintendent's professional standing and chances for promotion to a more "successful" institution. Power bases, of course, attract attackers and the nineteenth-century mental hospital was just such a bastion. Nancy Tomes has pointed out that "The asylum doctors' real genius consisted ... in their ability, as moral entrepreneurs, to accommodate and legitimate the social forces impelling the insane out of the household and community" and furthermore that they "succeeded in their bid for power largely because they devised an institution capable of meeting a deeply felt social need,"[13] By the late seventies, however, the monolithic, Kirkbride-design hospital and moral treatment both were under seige.

The legislators and the "young Turks" among the doctors not only attacked the results of asylum treatment by assaulting the statistical basis of "cures" on which it was built, but also by casting doubt on the very concept of hospital care in terms of its cost to society, the growing number of chronic, incurable insane that were showing up in institutional reports, and the small proportion of the mentally ill that were being reached.[14] In 1883, forty years after Dorothea Dix's report of the conditions in Pennsylvania, for example, the state commissioners investigating hospital care reported finding a man in Clearfield County who had been housed in chains in a box for thirty years. Such sensational findings were offered up as public proof that the present generation of superintendents were serving themselves more than the "indigent insane" they were charged with helping.

While it was the legislators who had insisted that the "indigent insane" shall have preference over paying customers, the need to build more and increasingly larger hospitals made it easy for those same legislators to attribute the growing number of permanent, incurable residents being housed to the ineffectiveness of the hospital's head. To the older superintendents these were management problems to be solved by building more and better facilities; to the public and their representatives these were indications that the physicians had not delivered on the promise to cure the sick.

To help alleviate the overcrowding problem and the growing number of chronic incurables being "warehoused" at the

Pennsylvania State Lunatic Hospital (as well as meet budgetary needs by retaining a significant number of higher paying private patients), John Curwen, as did the superintendents at other state hospitals, acquiesced in the practice of leaving some patients at, or even returning others to, the countypoor houses. This, of course, was contrary to the legislature's wish and Dorothea Dix's hope, but met fully with local approval. The Harrisburg newspapers reported as early as 1873 that among the 152 inmates at the Dauphin County almshouse were 15 insane men and 12 insane women. The reporter went on to explain that previously:

> The unfortunate poor and helpless were kept at the State Lunatic Hospital at a cost to the county of nearly $4,000. There are still a number of patients kept at the latter institution, but the cost to the county is only about $1,600. It is hoped in time all the patients may be accommodated in the almshouse, where the cost of maintenance would be reduced nearly one-half.[15]

*　　*　　*　　*

Curwen's obstinacy, in the face of change, apparently blinded him to the dangers that he faced—not only with the establishment of the Pennsylvania Board of Public Charities but with the appointment of Hiram Corson to the Pennsylvania Lunatic Hospital's Board of Trustees. He knew Corson well. He had written to Kirkbride of his own pleasure when the Pennsylvania Medical Society had successfully rebuffed Corson's efforts to get women certified as hospital physicians. But the Montgomery County physician would eventually have his way as well as get the superintendent dismissed.

Curwen's medical practices were never questioned but his management ones were; not only by the Montgomery County physician but also by the Pennsylvania State Legislature. There were several legislative investigations of wastefulness and extravagance at the hospital during the 1870s; all came up empty-handed. But there were so many that even one of Curwen's supporters in the legislature came to believe that there must be "something rotten out there."[16]

Among the specific charges that were leveled against the superintendent were the lack of accounting for funds that the state treasurer had given him, that he had too many paying patients at Harrisburg and gave preference to them over the indigent, and that he was frequently absent from his duties as superintendent.

This latter charge had more than an element of truth in it, although there is no direct evidence that his patients suffered from John Curwen's absences. Because of his reputation and the hospital's proximity to the seat of Pennsylvania government, he was called upon frequently by the governor to evaluate the "mental condition" of men condemned to death or of prisoners for whom physicians around the state had made commutation appeals. Even more time-consuming, the governor appointed him as a commissioner to help set up several new mental hospitals that the legislature had approved. During the late 1870s, for example, Curwen was frequently gone from the hospital when visitors came. Many of these trips were to Western Pennsylvania, where he was assisting in the building of the new State Hospital at Warren.[17]

The "charges" against John Curwen were never brought officially, so he had no chance to defend himself against them. The hospital trustees simply failed to reappoint him as the superintendent and instead in March 1881 placed his able First Assistant, Jerome Z. Gerhard, in charge. In a long letter to Thomas Kirkbride, Curwen poured out a somewhat disjointed and thus not completely convincing defense.[18]

The superintendent went to great lengths to explain that the two checks that the state treasurer had given him in August, 1875, for $15,000 had not been used to pay off old indebtedness [apparently the reason on which the request for money had been based] because "it would have left us just that much behind in the payment of our usual regular bills for household expenses." He then went on to state that "if the Board of Charities had visited this hospital as the law requires after the application for the appropriation had been made to them, they would not have been left to mere conjecture in regard to the application of the $15,000, but all the facts could have been made known to them."[19]

Apparently the hospital accounts were not kept too carefully, at least by today's accounting standards. The superintendent made no offer, for example, to exhibit them in his defense when he was accused in 1880. John Weir, the treasurer, also was replaced in the fall of that same year. His dismissal, after 30 years, without recognition or even explanation (rather shabby treatment it seems on the part of the Board of Trustees) appears to support the conclusion that Curwen's departure was based primarily on the "misuse" of these funds. D. W. Gross, of Harrisburg, was appointed treasurer "pro-tem."[20]

Regarding the charge that the hospital contained a "large preponderance of paying patients at unremunerative rates," Curwen claimed that "it has always been my aim to keep this Hospital in such a condition that anyone of moderate means could place their friends here for treatment. ... " He justified this position by stating that "insanity is no respecter of persons," and went on to write to Kirkbride that "I never could be made to believe that the members of the Legislature of Pennsylvania could refuse to make up the difference between the actual cost and what those who were denying themselves ... were required to pay for the board and medical attendance of their relatives."[21]

He had frankly written, moreover, in his annual report of 1877: "If those who are able to pay three dollars or three dollars and fifty cents a week, often at great sacrifice of personal comfort, are to be esteemed rich in this world's goods, then this Hospital has given accommodation to the rich in preference to the poor. ..."[22] Thus John Curwen played directly into the hands of Hiram Corson, who claimed that the superintendent was a bad manager as well as a "despot"—one that simply ran the hospital as he wished. The superintendent also resisted another important Corson wish, although it was not one of the informal charges that John Curwen related to Kirkbride.

*   *   *   *

The Female Medical College of Pennsylvania was founded

in Philadelphia in 1850 and in December 1851 graduated seven young women. The college classes increased and each year greater numbers were graduated and sent forth to practice. This movement of women, according to Corson, "was not agreeable to the profession in Philadelphia, ... and was opposed by good men and women outside of the profession, as being a business outside of woman's sphere and demoralizing to her. No combined action was taken against them until eight classes were graduated and the women established in practice. But in November, 1858 the Board of Censors of the Philadelphia County Medical Society reported their disapproval of any member of the society holding professional intercourse with the professors or alumni of the Female Medical College." This committee report not only was approved by the Philadelphia Medical Society but a copy was sent to each of the County Societies in the state.[23] Hiram Corson, a member of the Philadelphia Medical Society as well as of the Montgomery County Medical Society was the only one to oppose this resolution.

Thus began Corson's decades-long campaign to have women certified as physicians in state hospitals. He considered "the control over the female insane by young male physicians to be a shameful abuse." Year in and year out from 1860 to 1879, he introduced resolutions, first in the Philadelphia and then in the State Medical Society, and was "violently opposed by the superintendents for the insane everywhere." By convincing first the Montgomery County Medical Society and then the Lancaster County one, he finally was able to convince enough doctors in the state medical society to overturn the Philadelphia physicians' resolution.

In June 1879, largely through Corson's efforts, the Pennsylvania Legislature passed an "Act for the Better Regulation of the Female Insane."[24] This law, however, did not make the appointment of women physicians mandatory as Corson had originally written it, but only "encouraged" their appointment in state hospitals for the insane.[25] In many hospitals across the state the act was simply ignored, but with Corson on the Board of Trustees at Harrisburg, action was soon taken to hire them against the wishes of the superintendent.[26]

On July 8, 1880 the board elected Margaret A. Cleaves of

Davenport, Iowa to have charge of the female side of the house. Jane K. Garver was selected as her assistant.[27] Three of the trustees, Daniel Eppley, D. W. Gross, and Henry Gilbert escorted Cleaves on the first of September to the hospital. Curwen was in Warren. The first assistant physician, Gerhard, took them on a tour through the female wards. Then the trustees called the supervisor and the attendants in each of the wards and the watchwoman together. They informed them that "Doctor Cleaves now had the medical charge of this side of the house and that they were entirely under her control, were expected to obey her promptly and support her faithfully; in case they did not they would be discharged and the trustees would sustain her in so doing."[28]

The trustees declared that Margaret Abigail Cleaves was "eminent in her profession." She had been born in 1848 in Columbus, Ohio, in the "midst of illimitable space, on the western prairie," as she later put it. Her father, an early New England physician, had settled in what was then called the Indiana Territory, later moving to Iowa. Deciding to follow in her father's footsteps, the young woman graduated from the medical department of the Iowa State University in 1873. After graduation she was appointed to the State Hospital for the Insane at Mount Pleasant, Iowa.

Cleaves only remained in Harrisburg for three years, when she resigned for health reasons. She returned to Iowa where, having partially regained her health, she became in 1885 one of the examining commissioners of the Iowa State Medical University. In 1887 she went to Paris to study electro-therapeutics. She returned to New York, where she became the clinical assistant to the chair of electro-therapeutics in the Post-Graduate Medical School of New York. One biographer described her as "gentle of speech and manner with firmness of character." She was, moreover, a woman of "keen insight and quick sympathies, yet cool judgment." Her *The Auto-biography of a Neurasthene*, which was published in 1910 was a history of her disease, "nerve exhaustion," rather than of her life.[29]

Garver replaced Cleaves. The second head of the "female side of the house" had been born in Somerset, Pennsylvania in 1844. Her father was Judge Francis Kimmel and her mother Phoebe Forward Kimmel. She had been educated in the Somerset schools and at Mrs. Dixon's School in Harrisburg. After she was married, both Margaret and her husband undertook the study of medicine. She was graduated in 1872 from the Women's College and spent a year at the Women's Hospital in Boston. She and her husband then practiced together, first in Scotland and later at York, Pennsylvania. After she came to Harrisburg, she became active in the Daughters of the American Revolution and the Civic and the Wednesday Clubs.[30]

* * * *

While actions such as this and the establishment of the Pennsylvania Board of Public Charities and similar groups in other states were viewed as an attack on the authority, as well as the methods, of the hospital superintendents it was within the profession of hospital superintendents, that the real challenge to moral treatment lay. The first to criticize Kirkbride openly was John Galt, a member of the original 13 founders of the *Association of Medical Superintendents of American Institutions for the Insane.* In an article, "The Farm of St. Anne," he objected to the preoccupation with hospital design. He wrote that as long as "those entrusted with the supervision of the insane, and particularly those at the head of the most richly endowed asylums, shall deem the true interests of their afflicted charges not to consist in aught on their part but tinkering gas-pipes and studying architecture ... so long may we anticipate no advancement in the treatment of insanity ..."[31] By the 1870s and 1880s the young Turks had become increasingly vocal in their criticism.

The principal disagreement between the two groups concerned the method of treating the different classes of the mentally ill. One of the tenets of Kirkbride's moral treatment was that *all* patients should be housed in a single "linear" facility. In this fashion, he reasoned, the patients were more easily observed with a smaller staff, while the design provided for maximum social, even family-like, relationships among the patients. In his plan, the various classes of patients were accommodated by arranging them across the several wards.

The younger men believed that the chronically ill, who were beginning to fill American institutions (as state boards of charity moved the insane out of poorhouses), did not need the same amount of constant observation as the recent cases, and that they were a drain on the facility's financial and medical resources and should be housed separately. This would free up the medical staff to provide greater amounts of care for those that could be cured, at the same time permitting the hospital to engage more in research into mental illness. This group of doctors resented, moreover, what they felt was the intractable nature of their older brethern. On these issues, Kirkbride would not relent and with his widespread reputation was able to prevent the younger men from introducing changes. Within several years of his death in 1883, however, the *Association of Medical Superintendents of American Institutions for the Insane* voted "not to reaffirm" his principles on hospital design.

In the decade following the death of Thomas Kirkbride, psychiatry, as the specialty was now being called, also began to concern itself more "with the somatic as opposed to the psychological factors producing mental disease. Hereditarian explanations for insanity (which Kirkbride had always opposed) became much more popular." The new conception of the disease was increasingly as that of "a product of cellular pathology."[32]

The new profession of neurology, too, had been developed as a direct outgrowth of the Civil War. Surgeons had faced for the first time massive numbers of men suffering from gunshot wounds that affected the nervous system. As Deutsch states, many medical men emerged from both sides during the Civil War as "practicing neurologists."[33] Along with the new views of "psychiatry," this group was to become a formidable adversary for advocates of traditional moral treatment.

Although the winds of change were blowing briskly (perhaps we might say "warring"), Kirkbride's protege, John Curwen, was still elected president of the *American Medico-Psychological Association*, as the *Association of Medical Superintendents of American Institutions for the Insane* was being called by 1894. In his presidential address Curwen paid homage to the founders of the association—the thirteen men who introduced moral treatment to America. Of them he said:

> With high resolve and determined purpose these gentlemen aimed to impart correct knowledge and inaugurate a new system of treatment which would commend itself to the minds of all. They were the friends and promoters of progress; steady, consistent, persistent, not lured away from the true path by theoretical philanthropists and visionary schemers, but animated by a calm consideration in their adherence to justice, truth and right, and guided by a faith which enabled them to look beyond the cloud bank of temporary expediency to the ever-enduring realities.[34]

The memory of moral treatment and its advocates, moreover, was still strong enough that when the foundation of the original Pennsylvania State Lunatic Hospital was excavated in the early 1950s—one hundred years after the building's construction—a young resident, S. Philip Laucks, who later became a hospital superintendent, recalls that the remains of the structure were still referred to as those of the "Kirkbride" building.

END NOTES

1. Corson, Hiram, *The Corson Family, A History of the Descendants of Benjamin Corson*, Henry L. Everett, Philadelphia, 1906, page 127.
2. Ibid.
3. Nancy Tomes dismisses Corson as a "country doctor." Actually he followed much the same plan of training as did Thomas Kirkbride. He studied medicine first in the office of an uncle and then attended the lectures given at the University of Pennsylvania by Nathaniel Chapman and Philip S. Physick. Corson graduated from the University in 1828. Although his practice was a rural one, he maintained his contacts with Philadelphia physicians. He was a founder of the Montgomery County Medical Society, a member of the Pennsylvania State Medical Society from 1848 (of which organization he was president in 1853) and of the American Medical Association from 1862, a member of the Philadelphia Obstetrical Society, and was elected an Associate Fellow of the College of Physicians of Philadelphia in 1876.
4. Plymouth Meeting was the center of a strong anti-slavery movement and a key station on the Underground Railroad. The Corson name became a legend along the underground railroad, for virtually every member of the family participated. William Still, one of the black agents on the Railroad, claimed that there were few more devoted men than George and Hiram Corson. *The Bulletin of the Historical Society of Montgomery County*, Spring 1986, pages 76-77.
5. Corson, Hiram, op. cit.
6. Curwen, John, *Annual Report of the State Lunatic Hospital of Pennsylvania*, 1876, Theo. F. Scheffer, Harrisburg, 1876.
7. Tomes, Nancy, op. cit., page 303.
8. Deutsch, Albert, op. cit., page 153.
9. Among them were Dr. Pliny Earle of the Northampton State Hospital in Massachusetts. His 1887 book, *The Curability of Insanity*, had a significant influence on the course of statistical reporting in mental hospitals. (Deutsch, Albert, op. cit., page 155.) Earle, along with Kirkbride, was one of the outstanding men of mental health in mid-nineteenth-century America.
10. William MaClay Awl was born in Harrisburg, on May 24, 1799. He was a descendant of John Harris. Although he attended one course of lectures at the University of Pennsylvania in 1819, he was largely a product of the apprentice system. He was highly respected, however, and was one of the 13 founders, and later president, of the *Association of Medical Superintendents of American Institutions for the Insane*.
11. One of the few scientific studies of the mid-nineteenth century, however, concluded that "In round numbers, of ten persons attacked by insanity, five recover and five die, sooner or later, during the attack. Of the five who recover, not more than two remain well during the rest of their lives; the other three sustain subsequent attacks, during which at least two of them will die." Thurnam, John, Dr., *Observations and Essays on Statistics of Insanity*, 1845. Quoted in Deutsch, op. cit., page 154.
12. Curwen, John, *Annual Report of the State Lunatic Hospital of Pennsylvania*, 1876, Theo. F. Scheffer, Harrisburg, 1876.
13. Tomes, Nancy, op. cit., pgs 85-87.
14. It is estimated that American hospitals, which were handling about 3% of the need in 1844, were still, by 1870, only taking care of 10% of the nation's mentally ill. By 1890 and the end of the "golden age" of hospital care, the number of those being helped was still less than 40%. *International Encyclopedia of Psychiatry, Psychology and Neurology*, Vol. I, page 452.
15. Harrisburg *Daily Telegraph*, January 8, 1873.
16. Tomes, Nancy, op. cit., page 298.
17. During one two-month period in 1879, from May 23 until July 19, Curwen was gone each of the four times when the visiting trustees came to inspect the institution.

18. Both Kirkbride and Dorothea Dix sided with Curwen. In a letter to Dix, Kirkbride called his removal "an outrage of no ordinary kind and disgraceful to all concerned in it." Thomas Kirkbride, letter of January 7, 1881.
19. Curwen, John, letter to Thomas Kirkbride, March 26, 1881.
20. Curwen, John, *Annual Report of the State Lunatic Hospital of Pennsylvania*, 1880, Theo. F. Scheffer, Harrisburg, 1880. Gross was made the permanent treasurer the following year. Weir had started in the coach-making business, then moved into retailing medicine in Harrisburg, later became a clerk to Governor Ritner and eventually a director of the Harrisburg Bank. His departure as the hospital's treasurer may have been in part due to ill health. He died in October of the following year at age 79.
21. Curwen, John, letter to Thomas Kirkbride, March 26, 1881.
22. Curwen, John, *Annual Report of the State Lunatic Hospital of Pennsylvania*, 1877, The Patriot Publishing Company, Harrisburg, 1877.
23. Corson, Hiram, op. cit., pages 124-125.
24. Ibid, pages 128-129.
25. The law read: "may appoint a female physician." The struggle continued even after the law's passage. Curwen argued at the May 12, 1881 Pennsylvania Medical Society meeting in Harrisburg (after he had been dismissed from the superintendency there) that the hospitals at Harrisburg and Norristown were actually in "direct violation of the law" for having appointed more than one woman to the medical staff. He said: "I never knew any construction of the English language which gave a to mean two. When the Constitution of the U. S. said the people should elect a President it did not mean two." John Atlee, of Lancaster, tried to soothe the older members of the society by calling the appointment of women "only an experiment." Curwen, John, letter to Thomas Kirkbride, May 12, 1881.
26. Ten years later, as the Superintendent of the Warren State Hospital, where he moved in 1881, Curwen still had not appointed a female physician. He wrote: "While we are not opposed to female physicians, but rather recommend the plan, we are decidedly opposed to a divided authority and responsibility, and believe that they should act only as any other assistant physician, subordinate to the physician in chief." Hartz, Fred R. and Hoshino, Arthur Y., *Warren State Hospital, 1880-1980.*, Maverick Publications, Bend, Oregon, 1981, page 49.
27. There is today a "Cleaves" and a "Garver" room on the third floor of the hospital administration building.
28. "Minutes of the Executive, Local and Visiting Committees of the Board," 1851-1924, September 1, 1880.
29. Willard, Frances E. and Livermore, Mary A., editors, A Woman of the Century, Charles Wells Moulton, Buffalo, New York, 1893, page 182. *The Autobiography of a Neurasthene* was published in 1910 by the Gorham Press of Boston. It consisted of 246 pages of "metaphysical prose," as one reviewer described it. (Angelo, F. Michael, letter of December 24, 1990.) According to Angelo, Cleaves never mentioned a single date or name in her "autobiography."
30. The *Harrisburg Telegraph*, October 10, 1902.
31. Galt, John, "The Farm of St. Anne," *American Journal of Insanity*, Vol. II, 1855, pages 352-357. Quoted in Tomes, Nancy, op. cit., page 283.
32. Tomes, Nancy, op. cit., page 315.
33. Deutsch, Albert, op. cit., page 276.
34. Hall, J. K., ed. for The American Psychiatric Association, *One Hundred Years of American Psychiatry*, Columbia University Press, 1944, N.Y., page 72.

XI

MANY MEMBERS
BUT ONE BODY

On February 15, 1881 the Visiting Committee of the Trustees of the Pennsylvania State Lunatic Hospital went out to the institution in the afternoon and wrote in their log (almost as if it were a suprise): "We found Doctor Gerhard in charge." Jerome Z. Gerhard always seemed to carry out his duties in that way—quietly, efficiently and in the the most unassuming manner. When John Curwen was the superintendent, the first assistant simply seemed to be there silently, almost invisibly doing as he was instructed.

Within months, however, of his elevation to the superintendency, it became clear that Jerome Gerhard was a man of strongly held opinions (frequently different ones than those of his former boss) and that he would be a firm superintendent. Many of his approaches to treatment were based on the same premises of moral treatment that John Curwen held. His Letter Press Book, for example, is filled with letters to the family members and the friends of patients, which exhibit many of the same concerns as his predecessor. His first annual report, however, makes it clear that he only stood in John Curwen's shadow out of deference for his position. On many subjects he did not agree. One of these concerned the success rate of hospital care for the insane as it was being practiced in the latter half of the nineteenth century. Six months after he assumed charge, Gerhard wrote:

> Efforts have been made to create the impression that from seventy-five to eighty percent of recent cases recovered ... and that these persons were active, productive and useful members of society. ... The statistics of this Hospital do not warrant this assumption. ...[1]

He went on to write that "this Hospital has always been largely occupied by chronic and other incurable patients" and then stated bluntly that "of the 154 male patients who remain only about 17 are probably curable." He summarized this by boldly claiming that "Hospitals for the insane can only be, to a limited extent, curative institutions ... They serve another purpose, equally noble and humane, in furnishing homes and ministering to the needs of the insane, who otherwise would often be friendless and neglected."[2]

Gerhard also believed that "employment is one of the most essential features in the treatment of the insane" and stated that "we are making constant efforts to employ our patients to as great an extent as possible." He never seems, moreover, to have had difficulty with having been divested of the responsibility of the female side of the house. (He and Margaret Cleaves, for example, would attend meetings of the Pennsylvania State Medical Society together.) And in a major departure from moral treatment theories he very pointedly said:

> During former years, and also during the beginning of the present year [a direct reference to Curwen's term which ended in the middle of the year], it was the custom to have an entertainment in the Chapel every evening. ... We now have only three or four during the week, make them as interesting as possible and as a result our audiences have more than doubled. It is possible to attempt to entertain people to excess and fail in accomplishing the very object aimed at. [3]

The written style as well as the mind of the new superintendent was like a breath of fresh air; direct, even blunt at times, it offered little of the nineteenth-century effusiveness of his predecessor. Although he separated himself from John Curwen and his policies, the new head of the Pennsylvania State Lunatic Hospital still wanted it to be clear that he needed the authority to manage the facility.

> An institution will necessarily be moulded, to a very great extent, at least in spirit and general character, by the head or chief executive officer. A change in the

Superintendent, therefore, marks an epoch in the history of a hospital and is far reaching in its results. In order that an institution may be efficient it must develop moral force and power. This is a thing of evolution, and cannot at once reach its full growth. The Superintendent must have full power to make and change appointments or else he will be hampered in his work ... The Institution must be a unit, having many members but one body.[4]

*   *   *   *

Jerome Zwingli Gerhard was born in Northampton County near the village of Cherryville on November 6, 1842. He was one of five brothers and three sisters born to the Reverend William T. and Elizabeth S. Gerhard. Jerome's great-greatgrandfather, Frederick Gerhard, who was a master wheelwright, had emigrated from Germany in 1737 and settled in Berks county. There Frederick pursued his trade and farmed as well. He also continued his active involvement in the Reformed church.

Father William Gerhard, on the other hand, was not only a successful pastor and a preacher of considerable ability, but he was "firm and judicious in the ruling of his family." Jerome's mother, however, was of "a very reserved disposition, quiet and mild in her manner." "There was a simplicity in her faith, a single-mindedness in her devotion to her children, and to the work of her husband, that made her a tower of strength."[5] Jerome apparently inherited many of his mother's traits.

"Although the home atmosphere was a religious one, and one of rigorous devotion to learning, it was liberally democratic. When the question of [whether they were to remain on the farm near Allentown or move to Lancaster] where the boys were to be educated arose, the situation was placed under discussion and consideration by the entire family. Finally each one was requested to put down in writing an answer to the difficult question. ... The decision to move was decided in the affirmative and in the spring of 1859 the family relocated to Lancaster. The Reverend William Gerhard thus left a pastorate in which he had been 'signally successful' for fifteen years and took a call in the neighborhood of Lancaster where there were a number of weak Reformed congregations in need of a minister."[6]

Jerome, the second of the five sons, first attended a country school in Durham township until he was sixteen and then Franklin and Marshall College, from which he graduated in 1864. Each of the five sons in fact completed their undergraduate work at the same college. Each of the sons also then entered professional life: three became clergymen like their father and two became physicians.[7]

When he completed his work at Franklin and Marshall, Jerome began the study of medicine with John L. Atlee, the leading physician in Lancaster.[8] The Civil War, however, interrupted his apprenticeship. In March of 1865 he enlisted as a private in Company K, 195th Regiment of Pennsylvania Volunteers and served for a brief time in the Army of the Shenandoah. Although he had joined as a private, as soon as it was discovered that he had a medical background, he was assigned duties as the steward in the division hospital. He was discharged in Washington, D. C. in January, 1866.[9]

Jerome then returned to Lancaster and resumed study in the office of John Atlee. That fall he entered the Medical Department of the University of Pennsylvania, where he received his medical degree in 1868. He then entered private practice in Lancaster. Two years later the young doctor was appointed the assistant physician at the Pennsylvania State Lunatic Hospital.

John Curwen and Jerome Gerhard apparently got along well during their years in Harrisburg together. During Gerhard's tenure as an assistant physician, Curwen sent him to visit many of the hospitals for the insane both in this country and in Europe. During 1877, for example, the First Assistant spent five months touring the institutions in England and Germany. In this way the superintendent helped to equip him more fully for work with the mentally ill.[10]

*   *   *   *

Compassion, but with a new frankness, was a hallmark of the Gerhard years at the Pennsylvania State Lunatic Hospital. He, like his predecessor, regularly wrote to the families of patients. Some days there were as many as six or seven letters. The new superintendent tried to be hopeful whenever he could. To one family member from Ashland, Pennsylvania he wrote: "Your letter in relation to your father was received. He is about the same, in body and mind, as he was at the time of your visit. Whenever he is in a condition to be moved from the Sixth Ward we will cheerfully put him into a more quiet ward."[11]

The few available photographs of Jerome Gerhard are of a kindly, gentle-appearing man, one befitting our image of an early American country doctor. But he could be direct and blunt if there was little cause to hope for improvement. One Gerhard letter to a York woman contained only three short sentences. "Your son Eddie is about the same as at the time of your visit. It is not probable that he will ever improve his mind. His bodily health is good."[12]

It was a recurring trait of his letters to mention a patient's "bodily health," when he could offer little hope for one of his charge's mental health. This was about the only way in which Gerhard ever tried to mislead anyone. He was not given to moralizing or to making claims based on obscure theories or using literary analogies to convince (or perhaps to confuse?) his contemporaries about the probable success of a patient's treatment in the hospital. For example, in spite of Curwen's optimism several years previous over new treatment regimens for epilepsy, he seemed to offer little hope for such sufferers. The new superintendent wrote in 1883 to an Allensville, Pennsylvania, woman:

> Your son has grown to be quite a large boy but there is no change in his mind. He still is subject to epilepsy and I see no hope for any improvement. We can make him comfortable and take good care of him, but that is all we can do for him.[13]

*   *   *   *

When the visiting trustees had come to the hospital and "found Doctor Gerhard in charge," they had also inspected the vacated quarters of John Curwen and his family. They found them to be in a terrible state of disrepair. There was no indication that they blamed this on Curwen. After thirty years of occupancy, with no more than minimal maintenance, they could have anticipated little more. They immediately authorized Gerhard, however, to get the third floor rooms back in shape. Later that year, at 39 years of age, the new superintendent married Elizabeth Hill of Sunbury. As had John Curwen he apparently waited until he had reached a more secure position or perhaps until there were adequate quarters to live in. Elizabeth was the daughter of a prominent Sunbury attorney.[14]

Although some members of the legislature had viewed Curwen's use of appropriated funds with skepticism, in truth most of the maintenance expenditures had been for moral treatment improvements such as ventilating and heating systems, gas and sewer works, outbuildings for the farm, iron fire escapes and grounds beautification, not basic structural enhancements to the main building. The second year of his tenure as superintendent, Jerome Z. Gerhard, openly, and perhaps startlingly for some, called for replacement of the entire structure.

> The time has come, I most firmly believe, when it is our duty to press upon those in authority the necessity of reconstructing the entire institution. This hospital has served a good purpose for one generation, but the buildings have always been unsatisfactory. They were badly constructed in the beginning, have been a constant expense to keep in repair and can never be made secure against fire. ...[15]

Gerhard went on to compare the cost of the hospital at Harrisburg with that of the other three state hospitals that the commonwealth had built by 1882. He estimated the original cost of his facility at $150,000 plus repairs and construction of the infirmaries, wash house and gas works of $189,000. The total of $339,000 for the hospital at Harrisburg, over a period of 34 years, he asserted was negligible compared to the price for construction of the other three: $733,000 for Norristown, $985,000 for Warren and slightly more than one million dollars for Danville. He continued by appealing to the legislators' sense of pride:

> Here at the capital the State should have the best buildings, reflecting in their arrangements and construction, the most advanced ideas in the care and treatment of the insane. It is not necessary to build in an extravagant manner. Let everything be for use, and nothing for unnecessary ornaments, but the true character of the institution must be kept in view, so that the architectural arrangements will themselves produce a pleasing effect. Economy and humanity demand that the building should be substantial, secure against accidents by fire, and so arranged as to meet the various indications for classification, medical treatment, occupation and amusement.[16]

This, of course, was no more than a veiled suggestion to build a hospital constructed along the lines of the cottage system that the "young Turks" had been advocating. Gerhard would never live to see its completion and the plan ultimately adopted for the Harrisburg facility would be a modified version of the original cottage idea. Nonetheless, as Gerhard said, "the present outlook indicates that this state is about to enter upon a new era in relation to the care of the insane poor."[17]

While this may not have been true of the other state facilities, especially the State Hospital at Warren [where John Curwen had gone], by the end of the century the Pennsylvania State Lunatic Hospital would be transformed along entirely new lines. Originally it had been expected that the hospital would be a place where, with treatment, the number of acute cases and chronic insane would not increase. By 1880 it was generally recognized that these expectations were not being realized. Moreover, the realization had set in that such institutions as the one at Harrisburg had become largely "warehouses" for the chronically ill.

Thus it was proposed, and Gerhard was apparently in full

agreement, that the hospital should be reconstructed along segregated lines—it would be a place where patients exhibiting evidence of improvement could be helped, while the remainder could simply "be kept." They would be "made comfortable" and "taken care of" in the superintendent's words, but "that was all." They were to be housed, moreover, according to the severity of their malady.

Jerome Zwingli Gerhard then was clearly a man with one foot in the future. From a very religious family—all his life he continued to maintain close ties with the German Reformed Church (in Harrisburg he was a church elder)—he had no difficulty reconciling new ideas with the old. Religion and evolution were to him, for example, part of the same life fabric rather than antithetical ideas. The possibility that heredity influenced an individual's mental health, moreover, was a reasonable thought for him.

> It is a great mistake to teach that insanity is eminently a curable disease and that we can prevent the accumulation of the chronic insane by erecting hospitals and treating all cases early and promptly. If we wish to prevent the accumulation of the chronic insane, in our hospitals, we must aim at prevention rather than cure.
>
> In many families there is a weak strain, or "bad blood," and it takes only a slight cause for such a step across the line which divides sanity from hopeless insanity.[18]

He supported his claim by referring to two female patients at the Pennsylvania State Lunatic Hospital. Their grandfather was insane as were three of his children. Gerhard also explained that when insanity was looked upon as curable, if caught in time, "magnificient buildings had been erected, which were called hospitals, not asylums, because they were intended as curative institutions. But within a few years, we have come to look upon insanity as not so curable and the tendency has been to make cheaper provision and to increase the capacity of hospitals."[19]

His superintendency was to be one of transition; he seemed

to recognize this immediately. At the same time, he willingly, even actively, charted a course for those that were to follow, rather than attempt to place his own unique mark on the institution. Practicality as well as humanity, then, was the measure of the man.

*　　*　　*　　*

From his earliest years as superintendent, however, there were accomplishments for Gerhard to report. In 1881 he had called attention to the many sanitary defects existing at the hospital and the insecurity of the building against fire. The following year he was able to report that improvements had been made in both areas.

A new sewer was constructed during 1882 to carry off the waste from all the water closets, the kitchens, and the laundry, and most of the storm water from the buildings. This required a trench 2,787 feet long which ran between ten and sixteen feet deep. He proudly exclaimed that "all the excavating was done by patients, in charge of hospital attendants." "This employment," he went on to state, "was a benefit to the patients, who worked an aggregate 9,972 hours or 1,246 days of eight hours each." He estimated the value of the labor was at least $1,500. Furthermore, he claimed, "the work did not interfere with the various other means of employment."[20]

Gerhard was able to write, moreover, in 1883 that: "We take pleasure in reporting that no mechanical restraint was applied during the year, not because I believe that it is never justifiable, but because we were able to manage the patients without its use." He continued by pointing out that "a large number of patients admitted were vicious and dangerous. Some came to us in handcuffs or with hands confined with ropes ..." He claimed that one patient had been in solitary confinement in a county jail for nearly a year. "With us," Gerhard reported, "he has had the liberty of his ward from the first, and on a number of occasions has been out in the grounds."[21]

*　　*　　*　　*

In 1884, the name of John L. Atlee appears for the last time as President of the Board of Trustees of the Pennsylvania State Lunatic Hospital. The previous winter the Lancaster physician had had a stroke which left him with a facial paralysis. For a period of time he hoped that he might be able take up his duties as a trustee again but eventually came to the conclusion that this would not be possible. Atlee, who was a man of dignified bearing, and who commanded immediate respect, had been a trustee since 1856 and President of the Board since 1867. Jerome Gerhard felt the loss keenly. He called his mentor "a kind preceptor, a warm personal friend and in our official relations a devoted, wise and faithful counsellor."[22]

That year we also see the name of Addison Hutton associated for the first time with the hospital. In a rather ominous report, he confirmed the superintendent's earlier assessment of the building's condition. Hutton wrote, after an inspection designed to estimate the cost of lining the hot-air flues with metal (to reduce their chance of catching fire):

> I am struck not only with the appearance in the cellar of danger from fire, but also with the shallow, dark, ill-smelling, malaria-breeding vaults and passages, and the wretched arrangements of the heating pipes ... and with the total absence in the wards of the proper appliances for successful ventilation and the bad arrangements of the plan of the dormitories with reference to sunshine and pure air.[23]

The legislature had appropriated only $500 for this work, so the best the superintendent was able to do was to remove unnecessary walls and obstructions in the basement and to cut large windows in the outside cellar walls in hopes of admitting enough sunlight and air to reduce the chance for health problems. As to the potential for fire, there was little he could do.

During Gerhard's early years as superintendent, the name of H. L. Orth also appears in the hospital reports for the first time. He was not a permanent member of the staff but a Harrisburg physician who was called on whenever there were operations to be performed. In 1882, for example, Orth completed a successful operation for a patient who had a "strangulated hernia." The superintendent claimed that "we are under obligations to him for surgical services in this and other cases."[24]

*   *   *   *

While Jerome Gerhard was active in proposing a major revamping of the entire hospital, to the patients, their families, and visitors to the institution, life continued much the same as in previous years. In 1885 a brass band of eleven pieces was organized. It was composed of patients and attendants, and was directed by one of the physicians. The superintendent claimed that it "furnished diversion and entertainment for the household." That same year the reading-room on the grounds of the male side of the house was converted into a gymnasium and quickly became "a source of great pleasure and benefit to some of the patients." What the men who used to read did, once the gym was built, is not mentioned.

Since he continued to recommend each year that the old buildings should be replaced by new ones, the superintendent did not feel that he should ask the legislature for much money to be used on the old wards; however, by 1888 they were in such poor shape that he had them repainted, the corridors recarpeted and the furniture generally overhauled. As a result of this overhaul, they were "now more bright and cheerful and more comfortable."[25]

The patients, especially the male ones, were employed in increasing numbers each year during Gerhard's administration. They were kept busy doing "valuable work" on the pleasure grounds, on the farm, and in the garden and the workshops. The superintendent estimated that the work during 1888 on the pleasure grounds alone represented 5,050 days of labor—savings to the state, at $1.25 per day, of $6,312.50. The men were used not only to grade the grounds but also for digging drainage trenches and breaking up stones. Female patients, of course, worked in the kitchen and the laundry. More than half of the patients were so employed. As "an inducement to proper conduct and industry," the more trustworthy working men were given parole on the grounds on Sundays.[26]

The superintendent used work in a variety of ways; in one habeas corpus case even to gain freedom for a prisoner who had been sent to the hospital from the Eastern penitentiary. The man, a black, had come to Harrisburg on a court order, but to Gerhard "did not show any symptoms of insanity." Moreover he "seemed to have as much intelligence as other persons in his condition of life." The superintendent reported:

> As he was industrious and anxious to make money, I allowed him to work on the new building, and to keep all he could earn. After he had saved thirty dollars, I applied to court for an order to discharge him, which was granted and he left the Hospital a happy man.[27]

There is little doubt about where the Pennsylvania legislature stood on the issue of work. In the Act that established the Asylum for the Chronic Insane at Wernersville, they expressly directed that the hospital trustees were to "secure the safe and economical employment of the largest number of the asylum, for the purpose of enabling said inmates to contribute, to the extent of their ability, to the cost of their maintenance." The act even went so far as to instruct the Commissioners building the hospital to "transfer twenty able-bodied, harmless, chronic insane, from each of the hospitals for the insane, to the premises ... to engage in farm work, grading, macadamizing, excavating for buildings and such other employment as may be required. ..."[28]

One change in the life of the patients dealt with their meal taking. Beginning in 1888, the attendants started sitting down (at the head of the table) with the patients. The attendants and the patients then ate family style, each helping the other. The patients were required to remain at the tables until all were done. Then "at a given signal all rose and retired to the day room." This congregate meal plan was brought about because, according to the superintendent, there were "many objections to having patients eat in small ward dining rooms." Although the new scheme did permit central storage of food supplies as well as central preparation (in a newly constructed kitchen building) and also more economical and judicious distribution of meals, it also (and probably more importantly) permitted Gerhard to convert some of the ward dining rooms into dormitories for the growing number of patients. By 1891 the number being treated had passed the one thousand mark. The hospital residents (male patients and attendants) not only did all the excavation work for the new kitchen and the covered passageways from it to the boiler-house and the storeroom but also built an ice house in 1886 at the head of the ice pond.

In 1891, Jerome Z. Gerhard decided to return to private practice. He summarized his tenure in that year's annual report:

> During the past eleven years we have fortunately been exempt from loss by fire. The value of the property has also greatly increased. At the beginning of the decade we had one hundred and twenty-nine acres of land; now we have two hundred and twenty-six, and there is an appropriation of $20,000 available for the purchase of additional land. The grounds of the hospital have been greatly improved and beautified, at moderate expense, and much of the labor was performed by patients. The sewerage of the entire institution has been rebuilt; the water closets in the old buildings have all been reconstructed and greatly improved and the buildings, in most particulars, are in better condition than they were ten years ago. The capacity of the hospital has been increased three hundred and twenty beds by the erection of branch buildings, one for each sex.
>
> A new boilerhouse has been constructed, including coal vault, machineshop, laundry, and accomodations for a number of employees ... The out buildings, including the barn, house for the Steward, stable for driving horses and the gardener's house have been greatly improved; and the green house and icehouse entirely rebuilt.
>
> The institution is in sound financial condition, no

bills remain unpaid and the treasurer has in hand $14,349.80 for current expenses.[29]

In one last appeal to the legislature for a new hospital, he wrote: "Great advances have been made in the care and treatment of the insane. ... The style of architecture has changed and much more attention is now given to the classification and employment, as well as to the entertainment and amusement of patients." He then attempted to drive his point home by invoking the memory of Dorothea Dix:

As long as fifteen years ago Miss Dix, who helped to locate this hospital and was always interested in its welfare, and who was practical and economical in her recommendations in the construction of the hospital, said to me that she could not help but feel that it would be a good thing if it would burn to the ground, providing the patients and everybody connected with it were safely out of the building.[30]

He closed his final report by recommending that Pennsylvania adopt the policy which the State of New York had. He suggested a review of his 1888 report, which also referred to D. Hack Tuke's "Cane Hill." In 1890 the New York State Legislature had passed comprehensive legislation that called for the removal of all patients from almshouses and other county care facilities into state-run hospitals.[31] In 1883 the Pennsylvania legislature had passed a law with a similar intent, but left the decision to the Committee on Lunacy (of the Board of Charities) to be based on where the patients could be "better cared for."

First many patients were moved into the state hospitals. Then as these facilities became crowded, the boards of trustees of many, including the hospital at Harrisburg, began to refuse to admit new patients. In 1891 the legislature, at the suggestion of the Board of Charities, passed a new law authorizing the re-transfer of any or all patients from the State Hospitals to the county houses.[32]

* * * *

The trustees accepted Jerome Gerhard's resignation with regret. They expressed their confidence in his integrity and appreciated the zeal and fidelity which he displayed. They claimed that "under the experienced, judicious, and humane mangement of Doctor Gerhard, the general direction of the Hospital has been good and the medical management efficient." They then proceeded to elect Henry L. Orth as the third superintendent of the Pennsylvania State Lunatic Hospital. He was to take charge on November 1, 1891.[33]

Gerhard opened a practice in Harrisburg. There he worked principally with alcoholics (many of whom he took into his home for rehabilitation) and as an expert on insanity in medico-legal cases. He died on November 20, 1906 after a brief illness following a cold. The cause of death was given as "congestion of the brain." He had been a member of the Pennsylvania State Medical Association, the American Medical Association and of the Dauphin County Medical Society. He served as president of the latter organization in 1883. At the time of his death he was president of the consistory of the Salem Reformed Church. He was buried with his parents and his brothers and his sisters in Greenwood Cemetery in Lancaster.[34]

END NOTES

1. Gerhard, Jerome Z., *Annual Report of the Pennsylvania State Lunatic Hospital, 1881*, Theo. F. Scheffer, Harrisburg, 1881, page 8.
2. Ibid.
3. Gerhard, Jerome Z., *Annual Report of the Pennsylvania State Lunatic Hospital, 1881*, Theo. F. Scheffer, Harrisburg, 1881, page 9.
4. Gerhard, Jerome Z., *Annual Report of the Pennsylvania State Lunatic Hospital, 1881*, Theo. F. Scheffer, Harrisburg, 1881, page 11-12.
5. Dickert, Thomas W., editor, *Life of the Rev. Clavin S. Gerhard, D.D.*, Sunday School Board of the Reformed Church in the United States, Philadelphia, 1904, page 20.
6. Ibid., pages 22-23.
7. *Obituary Record*, Vol. 2, Part 5, No. 9, published by the Alumni Association of Franklin and Marshall College, June 1905, pages 203-206. One brother, Jacob Alfred, died at age 26, while finishing his theological training.
8. Atlee was the professor of Anatomy and Physiology at Franklin and Marshall between the years 1852 and 1870. In all probability Jerome Gerhard first studied there with the older physician.
9. Egle, William T., *Biographical Encyclopedia of Dauphin County*, J. M. Runk and Company, Chambersburg, Pa., 1896, page 372.
10. Ibid.
11. Jerome Z. Gerhard, *Letter Press Book*, 1883, February 5, 1883.

12. Ibid.
13. Jerome Z. Gerhard, *Letter Press Book*, 1883, letter of February 7, 1883.
14. Egle, op. cit., page 372. The Gerhards had two daughters, Elizabeth Hill and Alice Hill.
15. Gerhard, Jerome Z., *Annual Report of the Pennsylvania State Lunatic Hospital, 1882*, Theo. F. Scheffer, Harrisburg, 1882, page 10. Gerhard's assessment was based in part on the report of the architect, John Sunderland, who had been hired in 1881 to inspect the hospital. Sunderland found it "impracticable to alter or make it in any way safe except by the expenditure of a large sum of money." The architect also claimed that "you would only have an old building very expensive to keep in repair."
16. Gerhard, Jerome Z., *Annual Report of the Pennsylvania State Lunatic Hospital, 1882*, Theo. F. Scheffer, Harrisburg, 1882, page 10.
17. Ibid.
18. Gerhard, Jerome Z., *Annual Report of the Pennsylvania State Lunatic Hospital, 1887*, Theo. F. Scheffer, Harrisburg, 1887, pages 9—10.
19. Gerhard, Jerome Z., *Annual Report of the Pennsylvania State Lunatic Hospital, 1882*, Theo. F. Scheffer, Harrisburg, 1882, page 10.
20. Ibid.
21. Gerhard, Jerome Z., *Annual Report of the Pennsylvania State Lunatic Hospital, 1883*, Theo. F. Scheffer, Harrisburg, 1883, page 9.
22. Gerhard, Jerome Z., *Annual Report of the Pennsylvania State Lunatic Hospital, 1884*, Theo. F. Scheffer, Harrisburg, 1884, page 16. Although his practice was restricted to Lancaster, John Atlee's national reputation went well beyond his professional medical associations. He gained recognition early in his career as a bold surgeon. It was estimated that he performed more than 2,125 operations during his lifetime, including 78 ovariotomies, a precedure considered risky when he first did one in 1843.
23. Gerhard, Jerome Z., *Annual Report of the Pennsylvania State Lunatic Hospital, 1884*, Theo. F. Scheffer, Harrisburg, 1884, page 5.
24. Gerhard, Jerome Z., *Annual Report of the Pennsylvania State Lunatic Hospital, 1882*, Theo. F. Scheffer, Harrisburg, 1882, page 10.
25. Gerhard, Jerome Z., *Annual Report of the Pennsylvania State Lunatic Hospital, 1888*, Theo. F. Scheffer, Harrisburg, 1888, page ll.
26. Ibid., pages 9-10.
27. Gerhard, Jerome Z., *Annual Report of the Pennsylvania State Lunatic Hospital, 1887*, Theo. F. Scheffer, Harrisburg, 1887, page 10.
28. Curwen, John, "Provision For The Insane In Hospitals Specially Constructed For The Insane," report to the Pennsylvania Medical Society, *The Pennsylvania Medical Journal*, Vol. II, No. 4, September 1898, page 191. Curwen, of course, was objecting to the provisions on patient labor in the 1891 Act of the legislature.
29. Gerhard, Jerome Z., *Annual Report of the Pennsylvania State Lunatic Hospital, 1891*, Theo. F. Scheffer, Harrisburg, 1891, page 11-12.
30. Gerhard, Jerome Z., *Annual Report of the Pennsylvania State Lunatic Hospital, 1890*, Theo. F. Scheffer, Harrisburg, 1890, page 15.
31. Deutsch, Albert, *The Mentally Ill in America*, Columbia University Press, New York, 1937, pages 260-261.
32. Orth, Henry L., *Annual Report of the Pennsylvania State Lunatic Hospital, 1893*, Harrisburg Publishing Company, Harrisburg, 1893, page 11.
33. "Trustees' Report," *Annual Report of the Pennsylvania State Lunatic Hospital, 1891*, Theo. F. Scheffer, Harrisburg, 1891, page 8.
34. *Obituary Record*, Vol. 2, Part 5, –9, published by the Alumni Association of Franklin and Marshall College, June 1905, pages 203-206.

XII

A NEW HOSPITAL RISES

When the nine trustees elected Henry Lawrence Orth as the new superintendent of the Pennsylvania State Lunatic Hospital, they not only selected one of their own (he had been appointed to the board two years earlier) they also picked a man with ties to the hospital that went back to its earliest years.

Rebecca Orth, Henry Orth's aunt, was married to Luther Reily, who had been President of the Board of Trustees during the early years of the hospital's development and Edward Lawrence Orth, Henry's father, was in private practice in Harrisburg with his brother-in-law for many years. It was Edward who had maintained their patient load, while Luther Reily served in the state legislature. Edward, moreover, became the medical preceptor of his nephew, George Wolf Reily, Luther and Rebecca Reily's son. And it was the two older physicans who established the library that was to become the nucleus for the Luther-Orth-Reily Medical Library of the Harrisburg Academy of Medicine at the turn of the century. Young Henry probably consulted the books in this medical library during his student years.[1]

Henry Lawrence Orth was born in Harrisburg in 1842. His great-grandfather had emigrated from the Palatinate, Germany to Lebanon County, Pennsylvania, in 1730. For several generations the family was among the pioneers involved in the manufacture of iron. Several members also served in political offices: a county commissioner, a district attorney and as clerk in the state House of Representatives.

Young Henry attended the Harrisburg Academy (as had his father) and from there went to Yale College in 1859. His education was interrupted three years later, however, by the outbreak of the Civil War. In 1861 he was appointed a medical cadet and was commissioned in the regular army in 1863. During the next two years he developed proficiency as a surgeon. After his discharge in 1865, he spent one year of study in the medical department of the University of Pennsylvania. He graduated the following year.[2]

Henry returned to Harrisburg after graduation but rather than going into private practice he became the surgeon for the Northern Central Railway Company. In 1873 be was appointed as the surgeon of the Pennsylvania Railroad Company and in August of that same year also became the "visiting surgeon" for the Pennsylvania State Lunatic Hospital, a position he held for eighteen years.

*　　*　　*　　*

The struggle over the physical form that hospitals for the mentally ill should take had raged for several decades, not only in America but also in Europe. On the one hand stood the linear, monolithic Kirkbride structure. At the other extreme was the dispersed "Cottage Plan," as exemplified by Gheel in Belgium. By late in the nineteenth century, psychiatry had become an international discipline. (One of Orth's first assistants, J. J. Kindred, for example, left Harrisburg in 1892 to accept a position in Edinburgh, Scotland.) Visits and ideas were regularly exchanged in both directions across the Atlantic. And Gheel was one of the mandatory stops that doctors studying mental patient care facilities around the world would include in their itinerary.[3]

In Gheel the entire community took responsibility for the insane. Each patient was placed in a private home where the residents looked after their charge as if he or she were a member of the family. Although the Gheel concept was much discussed among the younger members of the American Association of Superintendents of Insane Institutions, and a trial effort was made in Massachusetts, the idea per se was never adopted in this country. Rather it became a rallying point in attacking the older physicians and their entrenched ideas on patient care and hospital construction.

Jerome Gerhard had led the push for change in Harrisburg for a decade. The hospital building was more than 40 years old. Curwen was at Warren; Kirkbride was dead. Now it was Henry L. Orth to whom the task was passed. He accepted the challenge.

*   *   *   *

Nearly four of the five pages of Orth's first "Report of the Superintendent" were devoted to the "deplorable and almost uninhabitable condition of the building" of which he was in charge. He described it as "totally inadequate for the care and maintenance, much less the treatment, of the insane of the seventeen counties of this district." Orth claimed that "the sure but gradual deterioration of the inferior materials in the house has been going on for years, and cannot be retarded." He closed his comments on the condition of the house by stating: "it becomes a grave question how long the walls will hold together."[4]

The 1891 legislature had appropriated $10,000 for repairs and, after much deliberation among the trustees and their superintendent, the ward floors had been replaced and repairs were made to the outside air ducts and drains. The grounds in the immediate vicinity of the buildings were also regraded to reduce the chances of surface water damaging further the foundations and running into the cellar. In his 1892 report the new superintendent, moreover, explained that, being forced to house 864 patients in a hospital with a capacity of 700, "no provision can be made for the necessary classification of the different grades of insanity, and scientific treatment cannot be adapted to their cure."[5]

Money was also expended that year in moving the pig pens, which by then were within the limits of the growing city of Harrisburg. For several years complaints had been made that the surrounding air was filled with foul odors. Although the staff made every effort to keep the pens clean, the ground had become saturated over the years and, being in a low part of the hospital grounds, were always damp. Therefore it was considered impossible to correct the offensiveness to the satisfaction of the hospital's neighbors. The trustees, with the approval of the "farm committee," finally agreed to move the pigs to a spot 150 yards to the rear of the barn. There the ground was excavated to three feet, the space filled with 2½ feet of stone and then the stone covered with Dykerhoff cement. Orth described the new location as "sweet for pig pens."[6]

There were positive things for Henry Orth to report, however, in 1892. The previous May contracts had been let for the erection of an electric light plant. By the time of his report most of the house had been wired and the "dynamos were being placed in position" in the laundry building, which had been adapted for their installation. One advantage of the electrification was that "an electric watch-clock, with stations in each ward," was installed so that "a reliable record of the order and time of the movement, through the house, of the night watches and nurses" could be secured. Larger water mains also were installed and patent fire extinguishers were distributed through the wards giving "every safe-guard that intelligence can suggest" to protect the house and its residents from fire.[7]

*   *   *   *

With the recommendation of the Board of Public Charities, the Pennsylvania Legislature finally appropriated $100,000 in May, 1893 for the "rebuilding of the central portion of the main building."[8] This was to be just "the first step." According to Orth, Addison Hutton, of Philadelphia, was hired to draw plans for not only this construction, but also for a new group of hospital buildings. The operating philosophy employed by Orth and Hutton in their planning was that Kirkbride's linear design (which had been constructed "to secure compactness and economy of administration") retarded the recovery of patients. A building with wings of three or four stories in height on each side of a large central administration building, and with bedrooms on both sides of long corridors, which were utilized for day use by patients, all made for "a dull monotonous structure" of "depressing influence."[9]

They claimed, on the other hand, that while the village or cottage plan permitted variety and opportunity for subdivision and classification, all of which would improve chances for recovery, "in the variable climate of this country an outright cottage plan was not desirable." Their plans called for combining certain features of the linear plan with those of the cottage. They proposed to build a new hospital where the buildings were "adapted to our location" and embodied "all that is best in recent hospital architecture." They estimated the cost at $400,000 and stated the following as "cardinal rules."[10]

> The buildings will not exceed two stories in height. Two stairways will lead from the second stories, for easy escape in case of fire.
>
> The buildings are to be fire-proof; and will be so constructed that they can be warmed at all times to a temperature of 70 degree Fh.
>
> They will be constructed to permit the conditions of domestic life. There will be diversity, and no operative department will be in basements.
>
> Ample cubic space will be provided for ventilation and with out materially increasing the cost of maintenance or sacrificing the essential appliances for proper treatment and custody of the several classes.

Orth went on to describe the plans as consisting "of a central building and four cottages on each side connected with corridors, but so constructed as to avoid their objectionable features. These cottages are respectively for reception, observation and convalescent and disturbed wards, and will accommodate about 200 patients; in the rear and attached by corridors, will be six wards to accommodate 500 patients"— apparently the chronic ones. The plans also included a bakery, congregate dining-room, chapel, amusement hall, dormitory for nurses, and the "numberless out-buildings" necessary for the economical administration of a hospital for 1,000 patients.[11]

The superintendent also had Hutton prepare a plan and an estimate for a reservoir to hold 1,000,000 gallons of water; enough for one week's storage. He further claimed that to give air, space and exercise room in a hospital, "it was well established" that "there should be one-half acre of ground" for the support of each insane patient." To support the expected 1,000 patients this would require the purchase of 210 acres in addition to the 292 acres the hospital owned in 1893. For this he estimated $63,000 would be required. Some of the furniture in the old building would be usable, but Orth asked for an additional $10,000 to buy new.[12]

These then were no small plans.

*   *   *   *

Addison Hutton knew Harrisburg well even before he became an architect. He had been born in Westmoreland County and as a young man often made the trip between the office of Samuel Sloan, the well-known Philadelphia architect, and his parents' home. In those days, before the introduction of railroad sleeper cars, an overnight stop in Harrisburg was usual for railroad travelers between Pittsburgh and Philadelphia.[13]

Addison was born to Quaker parents living on the frontier west of Pittsburgh—at one time along the Ohio River and at another along the Pennsylvania Turnpike. His formal schooling was confined to two brief periods totaling about eight months. As a young man of sixteen he began an apprenticeship as a carpenter with his father, Joel. The elder Hutton was an expert, proficient workman and with him Addison developed his skills with tools. During this period, a fellow workman, Robert Grimacy, gave the young man a few lessons in architectural drawing. From this beginning, Addison developed his direction for life.[14]

The young Hutton's hiring by Sloan was pure happenstance. Sloan was in Greensburg during the spring of 1857 in connection with the building of a courthouse he had designed and asked one of the County Commissioners to recommend someone to work in his Philadelphia office. The commissioner recommended his nephew, Addison, who had recently been working with Grimacy. Sloan was impressed with Addison's clarity of expression and his neat handwriting and hired him.[15])

By 1859 Sloan was sending his apprentice south to North Carolina and Mississippi to oversee the building of Sloan designs for private homes. The Civil War brought an abrupt end to this work, but by 1862 Hutton was receiving independent architectural commissions such as the one for Henry Morris's "cottage" at Newport, Rhode Island. In December of 1862 the young architect opened his own office in "the business heart of the city." A year later, after turning down several offers by Sloan, Addison signed a partnership agreement and the office of Sloan & Hutton was established.[16]

Among the many commissions the new firm received were ones for the State Hospital at Middletown, Connecticut; alterations and an addition to the State Hospital in Trenton; the Third Presbyterian Church in Pittsburgh and Parrish Hall, the first building of Swarthmore College. The partners also designed a number of Philadelphia residences.[17] In January 1868 Samuel Sloan moved to New York and their partnership was dissolved.

By 1875 Hutton had reached maturity as an architect. "His solidly constructed office buildings, hospitals, churches, banks, libraries and markets were scattered throughout Philadelphia." During this period, too, he built many Main Line houses. So many that J. W. Townsend claimed that Hutton was responsible for developing a distinctive Main Line style. Hutton, moreover, served as the architect for two Quaker colleges, Haverford and Bryn Mawr. Many of the original student dormitories and lecture halls on both campuses were designed and constructed by Hutton.[18] Packer Hall at Lehigh University was also one of his buildings.

"Though fond of finely executed work, Addison Hutton had little tolerance for the overly ornate. He was more in sympathy with ... strong, utilitarian construction." One example of this was the large residence he built for A. J. Dull on Front Street, Harrisburg. It was a solid and durable dwelling of brick. There was, however, a delicately sculptured design about three inches wide between the first and second floors. The interior, with its mosaic floor in the small entrance porch and the elaborately carved mantels and Italian tiles around the fireplace, all gave evidence of the architect's attention to detail.[19]

It was probably as a result of his various trips (fourteen times in 1881 alone) to work on the Dull residence that Hutton first became involved with the trustees of the Pennsylvania State Lunatic Hospital. Now demolished, the Dull residence was a prominent city landmark for years and Dull, if not a close friend, would certainly have been known by Charles L. Bailey or L. W. Hall of Harrisburg, both of whom were trustees of the Hospital. It may have been through them that the introduction was first made.

Hutton seems to have had a special fondness for designing hospitals. "I plead," he wrote of such institutions, "that the skill of an architect can modify the appearance of almost anything, ... so as to render it a thing inoffensive and, with perhaps a slight addition to the expense, a thing of beauty." The topic of one 1894 lecture he gave at the University of Pennsylvania was titled "The Planning of Hospitals." Among the many observations he made was one that summarized the late-nineetenth-century view of state care for the mentally ill:

> The Middle Ages were the Cathedral building centuries. The Nineteenth Century is the era of railroads and high buildings. The Twentieth Century, with the growing tendency of the strong to help the weak and the unfortunate, ... may prove to be an age of scientific healing, and more universal, enlightened and charitable work than has ever before been seen in the world.[20]

*   *   *   *

One of the more original designs that Hutton produced— certainly the most imaginative one for the Pennsylvania State Lunatic Hospital—was done in 1900. It was the building for the Chronic Insane.[21] Two buildings in one, each structure (one was for the men and the other for the women) was rotated 45 degrees so that its corners were to the front, back and sides. The two were then joined together, at the corners where the buildings sided each other, by a large congregate dining room. The architectural drawing gives the appearance today of a design for a giant space station.

Each of the dormitory buildings opened in the center to a large "airing court." Ringing this airing court, two of the four sides of each structure were devoted to dormitories and two to day rooms. The front and back corners of each were devoted to facilities for bathing, laundry and storage. In the extreme end corners of each building were the infirmaries—one for the men and at the other the one for the women. The whole structure thus provided maximum ventilation and sunlight for the patients but afforded adequate separation of the men and women as well as privacy. It admirably fulfilled his hope that "on every day of the year in which the sun shines, at least three walls will be bathed in sunshine."

The Orth-Hutton plans were still based, however, on the premise that "treatment of insanity implies far more than treatment of the disease affecting other organs, ... and comprises [both the] bodily and mental. ... The former is therapeutical and hygienic, the latter is psychical and has definite relation to construction and surroundings." The design of the new Pennsylvania State Lunatic Hospital followed principles suggested in a report of the Commission for the erection of the St. Lawrence Hospital in New York. The plans were both "sanitary and aesthetic" and were designed to "bear upon the bodily and mental welfare of the patients subjected to their influences."[22]

*   *   *   *

While the first of the new buildings were going up, Orth continued to report problems with the existing structures. Both the male and the female "branch buildings" which had been erected in 1887 to house the overflow of patients gave trouble and during the spring of 1894 "diarrhoeal and dysenteric diseases prevailed." Orth attributed these to "filth due to imperfect ventilation." This problem was corrected by "placing steam coils in iron chests" in the attics with outlets on the roof. From these chests large ventilation pipes were run to each closet, thereby securing a continuous downward ventilation through the closets. He reported "there has not been a single case of dysentery ... since the introduction of this apparatus."[23]

The hospital was generally free of serious diseases during the next few years. In 1897, however, two attendants were "seized with typhoid fever." On investigation it was found that the creek water was contaminated with typhoid bacilli. Although drinking water was supplied to the hospital from an artesian well, the creek water came through spigots, which were controlled by keys in the possession of the attendants.

It was intended for general use only; not for drinking. The two men had been consuming it persistently and had become ill. The artesian well was also a problem during dry summers. The pump, which had originally gone to 195 feet, had to be "dropped to 400 feet" that year to maintain an adequate supply. After this improvement, the water from the well was "abundant and of good quality."[24]

A more serious problem occurred that year, however, with the dairy herd. The State Veterinarian from the Board of Agriculture had been called to examine the cows to determine if they were affected with tuberculosis. They were inoculated with tuberculin. In "two bulls, thirty-eight cows and six heifers they found diseased glands, or large masses of caseous matter thus verifying the tuberculin test." All were destroyed.

The large number of diseased cattle made it obvious, moreover, that the hospital's stables were contaminated and demanded a thorough cleaning and disinfection. The stalls and wooden floors were removed, six inches of earth floor scraped away and removed. Then the ground was treated with sulphate of iron solution, fresh earth installed and the walls and ceilings carefully scrubbed with a solution of green soap. All the wood was then douched with a solution of mercuric bichloride and whitewashed. New cedar wood stalls were erected. After much difficulty, "milch-cows" that would resist the tuberculin test were finally found and in May Orth purchased a bull and forty new cows.[25]

Reports of tuberculosis among the hospital's patients, on the other hand, had been made as early as 1888. Periodically in the years following there would be reports of death from tuberculosis. Each of these patient deaths was attributed, however, as occurring to individuals who were infected at the time of their admittance. The threat of an epidemic, though, always existed in an instituion such as the Pennsylvania State Lunatic Hospital.

Tuberculosis, which is still a scourge, received a great deal of attention in the late nineteenth and early twentieth centuries when the outbreak worldwide grew to significant levels. Sanatoria, great structures not unlike asylums for the insane, were built around the nation.[26] These were usually in high places with lots of fresh air. With rest, good food, and nursing care, many patients could build up resistance against the tubercle bacillus and eventually seal it off. The development in the twentieth century of antituberculous drugs, such as streptomycin and isonicotinic acid, has brought the disease under control in developed countries but it continues to flourish in many underdeveloped nations.

In 1894 there were three deaths at the Pennsylvania State Lunatic Hospital from tuberculosis; the year before there had only been one. By 1897 the number had grown to 12 and the following year the superintendent reported that 16 patients had died from the disease. A decade later Orth reported that "fully twenty per cent of our admissions suffer with tubercular trouble." Part of this accounting was attributed to improved methods of examination. Infected patients were isolated, subjected to large amounts of fresh air and sunlight, as well as with careful feeding. These efforts retarded the advance of the disease, yet the number of recoveries was small. [27]

During the Orth years the longstanding Pennsylvania State Lunatic Hospital practice of treating patients with alcohol, especially to help them sleep at night, was finally discontinued. In 1903 he wrote that its use previously "may have had some influence in warding off death," but that its discontinuance for one year proved that the claim of benefits were mistaken, and that the results were "so pleasing and so in accordance with expectations, that this method of treatment will be continued."

* * * *

From early in Jerome Gerhard's years as superintendent, occasional use had been made of a pathologist. The results of autopsies, for example, were being reported (rather sketchily) by 1888.[28] Autopsies were only performed on indigents, however, so there was no need for the services of a full-time pathologist. Gerhard had recommended that, important as the work was, the position should be shared with the other state hospitals. This suggestion was never implemented. Rather, beginning with the Orth years, it was the practice to hire as an assistant, a physician who also served as pathologist.

In 1894 Orth had hired W. H. Harrison away from the Pennsylvania Hospital for the Insane, where he had served several years as the Assistant Physician and Pathologist. Harrison began working at Harrisburg in the same two positions, conducting ten post-mortem examinations during his first six months. These were investigations, not so much into reasons for the death of the patients, but rather into those for their insanity. He reported that "in all there were evidences of disease in the brain and its membranes as well as in other parts of the physical system." The pathologist examined microscopically the waste and degeneration of the cells of the brain and cord as well as of the nerve fibre.

The pathologist also conducted a urine analysis of each new patient admitted and of selected older residents of the hospital. His report stated that "we believe that the quantity and quality of urine are commonly altered in insanity." It was also Harrison's plan to start making "systematic examinations of the blood" ... to be "able to learn much of the effect of food and medicine on the human economy." If these investigations were fruitful, the results would be used to "guide the the hospital's medical and dietary treatment of the insane."[29]

Harrison had been hired only because Orth was a firm superintendent in the Curwen mold as well as a forward-looking one. J. T. Sprague, who had been appointed in April 1893 had "found hospital life uncongenial." At Orth's request, he "severed his relations with us." Thus there was a vacancy. In spite of his toughness, the superintendent had a sense of humor. He wrote in one annual report: "During the winter months five boilers are fired and sometimes six, though this is avoided as far as possible, ... a boiler, like a human being, requires rest, unless a short life and a merry one is desired."[30]

The superintendent also continued to perform operations after his appointment as the head of the institution. Jane Garver described one successful laparotomy he performed in 1892 as very complicated and difficult. She called it a case of a fibro-cystic tumor.[31] In another instance the next year a male patient, who suffered an attack of petite mal while eating, started to choke on a piece of beef. With the man lying on the floor of the dining room, Orth performed a tracheotomy using his pocket knife. No reason was given for why the superintendent of a major hospital carried a pocket knife—whether he whittled sticks with it, as he had as a boy, or as is more likely, simply used it to cut the ends off of his cigars.

Orth, as had Gerhard, also apparently believed in the influence of heredity on insanity. Beginning in 1894 he reported detailed statistics of each admission's history of family insanity. He collected the data in nine categories including: Father, mother, both parents, brother, sister, brother and sister, and cousins. The statistics for that year also are broken down for the first time to show the number of "white" and "colored" in the hospital. Of the 815 patients, 25 were black. These were probably not all new admissions, but there is no record of when the first black was accepted at Harrisburg.[32] The first reference to one, of course, was the prison laborer that Jerome Gerhard had helped to gain his freedom in 1887.

*   *   *   *

The name of the York, Pennsylvania architect, John Augustus Dempwolf, became associated with the Pennsylvania State Lunatic Hospital about the turn of the century. It is not clear when or how, since most of the drawings for the new buildings at Harrisburg contain the name of Hutton while a few are labeled with the names of both Hutton and Dempwolf. More than likely Hutton grew tired of commuting between Philadelphia and the hospital on a regular basis and first approached Dempwolf to oversee the actual construction. Finding Dempwolf eminently reliable, the trustees and Hutton then probably turned over to him gradually the responsibility for the design of the hospital outbuildings as well as the construction of some of Hutton's designs for the main structures.

Dempwolf had been born in Brunswick, Germany, in 1848 and had come to York in 1867 as a young man. He began as a carpenter and in 1870 started to work for Nathaniel Weigel, a York building contractor. With Weigel he made most of the full size detail drawings of St. Paul's Lutheran Church in the city. The church had been designed by Stephen D. Button of Philadelphia. After two years of study at the Cooper Union Institute in New York, John Dempwolf joined Button in the design of some of the buildings for the Centennial Exposition of 1876. He then returned to York and established a successful architectural firm with his brother Reinhardt.[33]

Over the next fifty years the Dempwolf firm built many of the schoolhouses, banks and public buildings in the central Pennsylvania area. Among these were the York Trust Company, the National Bank Building in the same city, the Carlisle Hospital and the York County Court House. Churches, such as Saint Mary's Catholic in York, and the Evangelical churches in Johnstown and Steelton, Pennsylvania also figured among his many commissions. Several of the buildings on the campus of the Gettysburg College also were of Dempwolf design.

John Dempwolf also constructed and enlarged a significant number of personal residences, especially parsonages. The most impressive of his private designs, however, were the twin residences (East and West Hill) of the two Glatfelter brothers of Spring Grove, Pennsylvania. Dempwolf, together with the well-known landscape architect F. L. Olmsted, studied the area around Spring Grove throughout the four seasons of the year before selecting the site and positioning the houses. The estate included a greenhouse, a stable, houses for servants, a garage for ten cars and an enclosed swimming pool.[34]

Among the distinctive brick buildings he built at the Pennsylvania State Lunatic Hospital were the Chapel, the Sun Parlor and several ward buildings. This was a period in American achitecture often referred to by the general term of "Victorian." A more precise description of Dempwolf's style, however, would be that of "restrained classicism," although he originally exhibited strong Queen Anne tendencies.[35]

*　　*　　*　　*

Each year during the last decade of the nineteenth century, the Pennsylvania governor continued to come for the hospital's Christmas exercises. The board of trustees would be there too. The Governor and the President of the Board would make short addresses to the patients. There would be music. The hospital choir would sing and often a musical group from Harrisburg, usually a string or brass band, would give "delightful music." The wards would be decorated with spruce, ferns, and by 1897 with colored electric lights. Candies, oranges and cakes would be distributed to all the patients in the hospital.

The farm and the garden continued to produce abundantly in most years, although on occasion there were lean seasons due to a lack of rainfall. By the nineties, moreover, the steward's report of J. B. Livingston showed that the hospital was consuming huge amounts of food each year. In addition to the meat and produce raised at Harrisburg, in 1892 25,710 pounds of butter, 9,855 dozen eggs, 192,443 pounds of fresh beef, 12,399 pounds of fish, 37,288 pounds of sugar and 1,300 barrels of flour were purchased.

Five years later the figures for these items were all at least 15 to 20 percent higher. The staff, if not the patients, had a varied diet.[36] In addition to beef, there were ham, chicken, sausage, veal, mutton, liver and tongue. For fruits there were apples, bananas, cranberries, grapes, melons of all kinds, oranges, peaches, pears and quinces. Although nearly five thousand pounds of rice was being consumed each year, potatoes were still the hospital's staple.[37]

The women, too, were as busy in the house as the men were on the farm and about the grounds. They worked primarily in the laundry and in the kitchen, but also did housework throughout the building. One very important job, apparently done in the day areas of the house, consisted of sewing, knitting and fancy needlework. In 1893, for example, Jane Garver reported that they made 2,651 dresses, 4,162 articles of other types of wearing apparel, and 5,246 articles of household furnishings. The sheets, pillowcases, tablecloths, napkins, and towels for the entire household as well as the women's undergarments were made by the female patients.[38] Henry Orth claimed that the sewing room, where all the linen of the house is prepared and kept in repair, "gives employment to many, but does not amuse and seldom arouses them."[39]

It was not all work for the women. They did enjoy a variety

of amusements, including walking, tennis and croquet. There were singing groups to join (one winter evening the group "rendered a semi-operatic version of Cinderella"), an occasional dance or a summer's day picnic on the hospital grounds, as well as games to be played and books to be read. There were also trips to the "wild woods" to pick flowers or hunt for chestnuts. Garver reported that these afforded "keen pleasure" to those participating. On a few occasions a select number of female patients were invited, by the family of a fellow inmate, to spend a day in the country. The head of the Female Department also hired a woman in 1894 whom she described as "skilled in massage and Swedish movements" but reported that the patient's "mental improvement has not been commensurate with the physical gain observed."[40]

Early in Orth's administration the rate for care and maintenance of patients was down to $3.63 per week, "the lowest weekly rate but one since the organization of the hospital," he claimed. By 1894, moreover, there was an unexpended balance of $9,751.33 on the treasurer's books, which was being used to pay the hospital tradesmen's accounts as soon as the bills came in. That year. however, they were required to start returning all excesses to the State Treasury. Since the Auditor General only paid the hospital quarterly, the superintendent reported, "this deprivation of a working balance necessarily makes us dilatory in our payments."[41]

END NOTES

1. Laverty, George Lauman, *History of Medicine in Dauphin County, Pennsylvania*, The Dauphin County Medical Society, 1966, pages 154-155.
2. Egle, William H., *Biographical Encyclopedia of Dauphin County, Pennsylvania*, J. M. Runk & Co., Chambersburg, Pa., 1896, page 370.
3. Whether Gheel was one of the stops that Jerome Gerhard made during his European trip is unknown.
4. Orth, Henry L., "Report of the Superintendent," *Forty-Second Annual Report of the State Lunatic Hospital, 1892*, Harrisburg Publishing Company, Harrisburg, 1892, pages 10-12.
5. Ibid.
6. Orth, Henry L., "Report of the Superintendent," *Forty-Second Annual Report*

of the State Lunatic Hospital, 1893, Harrisburg Publishing Company, Harrisburg, 1893, pages 12-13.

7. Ibid.
8. Ibid., page 8.
9. Orth, Henry L., "Report of the Superintendent," *Forty-Second Annual Report of the State Lunatic Hospital, 1894*, Harrisburg Publishing Company, Harrisburg, 1895, pages 13-14.
10. Ibid.
11. Ibid.
12. Orth, Henry L., "Report of the Superintendent," *Forty-Second Annual Report of the State Lunatic Hospital, 1894*, Harrisburg Publishing Company, Harrisburg, 1895, pages 14-15.
13. Yarnall, Elizabeth Biddle, *Addison Hutton, Quaker Architect, 1834-1916*, The Art Alliance Press, Philadelphia, 1974, page 24.
14. Yarnall, Elizabeth Biddle, op. cit., pages 24-25.
15. Hutton, Finley, Memoir, 1916, unpublished, page 6.
16. Yarnall, Elizabeth Biddle, op. cit., pages 38-39.
17. Yarnall, Elizabeth Biddle, op. cit., page 39.
18. Yarnall, Elizabeth Biddle, op. cit., pages 51-52.
19. Yarnall, Elizabeth Biddle, op. cit., page 54.
20. Hutton, Addison, "The Planning of Hospitals," lecture given at the University of Pennsylvania, April 5, 1894, quoted by Yarnall, Elizabeth Biddle, op. cit., page 60.
21. The structure has been greatly modified for its current use as a Department of Welfare office building.
22. Orth, Henry L., "Report of the Superintendent," *Forty-Second Annual Report of the State Lunatic Hospital, 1894*, Harrisburg Publishing Company, Harrisburg, 1895, pages 12-13.
23. Ibid., page 15.
24. Orth, Henry L., "Report of the Superintendent," *Forty-Second Annual Report of the State Lunatic Hospital, 1897*, Harrisburg Publishing Company, Harrisburg, 1898, page 11.
25. Orth, Henry L., "Report of the Superintendent," *Forty-Second Annual Report of the State Lunatic Hospital, 1897*, Harrisburg Publishing Company, Harrisburg, 1898, page 12.
26. There were many celebrated cases of "consumption," as the disease was usually called in the nineteenth century—among them Chopin. In literature, too, there are books as well as novels, such as Thomas Mann's *Magic Mountain*, which dealt with the subject.
27. Orth, Henry L., "Report of the Superintendent," *Annual Report of the State Lunatic Hospital, 1907*, J. H. McFarland Co., Harrisburg, page 8.
28. The trend was apparently nation-wide. Deutsch states that "the first great step toward organized psychiatric research in this country was taken in 1895 with the establishment of the Pathological Institute of the New York State Hospitals." Deutsch, Albert, op. cit., page 285.
29. Harrison, W. H., "Report of the Pathologist," *Forty-Second Annual Report of the State Lunatic Hospital, 1894*, Harrisburg Publishing Company, Harrisburg, 1895, pages 58-60. No credence is given today to detecting mental illness by a urinalysis.
31 Garver, Jane K., "Report of the Physician-Female Department," *Annual Report of the State Lunatic Hospital, 1892*, Harrisburg Publishing Company, Harrisburg, 1892, page 17.
32. During his first year as superintendent, John Curwen had asked the Board of Trustees for a decision concerning the admittance of blacks, and was told: "We are not prepared to handle them."
33. "The Life Story of John A. Dempwolf," *Christ Lutheran Messenger*, Vol. 5, No. 10, January 1927.

34. "East and West Hill," article in *Architecture*, Vol. XXXII, No. 6, December 1915, pages 292-295.

35. Forness, Norman, interview March 28, 1990.

36. S. Philip Laucks stated that when he arrived at the hospital in the 1940s, the staff dining room was regularly filled with a wide variety of roasts and steaks while the patients often ate little more than potatoes.

37. Livingston, J. B., "Steward's Report," *Annual Report of the State Lunatic Hospital, 1892*, Harrisburg Publishing Company, Harrisburg, 1892, pages 39-40.

38. Garver, Jane K., "Report of the Physician-Female Department," *Annual Report of the State Lunatic Hospital, 1893*, Harrisburg Publishing Company, Harrisburg, 1893, page 19.

39. Orth, Henry L., "Superintendent's Report," *Annual Report of the State Lunatic Hospital, 1897*, Harrisburg Publishing Company, Harrisburg, 1898, page 13.

40. Garver, Jane K., "Report of the Physician-Female Department," *Annual Report of the State Lunatic Hospital, 1894*, Harrisburg Publishing Company, Harrisburg, 1895, page 20.

41. Orth, Henry L., "Superintendent's Report," *Annual Report of the State Lunatic Hospital, 1894*, Harrisburg Publishing Company, Harrisburg, 1895, page 16.

XIII

THE CITY ON THE HILL

It is not clear whether their contemporaries understood; Orth, Hutton and Dempwolf were not simply erecting "cottages" on a hill northwest of the state's capital, or haphazardly putting up great brick buildings on the nearly square mile site; they were constructing an entire city.[1] A city designed on a pattern of classical—but not slavishly adhered to—symmetry; one in which each side of the community (the men's and the women's) mirrored the other. The site, moreover, was laid out in the form of a giant rectangle surmounted by a semicircle. When the eighteen buildings were finished by 1912, even the floor plan of the Sun Parlor in the center of the grounds, as well as the main entrance door of the Administration Building, echoed this Italianate window design theme. Perhaps its creators consciously intended that the layout of the hospital grounds be symbolic of a "window to the mind."

"Make no little plans; they have no magic to stir men's blood and probably will not be realized. Make big plans; aim high in work and in hope. ... Let your watchword be order and your beacon beauty." With these words architect Daniel Burnham had challenged the nation with his magnificent plan for the Chicago Columbian Exposition in 1893. Undoubtedly Addison Hutton knew of Burnham's words. The buildings at Harrisburg were less ornate, less grand than Burnham's at Chicago, but the plan was no less imaginative, no less bold.

Whose vision was the hospital ground plan? Probably Hutton's, as the earliest drawings are signed by the Philadelphian, not by Dempwolf. The scheme must have existed in the builder's (or Orth's) imagination before the second structure, the Chronic-Ill Building, was started since, although it followed the Administration building in order of construction, the two were at opposite ends of the site. The rotated portions of the Chronic Ill Building, moreover, beautifully, consciously complete the arch of the "window" design. Today the hospital grounds are so cluttered with extraneous and unsympathetic structures that the architect's elegant scheme is lost to all but the most careful of viewers.

Hutton apparently laid out the overall plan after 1895, when the Administration Building was put up, as the first Orth structure is not quite centered on the "sill" of the window. The architect, beginning in 1900, then completed the Chronic-Ill Building, the Kitchen building and the Dangerous and Destructive Building for Men.[2] The remaining structures, including the Nurses Home, the Convalescent and Psychopathic Wards both for the men and the one for women, the Chapel and the Sun Parlor all appear to have been the work of Dempwolf. We cannot be certain that he was responsible for all of them, but it is a reasonable conclusion based on the available evidence.[3]

Whether he designed or only built them, the York architect followed through carefully on the Hutton scheme of symmetry. The Convalescent Building for Men (which was certainly by Dempwolf) and the one for Women, for example, with their turrets, serve as magnificent anchors for the corners of the "sill" of the site's "window." Inside both floors of the two buildings, these turrets with their southern exposure provided extra air and light for the large day room into which they opened. Each building also included a substantial "amusement" room on the first floor as well as a "rain bath" on both floors.

Hydrotherapy was one of the principal regimens used for the mentally ill at the turn of the century. It had an important place in the therapeutic arsenal available at the Pennsylvania State Lunatic Hospital. In addition to "rain baths,"[4] such procedures as colonic irrigation, fully submerged baths, and the wrapping of patients in wet packs or wet sheets were available. The various techniques were used on a wide variety of patients. They were intended to accomplish two ends: to calm the excited and to restrain them. As the wet sheets dried they, of course, tended to shrink, thus further restraining the patient. Abuses of patients by the use of this technique were reported in Pennsylvania state hospitals, although never at Harrisburg. By the 1950s, however, use of hydrotherapy as a major means of therapy for the mentally ill had been replaced by other more "modern" methods.

Except for two dormitories on the second floor of the Convalescent Building for Men, the rooms for patients were approximately 8½ by 15 feet—designed for no more than double occupancy. Each of these patient quarters had separate ventilation and heat ducts. A dumbwaiter led from the basement pantry (which was near the underground walk), to the first floor serving room adjacent to the dining room.

The Psychopathic Ward buildings also exhibited many of these same internal characteristics as well as their external symmetrical placement on the property. In addition, as protection against fire the floors and the partitions in the Psychopathic Wards were made of terra cotta. The stairs also were constructed of iron posts with iron risers and slate treads. The only concession to relieve the cold look and feel of the slate and the iron was the addition of a wood hand rail to each set of stairs. Two unique features of the Psychopathic Ward for Women were an operating room on the second floor and a "hydro-therapeutic" room in the basement. According to Orth both rooms were "equipped with the latest and best instruments of precision."[5] The men's building did not contain either room. The hospital underground also included a branch from the Convalescent Building for Women down the incline to the Morgue, which was located in the hollow through which Asylum Run flowed.

By 1907, when the two Psychopathic Ward Buildings were completed, the superintendent reported that "the gradual maturing of our plan has been a source of constant anxiety but as it approaches completion, the smooth working of the different parts more than compensates for the time and labor expended to secure a perfect whole, and it is a source of gratification that a kind Providence has permitted us to practically complete our plans. ..."[6]

Much construction, however, still lay ahead, including the Sun Parlor and the Chapel. The Sun Parlor, which was completed in 1912, was surmounted by a large copper dome. The dome, in turn, was topped by a handsome Belvedere.[7] The small mansard-like portion of the roof was made of "slag," but all the rest, including the Belvedere, the cornices, the gutters and the downspouts were of copper. A visitor entered a large vestibule or corridor, which ran the width of the building's front. Across this vestibule there were two sets of double doors that permitted entry into the main part of the first floor. These were located on either side of a "drug room." There were also two sets of wide stairways on each side, which led down to the basement.

The first floor of the Sun Parlor, or Solarium, as it was later called, consisted of a large round open area. Looking up at the axis of the dome at night, the observer saw a cluster of ten lights, while forty more lights ringed the outer edge of the clerestory like stars. The annual "masked ball" would have been held here and it was probably in this large area each winter, when croquet, walking, tennis and outdoor carriage riding were no longer possible, that the weekly calisthenic exercises were held. It was here also that the dancing master employed by the hospital would have conducted his weekly classes.

The basement of the Sun Parlor was an open 60-foot semi-circle, which was divided into pie-slice-shaped sections described as "work areas." This floor also included a drug room immediately below the one on the first floor. The presence of the drug rooms in this building suggests that it might have been used for mass inoculations or perhaps it was simply a central and secure location for storing medicine. Lying on the center line of the hospital site, the Sun Parlor was the one building that was designed with toilets for both men and women. (They were, however, on the appropriate sides of the institution.) Although the sexes may have time-shared the lower level for craft work, the upper floor most likely was used for joint social occasions.

All of the hospital's food was prepared in the central Kitchen Building, which had been completed in September 1903. The structure had been placed at a point on the grounds midway and at equal distances from each of the buildings to which food was distributed. From the kitchen food was carried via the concrete underground to the basement of each of the living structures. All incoming material used in the kitchen was delivered to the cold storage building. In this way economy in handling the raw materials was achieved. The cold storage building, which was adjacent to the kitchen, was finished in 1904. It supplied the hospital with two tons of ice daily, provided capacity for storing 20 beef carcasses, and furnished boxes for vegetables, milk and butter. It was equipped with a system of electric elevators for ease in moving material.

The kitchen used prodigious amounts of food. In 1904 173,793 pounds of beef, 29,109 pounds of butter, 12,162 dozen eggs, 17,159 pounds of ham, 51 barrels of salt fish, 9,025 pounds of coffee, 1,699 barrels of flour and 205 gallons of oysters were consumed. Smaller amounts of clams, crabs and lobsters also were used, although most of these probably ended up in the staff dining room. Orth attempted to introduce Oleomargarine as a more economical substitute for butter ("I have used it upon my own table and can testify to its value and harmlessness"), but was rebuffed by William Hargest, the Deputy Attorney General. The dairy industry (as it did later nationwide) had gotten a law passed in 1905 that made use of any "imitation dairy product" in a state charitable institution illegal.[8]

J. B. Livingston, the hospital steward, who kept such detailed records as those on food consumption, retired in 1906. Orth regretted his departure as he had "filled all his positions with credit to himself and us." Livingston's employment record was a success story typical among employees who stayed at the hospital for a long time. He had entered duty as a nurse in 1884, slowly won his way up first in charge of a ward, then as supervisor and finally was appointed steward in 1890. Orth's regrets apparently were sincere. Unable to find a suitable replacement, the superintendent hired Livingston back not too long after he left. In March 1927, after perhaps the longest appointment as a hospital officer (37 years as steward), Livingston retired again. He logged a total of 51 years as a hospital employee.[9]

In addition to being used to transport food, the hospital underground (or incline as it was sometimes referred to) also was used in inclement weather for the staff to go from building to building. It is unlikely that patients were permitted to roam through these halls indiscriminately. Of all the portions of the hospital that may have been constructed with patient labor, however, this system of underground passageways and possibly the basement excavations of some of the buildings are the most likely items.

The new Chapel was finished in 1913 and formally opened on February 15, 1914. Religious services were held there every Sunday and prayer meetings four times a week.[10] Every fourth Sunday the services were conducted by the Catholic Church, although they were attended by both Catholics and Protestants. A pipe organ costing $1,467.24 had been installed. The new Nurses Home on the female side was an especially welcome addition to the hospital. In the annual reports of prior years, Jane Garver spoke several times about the deplorable conditions under which the attendants worked and lived—"disadvantages," she called them.

> They are confined in crowded wards by day and sleep there at night, and take their meals among the patients. Under better conditions they would suffer less from nervous strain and from illness, and thus be able to do better work for the patients.[11]

Henry Orth claimed that the rooms of the new buildings "are beautifully lighted and well ventilated," and also that "the resulting diminished death rate demonstrates in a small way the advantages of fresh air and sunshine." He went on to state that "improvements in heating and ventilation, and the introduction of sunlight into the wards, in connection with our pure filtered water, is slowly but surely giving results."

The grounds around the buildings also received refurbishment. Based on suggestions made by the State Forestry Department, trees that had died or been damaged by storms were replaced. The Forestry Department furnished 6,000 seedlings for planting. These were placed mainly on the unproductive hillsides and along the streams. The Harrisburg Department of Parks and Public Property also furnished a number of young trees for the grounds. (It was not until 1915, however, that the stone-work for the gateway entrance and the iron-work was completed around the hospital property. That year, too, the city of Harrisburg paved Maclay Street from the hospital to the Pennsylvania Railroad bridge.)

There were acquisitions of additional farmland, too, which

helped to contribute to the annual yields of produce. The Fisher farm, for example, which adjoined the hospital property on the north side, was purchased in 1903 after the legislature appropriated the $10,000 being asked for it.[12] This purchase brought the hospital acreage up to 412 from the original purchase of 127 acres.[13]

Although there were lean years, especially when the rainfall was slight, in general the farm and garden yields were good. Potatoes were still the hospital's staple, but abundant amounts of wheat and corn were also grown. By the turn of the century more than a hundred tons of hay were being produced each year—enough to supply all of the farm's needs. The hospital by then was largely self-sufficient. In 1903 expenses including feed and the purchase of new stock were $18,392.26, while income was $21,862.00. That year, for example, J. B. Livingston reported that 4,800 bushels of potatoes, 1,139 bushels of corn and 39,328 gallons of milk were sold. Ten years later, income had risen to $58,208.46 against $41,220.49 for expenditures.

While potatoes, wheat and corn were the main crops, they were only the big money items. In addition to vegetables such as beans, cabbage, carrots, cucumbers, lettuce, onions, squashes and tomatoes, the garden also produced asparagus, eggplants, kale, parsnips, parsley, rhubarb, rutabaga, radishes, spinach, salsify, turnips and mushrooms. Grapes and raspberries also were raised and a separate herb garden provided most of the kitchen's spice needs. Even the hospital's "chore horses" were used to make money. When they were not busy working in the fields, they were employed to haul coal from the hospital's wharf at the canal to neighboring businesses. During 1903 they moved 5,776 tons of the black gold, thus raising an additional $1,444.00 for the hospital coffers.

It was the legislature's intent not only that the hospital's team of horses be employed to raise money, but also that the best use be made of patients as laborers. By the Act of 1907, all state hospitals for the insane "were given permission to make, manufacture, or produce such supplies, manufactured articles, goods, and products, as may be used in any State hospitals."

In an answer several years later to a letter from Governor Brumbaugh, who had desired the information for "his personal use," Henry Orth acknowledged that occupation is the best means of cure in mental disorders and that a large amount can be and is accomplished by our inmates. He mentioned specifically brooms, brushes, knit stocking, rugs and woven carpets, but claimed that he was "unable to give an estimate of the quality of the goods manufactured." He went on to describe the work of inmates of hospitals for the insane as "uncertain, often untrustworthy—as a business proposition, it is not feasible. ..."[14] A few years later, in support of the war effort, the patients were even busier making blankets, comfort kits, helmets, sweaters, shot bags, and "housewives" (pocket-size rolls of cloth for carrying small articles such as needles and thread) for the men in France.

* * * *

The institution had become a city, a largely self-sufficient combination farming and "manufacturing" community, but it still was a hospital. In December 1908, Henry Orth had to contend with an epidemic of diphtheria. The disease was brought into the hospital by an attendant. Not realizing the gravity of the disease, she did not give any attention to it for two or three days and the damage was done. Many patients and attendants succumbed to the disease. At one time over one hundred and fifty individuals were in isolation. Antitoxins were used but it was not until after three months that the epidemic was under control. As the superintendent reported, "the only satisfaction we enjoyed for our hard and persistent work in fighting the disorder was our freedom from mortality, due not to our care but to the innocuous character of the bacilli."[15]

Preparations for the First World War also took a heavy toll on the hospital staff. Dozens of male attendants were drafted and Orth had to replace them, for the first time in the hospital's history, with "foreign born" help. He was not more specific but claimed that they were "inferior." He mentioned that there was also "a spirit of unrest especially among the recent employees." In 1916, for example, he fired sixty-five male and twenty-one female attendants for charges of "inefficiency, indifference to work, cigarette smoking, utter worthlessness, and abuse of patients."[16]

There were other problems to report. In 1915, the superintendent complained about the "tendency to commit aged feeble patients to the hospital instead of caring for them in their homes or local hospitals." He pointed out that eight of the patients who died that year were in the house less than 30 days, while eighteen more were in such a poor state when they arrived that they died in less than 3 months.[17] To further support his claim he mentioned that 66 of the patients admitted that year were over 50 years of age. That same year, too, eighteen patients and eight attendants suffered broken bones from falls, altercations with other patients or while playing baseball.

One patient death that year was of a man who was restless, noisy and continually interfering with the others, especially with those confined to bed in their rooms. Thirty-three of the 69 patients in his ward took their meals in the dining room, while the others ate their meals from trays served in their rooms or in the corridors where some of them lived. While the meals were being served one evening, the man eluded the attendants, slipped into the room of a very dangerous patient, pulled off the bed-clothes and attempted to get into bed with him. In the ensuing altercation he was thrown across the room and struck a heavy commode. Several bones were broken but he seemed to be mending until inflammation of the pleura set in. The man died a few weeks later.[18]

*   *   *   *

In spite of his heavy involvement with new construction, Orth did take an interest in the clinical aspects of the institution. He continued to upgrade the pathological work being performed at the hospital. Walter E. Kiefer, the pathologist, reported in 1915 that a "new era in laboratory investigations" occurred here late in the fiscal year, when "adequate reagents, glassware, a centrifuge of 3,000 revolutions per minute, guinea pigs and a sheep were secured and Wassermann tests were performed on the blood and the spinal fluids of 78 cases."

Kiefer also conducted 200 more urinary tests that year than in former years. He seemed pleased to mention, moreover, that "new modern books on laboratory methods had been added to the hospital library." Among them were Kolmer's *On Infection, Immunity and Specific Therapy*, McFarland's *Pathogenic Bacteria and Protozoa*, Kaplan's *Serology of Nervous and Mental Diseases* and Wood's *Chemical and Microscopical Diagnosis*.

One of the pathologist's more responsible jobs was to see that the Sewage Disposal Plant was doing its job. The state had adopted a new "official method" of determining this in January, 1915 and Kiefer was pleased to announce that the hospital's filtration beds had retained their high degree of efficiency.

*   *   *   *

Earlier, quietly in 1903 Orth had pushed through significant changes in the hospital's administration. The portion of the by-laws which provided for "medical control of female patients by a female physician" was annulled. Rule one of Chapter IV thereafter read:

> The officers of the hospital shall consist of a superin-
> tendent, who shall be a skillful physician, of one first
> assistant male physician, and three assistant physi-
> cians, two of whom shall be women, a steward and
> a matron, all of whom shall reside on the premises
> and devote their whole time to the interests of the
> institution, under the direction of the superintendent.

W. E. Wright, who had been assistant on the male side, was made the new First Assistant and Claude W. Gillette, Grace Wintersteen and Charlotte E. Goodman were appointed assistant physicians.[19] Goodman was Jane Garver's replacement. Earlier that year Garver had died after 22 years of service to the hospital. She had not been in good health for several years, but her condition was not considered serious. In July 1902 she took a leave of absence from her duties and went with her daughter to Chambersburg, Pennsylvania for a rest. There she became ill in August and died two months later.[20]

Although he "lamented" her death, in all probability Orth had wished to restore the superintendency to its previous level of importance for some time, and simply took advantage of Garver's passing. Thus, almost imperceptibly the movement to eventually integrate the hospital began with these staff changes. While Hiram Corson's efforts appear to have been reversed by this action, in one sense they were being extended. Women were now full partners on the medical staff, not simply in charge of women patients. Although it would be years before they would be assigned to actually work on the male side of the house it was a beginning as well as an ending.

Both Cleaves and Garver seem to have run the women's side of the house with "entire satisfaction"—words that John Curwen might have used, if ever he had a female physician on his staff. There is every indication that the two women were fine physicians, but neither woman appears to have had the managerial or political instincts to actually challenge the male role as the authority for the institution. The woman who had would have been a most remarkable one.

The female side of the house had been an equal then of the male side but it was an equality in which, as Orwell might have said, the male side was more equal. The two physicians' subservient position also probably was a recognition that control of the purse strings ultimately meant control of the institution. More important, the changes that were occurring at the hospital were symptomatic of the new century—one in which the specialist, architect, engineer, or physician, whether male or female, in hundreds of disciplines would come to dominate, but not ultimately to control. That would be left to the administrators, especially those who possessed political sensitivities.

The beginning of the twentieth century then marked the end of the centuries old apprentice system. Only in the skilled trades such as carpentry or plumbing would it continue. No more could a young man such as Addison Hutton go to work for a practicing architect for a few years and then open up a business for himself. No more could a Luther Reily study with an older physician for a few months and then proclaim himself a doctor. Medicine, of course, is the one profession in which the apprentice system still does persist, after a fashion, but there it is in the form of resident internships. These, however, are only permitted after years of formal training are complete.

*   *   *   *

While little was written about Orth as a man, it appears obvious that he was a strong leader—one with an administrative as well as a political bent. His longevity at the helm, his success in getting the state to give him the money to rebuild the entire facility, his restoration of the "imperial" superintendency, and the fact that he was so confident of his position that he seldom wrote more than two or three pages of narrative in the hospital's annual reports all bespeak a man of self-assurance and consummate political skill.

On November 30, 1917, Henry L. Orth, who had served first as a visiting surgeon, then as a Trustee and finally for twenty-six years as Superintendent, retired "on account of impaired health and advancing age." With the possible exception of John Curwen, no superintendent had a greater impact on the life of the Pennsylvania State Lunatic Hospital. As the new superintendent reported the following year, Orth "had the satisfaction of carrying to completion his plans for rebuilding the whole hospital, ... an ambitious labor which will remain as a monument to his genius as an executive and an organizer."[21] To the discerning eye it still is!

That same year we also see the coming of several modern conveniences to the hospital. In order to secure better fire protection for the institution, a centrally placed alarm box was installed. This box was connected directly with the Harrisburg Fire Department. That year, too, a contract was signed with the Bell Telephone Company for the installation of telephones throughout the hospital.[22]

Orth retired to a residence on Pine Street in Harrisburg, wintering in Florida each year until he died in May 1920.

*   *   *   *

Edward M. Green, of the Georgia State Sanitarium, was elected to succeed Orth. A native of Washington, Georgia, he was the son of Edward Melvin Green and Sarah Emily Howe Green. The elder Green, a renowned Presbyterian minister, had served as a chaplain in the Confederate Army of Tennessee from 1863-1865. Following the birth of her first son in 1869, Sarah never regained her health and remained an invalid throughout the rest of her life.[23]

Young Edward was educated first in the private schools of Danville, Kentucky and then at Center College, where he received his A.B. and M.A. degrees.[24] He attended the Medical School of Tulane University as well as the University of Pennsylvania from which he received his medical degree. After a short stint in general practice in Danville and Versailles, Kentucky, Green served for several years in the State hospitals of Kentucky, Oklahoma and Georgia in a variety of positions including those of Physician in Chief and Clinical Director. For a period of time he taught at the Louisville Kentucky Medical College. Green apparently came to the attention of the Board of Trustees of the Pennsylvania State Lunatic Hospital through the consulting work he did at the Lancaster County Hospital, the neuro-psychiatric clinic of the York Hospital and at Harrisburg's Polyclinic Hospital.[25]

The new superintendent inherited a going concern, a mature institution. He was to run it for seventeen years. While there would be a few additional changes in the plant facilities during his administration, his real impact would be in the area of changes related to the institution's mission as a healing facility. This apparently was the result of his strong clinical background.[26]

In 1919 Green inaugurated a system of semi-weekly hospital staff meetings. Each newly admitted individual to the Pennsylvania State Lunatic Hospital thereafter received a thorough mental and physical examination, after which the patient was presented before the medical staff. In these meetings each case was discussed freely and a diagnosis arrived at if possible. (Only those patients who were too ill to come were excluded.) Any doubtful cases were represented after an interval of a few weeks. By this means, the new superintendent hoped that "the personal factor in diagnosis is avoided." The advisability of parole or discharge also was considered at these meetings.[27]

In his first year the new superintendent also expanded considerably the size of the consulting staff. In addition to two surgeons, George B. Kunkel and H. F. Smith, and two internal medicine members, J. W. Ellenberger and J. B. McAlister, the visiting staff under Green also included specialists in Neurology and Ophthalmology, as well as one in "Otology," Rhinology and Laryngology.

Following the war in Europe there were also several changes in the mix of the hospital's patient population. The U.S. Bureau of War Risk Insurance requested that the hospital admit Pennsylvania veterans that the Bureau was unable to care for. In the year following Armistice, there were 25 of these patients. The hospital also was continuing to accept criminals from the courts. In 1920 five such men and one woman were sent to Green. The superintendent was able to get one of these patients transferred to the Hospital for the Criminal Insane at Farview but two of the others escaped. And in 1921 the legislature passed a law providing for the commitment to state hospitals of non-insane drug addicts. Between 1921 and 1923 Green received 11. All but one were soon discharged[28]

Under Green's urging the hospital began to make greater use of the parole system in order to reduce the size of the hospital's resident population. Any patient who had improved sufficiently to make it safe for him or her to return to friends able and willing to assume his or her care, was considered for parole. The crowding was serious enough that Green even discharged "unimproved" patients, "who had shown no disposition to injure themselves or others," and "who would not be disturbing elements in the communities in which they lived."[29] Even in cases where patients were considered to have recovered, he "thought it best to grant paroles rather than to discharge them outright." In this way "legal formalities might be avoided in the event that it should be necessary for them to return within a few months." By 1919 fully one third of those he considered as "possibly curable cases" he placed on parole.[30]

In 1921 the hospital established Mental Clinics in several nearby cities. That first year there were only four, but by 1926 two more were added. They were held at Carlisle, Chambersburg, Gettysburg, Lancaster, Lebanon, York, and occasionally at Waynesboro. By then the medical staff of the Harrisburg State Hospital—the word lunatic, which had become a term of derision, was dropped from the hospital's name by an act of the legislature in 1921—was seeing more than 400 clinic patients annually. Unfortunately they were only able to get to each clinic once a month. The hospital's outreach program also included a series of lectures on nervous and mental diseases, which was given to the nurses at the Polyclinic Hospital of Harrisburg. According to Green, these included demonstrations of the more common forms of mental disorders.[31]

The medical staff, the Directress of Nurses and the Dietitian also began giving lectures, quizzes and demonstrations for the hospital attendants. The previous year the State Board of Examiners for Registration of Nurses had recommended that a school for licensed attendants be established in the hospital, so the superintendent set one up in the fall of 1922. The course covered the period of a year and was designed to "fit the pupil to care for simple cases of illness, ordinary emergencies, the preparation of food and to qualify them to render more intelligent service in all departments of the hospital." Attendance at the school was made obligatory. That first year ten of the hospital's employees not only completed the course but passed their State Board exam.[32]

Life at the hospital, by the early decades of the twentieth century, truly was a community affair. Not only were workers in the shops located in the basement of the Chapel busy caning chairs, making brooms and settees and arm rockers, but patients in the tailor shop, which was established in 1926, also were active sewing together overalls, canvas suits, trousers and coats as well as doing a large amount of clothing repair work. In some of the older shops, moreover, patients were employed in repairing shoes, making mattresses, pillows, awnings, window shades and indestructible blankets. By the late twenties, too, a "Toy Factory" had been established in the basement of the Male 9 & 10 Building. There a large number of wooden toys of good quality were produced. Seven hundred and thirty-four patients were regularly engaged in some form of work by 1928. Among the new occupational and recreational activities that were established during the Green administration was that of a nursery. At the request of the Commissioner of Forestry, a plot of ground was set apart for the cultivation of trees. The department of Forestry furnished the seeds and trees and the hospital furnished the labor.

In addition to such group activities as the weekly dances, the residents also enjoyed moving picture shows ("talkies" were introduced in July 1935). During this period, too, Mrs. Florence Ley, the Director of the Community Service Bureau of the Harrisburg Chamber of Commerce, visited the hospital each week and instructed the patients in community singing. The hospital band and orchestra, which were made up of patients and attendants, also continued to perform. Each ward of the institution, moreover, was supplied with an organ or a piano. Many also had phonographs and radios which were in "more or less constant use." With all these opportunities the superintendent felt that "the musical needs of the hospital are adequately met."[33]

The hospital patient library also had expanded, both through the purchase of new books and through the gifts of friends. Green reported that it contained 3,600 volumes at the end of 1928 (by 1935 the number of books had grown to 4,355.) The call for reading matter had grown steadily and during the previous year 8,856 books and 31,669 magazines had been distributed to the wards. Male patients were privileged to visit the library two days a week and female patients to visit it on two other days of the week. The facility, which was located in the Female Convalescent Building, was unique—no other state hospital had such an "extensive, attractive library."[34]

Despite his efforts at increasing the number of paroles and the continued expansion of facilities, overcrowding always seemed to be a problem. Green, however, was not convinced that increasing the size of the facilities at Harrisburg was the answer. He suggested to the Department of Welfare, as the Pennsylvania State Board of Charities was then being called, that transfer of the excess population to other hospitals should be considered. Not only was the lack of buildings at Harrisburg an issue, but so too was the lack of furniture. In an urgent request in 1927 for beds and mattresses the superintendent advised C. W. Hunt, the Deputy Secretary of Public Welfare, that 75 patients were sleeping on pallets spread on the floor.[35]

In the decade from 1919 to 1928 the hospital's annual expenditures rose from $350,501.78 to more than a half a million dollars, of which $201,261 was required for salaries and wages.[36] Since the hospital's income was usually less than the amount of the expenses, the legislature had to provide the hospital with special appropriations each year. In 1919 the state's share was $45,000. By 1928 the amount had risen to $188,561.45. In 1919 the superintendent reported that the $49,000, which had been appropriated that year, had been expended on outstanding bills with the exception of $6.24. This he stated he would return to the state treasurer. A decade later the amount he returned was given as "none."

Statistics on patients also seemed to take on a new dimension under E. M. Green. Not only was he interested in the place of birth of his first admissions, but also such things as their citizenship status, their degree of education, their marital status and their economic condition. The latter he broke down into "Dependent," "Marginal," "Comfortable" or "Unascertained." He reported, moreover, that sixty percent of the hospital's admissions had a common school education while eight percent had gone to high school. Of the twenty-three percent who had no formal schooling, the superintendent claimed that sixteen percent could read and write.[37]

In his 1928 annual report Green also provided some employment statistics for the hospital. There were a total of 248 officers and staff members. Nearly half of this number, 118, were nurses and attendants. The 118 were almost evenly divided between male and female. That year the professional staff included 6 physicians, one dentist, a full time pathologist and 6 occupational therapists.[38] In seeking a wage increase for the professional staff a few years earlier, Green described the duties of his physicians as follows:

> Forty years ago the population was 402 and the number of assistant physicians was four. At the present time our population is 1370 and the number of

assistant physicians is still four. The work of these physicians, irrespective of the number of patients under their charge, has changed materially, we are no longer merely to make a few brief notes on the condition of newly admitted cases supplemented by a word or two at long intervals to indicate any improvement or the reversal that may have taken place. Each patient is now thoroughly studied throughout the first month of his or her stay in the hospital, the blood, spinal fluid, urine and other secretions tested, and a full record kept of the progress of the case.[39]

After the arrival of Green from Georgia, the hospital staff was beefed up by an influx of individuals from the South. Prominent among these was the physician Julius H. Anderson, the only one who came at the specific request of the new superintendent. Anderson, a recent graduate from the University of Georgia Medical School, was recommended to Green by a friend on the staff of the hospital. The young doctor and his bride, Dorothy, came to Harrisburg in July, 1931. He was interested primarily in surgery and did not anticipate staying at the hospital more than a year or two.[40]

In spite of the new physician's restlessness, somehow Green and the superintendents who followed him were able to find interesting jobs for Anderson to do—assisting in surgery, helping with autopsies, experimenting with new treatment methods—so that he spent his entire professional life in the same job. Taciturn almost beyond belief, he would sit talking with a patient for an hour or more, saying no more than a few words. He was a good listener and communicated with his patients mostly with nods of the head. When it came time for him to make presentations at the morning staff meetings, he simply read the one or two pages he had written concerning a patient's diagnosis and treatment.[41]

One of the several attendants that migrated north was Basil Long, from Virginia. He started as an aide, later became an attendant and eventually ended his career in rehabilitation service. When Long arrived at the hospital, he found that attendants worked from 6 A.M. to 6 P.M. each day and every other night until eight P.M—seven days on and then one day off. If an attendant's day off was Saturday he was also given Sunday off. If, however, he was caught smoking it meant suspension; if he lost his keys, he was relieved from duty without pay until they were found. If any employee struck a patient, it was an automatic discharge. And whenever a doctor or a supervisor entered the ward, every employee had to stand at attention.[42]

* * * *

Edward Green was a man of striking appearance, his white goatee always neatly trimmed, his three-piece suits immaculately tailored. His appearance was that of a distinguished Southern gentlemen. He possessed a natural dignity that masked a kindly and friendly personality. A sense of deep sincerity marked his unselfish nature. In his dealings with people, however, he had a down-to-earth touch about him. He was fond of using short homilics to gently admonish erring employees. One such Green reproof to a secretary, who was whistling in the hallway, was that "whistling women and cackling hens all come to a bad end."[43] The state provided him with an automobile and a chauffeur. It must have been an impressive sight for bystanders to see such a distinguished-looking doctor being driven around central Pennsylvania in his handsome convertible Cadillac Touring Car.[44]

Ann Green, the superintendent's wife, was, like her husband, reserved and formal. She would entertain the wives of the physicians with afternoon tea in her third-floor parlor and although sometimes she would come to the second floor to visit in their quarters, she would always send a note down first with one of the house maids. On occasion she would invite one or two of them to go with her in the car to Philadelphia for a day of shopping at Wanamaker's Department Store.

Green served as Superintendent until 1934, when he resigned to go into retirement. He continued to do psychiatric consulting work after leaving the hospital. In 1942 he returned to the hospital as a staff psychiatrist to help Howard K. Petry fill the void left by the call-up of doctors for World War II. He died in his quarters on the hospital grounds on September 30, 1944. His remains were returned to Danville, Kentucky.[45]

END NOTES

1. The first written use of the expression "The City on the Hill" was by H. K. Petry in his biennial report of 1950-1952. Petry attributed the source of the name to a series of thirteen radio programs on the hospital that were presented by the patients during that biennium.

2. Of those structures for which specific contract information is available, we know that the building contractor for the Dangerous and Destructive Building for Men and for another building described as the "Treatment Building" (possibly the Male Admission Ward) was awarded to John K. Ness of Harrisburg for $124,054. The cold storage plant was built by Coder and Miller for $15,542. We also know that thirteen bids were received for the construction of the Convalescent Building ranging from $67,800 to $106,517. With the unvarying regularity that the trustees from the time of John Curwen to that of Henry Orth had exhibited, the contract was awarded to the lowest bidder, Wildman of Harrisburg, without regard to any other criteria than that it was the lowest one. Two weeks later Wildman reported that "he had made a serous error in his computation, which would involve him in great loss." The trustees released him for $60 (which covered their expenses) conditioned on the next lowest bidder's willingness to still meet his bid. Thus Henderson and Company, Ltd. of Philadelphia ultimately built the structure for $75,467.

3. More than 60 detailed drawings by Dempwolf exist for the buildings listed below. Most of these structures are covered by sets of drawings for each floor from the basement to the roof. Some have detailed plans covering not only the interior and exterior, but also the mechanical and electrical layouts including the design of attic ventilation systems. Dates shown are for H. L. Orth's approval. Browley Wharton, the General Agent and Secretary of the Board of Public Charities, Dempwolf and two witnesses also signed each set. (Some of the drawings indicate the name of a general contractor, others do not.) We cannot be certain either to what extent Dempwolf's brother Reinholt may have participated in the design. The drawings, however, are signed by John. It was he, moreover, who had the national reputation. Shermeyer, Mark D., *Collection 11022*, Historical Society of York County, November 15, 1989.

Dangerous & Destructive for Women	September, 1905
Nurses Home	November, 1905
Boiler House	July, 1906
Convalescent Building for Men	August, 1907
Psychopathic Ward for Women	August, 1907
Convalescent Building for Women	October, 1907
Chapel	April, 1912
Sun Parlor	No date shown

4. A "rain bath" was a theraputic shower, in which the attendant could vary the spray effect being administered to the patient through the choice of nozzles. There were "fan," "jet," "vapor," and "Scotch" douches. In the Scotch douche, for example, the water was sprayed on the patient from two nozzles: the path of one stream was directed to the patient's body and the other bounced in a spray off the floor.

5. Orth, Henry L., *Annual Report of the State Lunatic Hospital at Harrisburg, 1907*, J. H. McFarland Company, Harrisburg, Pa., September 30, 1907, page 11.

6. Ibid.

7. The building is now called the "Vista Dome" and adjoins the Petry Building, which was not part of the original Hutton/Dempwolf design.

8. The Pennsylvania Act set the punishment at $1,000 and two years in prison for any hospital steward or official who would knowingly buy or use such products on inmates.

9. On July 1, 1952 matron Grace Hostetter retired after logging a total of 50 years and 11 months as a hospital employee.

10. The old chapel had been torn down in 1895 on order of the legislature as too dangerous for use.

11. Garver, Jane Kimmel, *Forty-Eighth Annual Report of the State Lunatic Hospital at Harrisburg, 1898*, Harrisburg Publishing Co., Harrisburg, Pa., 1898, page 17.
12. The Fisher farm was none other than "Spruce Run Farm," the original property that the trustees had first attempted to purchase in 1845. It had been bought from Jacob Ridgeway by Peter Fisher, who then later sold it to the hospital.
13. By 1932 the size of the hospital grounds had grown to 717.15 acres. Within a few more years, however, the losses started. There was 39.7 acres for the State Farm Show, 10.45 acres for the Cavalry Post and 82.28 acres for the City Parkway Project.
14. Orth, H. L., letter to Governor M. G. Brumbaugh, February 11, 1915.
15. Orth, H. L., *Fifty-Ninth Annual Report of the State Lunatic Hospital at Harrisburg, Pa., 1908*, J. H. McFarland Company, Harrisburg, Pa., 1909, page 9.
16. Orth, H. L., *Sixty-Sixth Annual Report of the State Lunatic Hospital at Harrisburg, Pa., 1916*, J. H. McFarland Company, Harrisburg, Pa., 1916.
17. As early as 1903 the Attorney General had advised the hospital trustees that they had a "right to fix the number of patients whom they may safely treat." They were reluctant, however, to exercise this right in most cases, thus overcrowding continued to exist. *Fifty-Third Annual Report of the State Lunatic Hospital*, op. cit., page 6.
18. Orth, H. L., *Sixty-Fifth Annual Report of the State Lunatic Hospital at Harrisburg, Pa., 1915*, J. H. McFarland Company, May 31, 1915.
19. Orth, H. L., *Fifty-Third Annual Report of the State Lunatic Hospital at Harrisburg, Pa., 1903*, Harrisburg Publishing Co., Harrisburg, Pa., 1903., page 11. C. W. Gillette previously had been the pathologist.
20. The Harrisburg Telegraph, October 10, 1902.
21. Green, E. H., *Sixty-Eighth Annual Report of the State Lunatic Hospital at Harrisburg, Pa., 1918*, page 24. In 1907 Orth claimed that in 15 years of construction not once had he exceeded the legislature's appropriations. Orth, H. L., *Fifty-Seventh Annual Report of the State Lunatic Hospital at Harrisburg, Pa., 1907*, J. H McFarland Co., Harrisburg, Pa., 1907, page 11.
22. Green, E. H., *Sixty-Eighth Annual Report of the State Lunatic Hospital at Harrisburg, Pa., 1918*, pages 22-23.
23. Green, Edward M., *Memoir, Edward M. Green, D.D.*, October 1, 1941, page 6.
24. "Edward M. Green, The Beloved Physician," memorial service bulletin, The Market Square Presbyterian Church, October 8, 1944.
25. Harrisburg *Patriot*, October 2, 1944.
26. Green did build the Hospital for the Physically Ill, now the Slothower Building, the Married Employees' Building, a new Dairy Barn and various other outbuildings.
27. By 1923 the frequency of these staff meetings had been changed to three times weekly. One of these meetings was devoted solely to discussion of paroles or discharges.
28. Green, E. H., *Biennial Report of the State Hospital at Harrisburg, Pa., 1921-1923*, page 7.
29. Green, E. H., *Biennial Report of the State Hospital at Harrisburg, Pa., 1921-1923*, page 11.
30. Green, E. H., *Sixty-Ninth Annual Report of the State Lunatic Hospital at Harrisburg, Pa., 1919*, pages 10-11. Parolees were required to return to the hospital at least once each year.
31. Green, E. H., *Biennial Report of the Harrisburg State Hospital, 1921-1923*, Harrisburg, Pa., page 12.
32. Green, E. H., *Biennial Report of the Harrisburg State Hospital, 1921-1923*, Harrisburg, Pa., pages 13-14.
33. Ibid., page 13. The orchestra of patients and attendants had been organized in 1923.
34. McCauley, E. Grace and Hunt, Clement W., Department of Public Welfare, "Inspection Report," February 6, 1930.
35. Green, Edward M., letter to C. W. Hunt, February 18, 1927.

36. Green, E. M., *Biennial Report of the Harrisburg State Hospital, June 1, 1926 to May 31, 1928*, page 23.
37. Ibid., page 50.
38. Ibid., page 22.
39. Green, E. H. *Biennial Report of the Harrisburg State Hospital, 1924-1925*, Harrisburg, Pa.
40. Anderson, Dorothy, Interview, January 14, 1991.
41. Logan, John, Interview, October 17, 1990.
42. Long, Basil, *Reminisence*, undated (probably prepared about December 1971)
43. Mumma, Ingrid, Oral History, July 23, 1990.
44. The car, which was supplied by the state for his use, was so impressive that Green was directed in March, 1925 to send it, along with his chauffeur, to Washington for use in President Coolidge's Inaugural parade. (C. W. Hunt letter of February 25, 1925.) Because of the difficulty of finding suitable housing, Hunt, Deputy Director of the Department of Welfare, did seek Green's assurance, however, that his chauffeur was not black.
45. Harrisburg *Patriot*, October 2, 1944.

Italianate entrance to the new Administration Building constructed during Henry Orth's superintendency.

New Administration Building with the old Kirkbride Building in the background, about 1895.

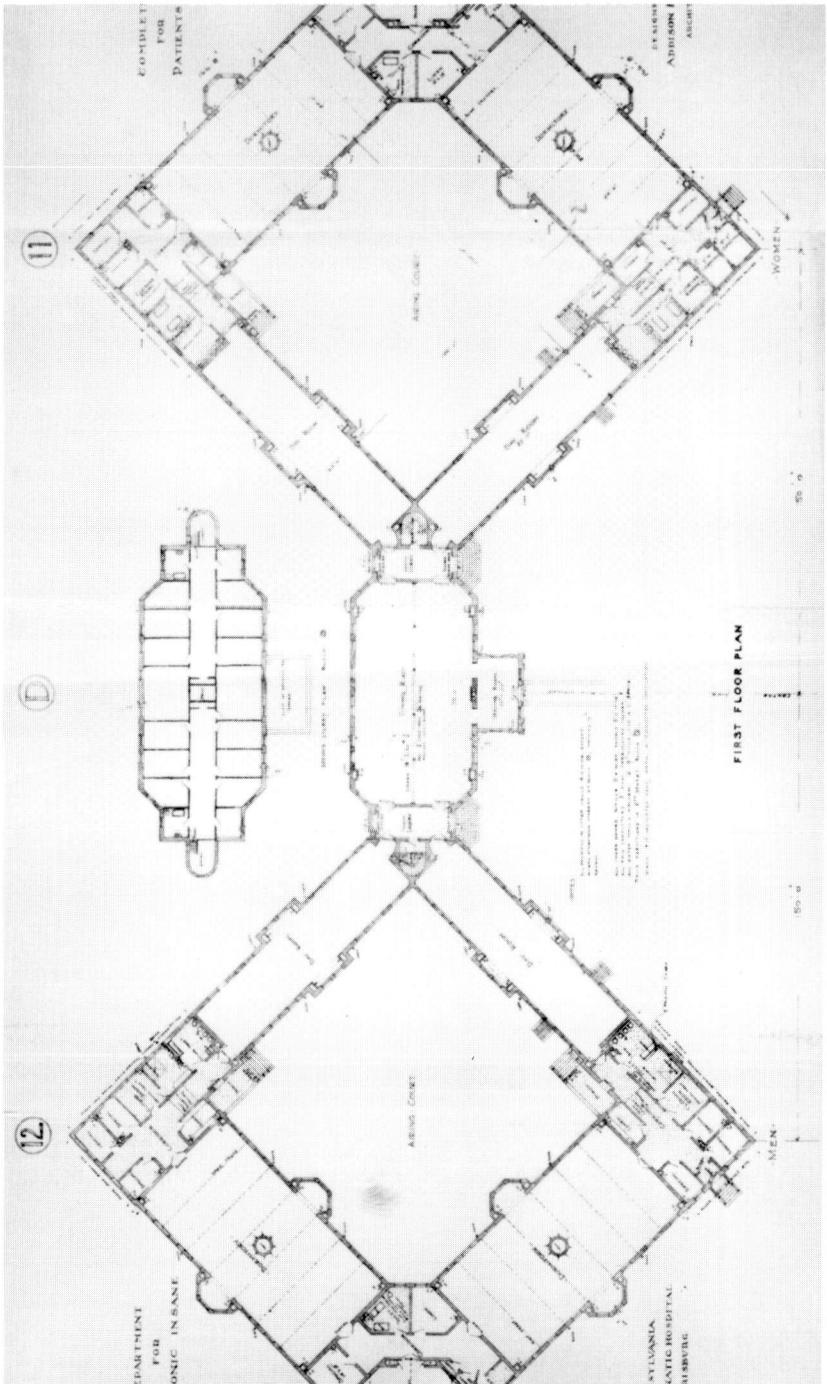

Addison Hutton's architectural floor plan for the Chronic Insane Building, 1900.

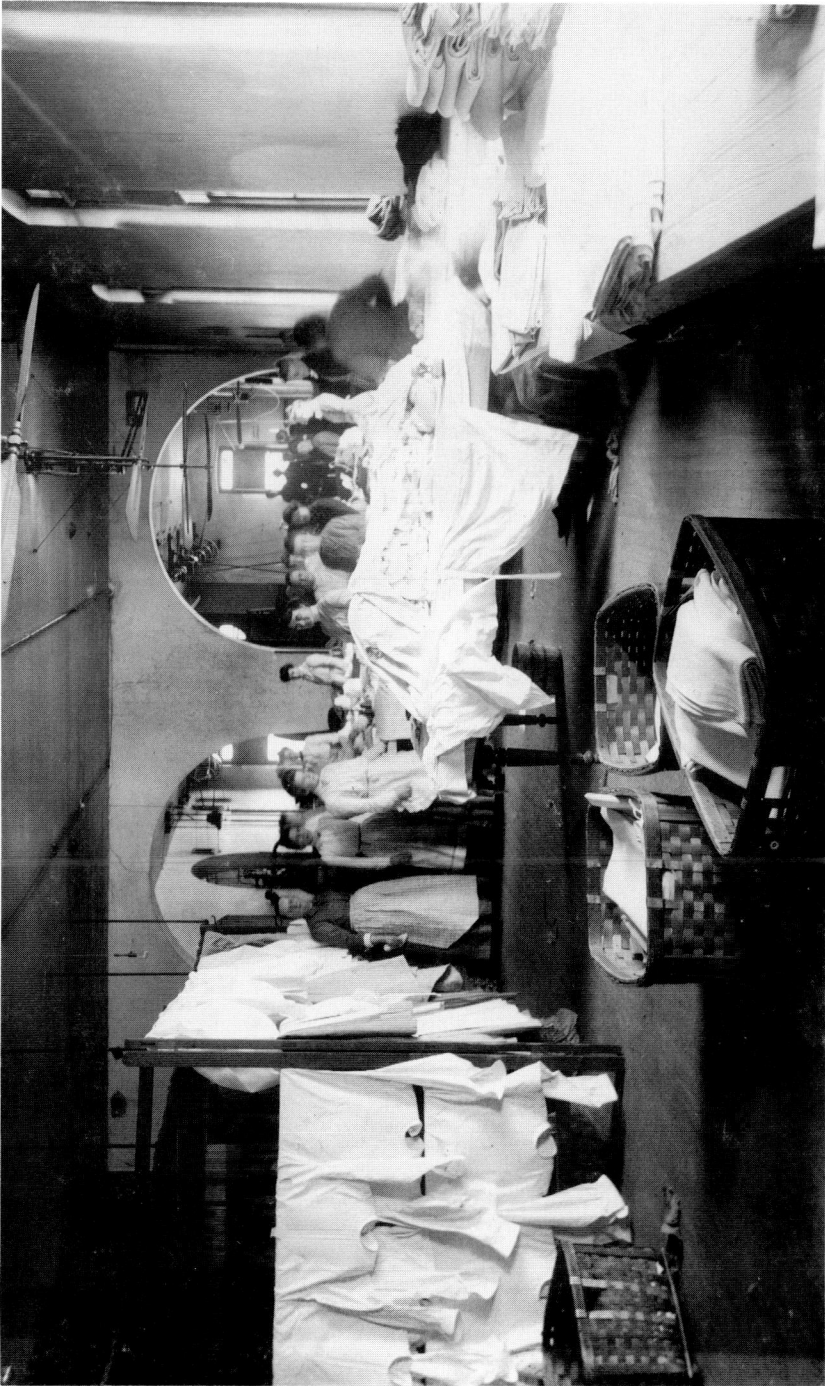

Interior of old Laundry, about 1910.

Interior of Female One showing one of the day areas, about 1910.

Henry L. Orth
Hospital Superintendent
1891-1919

Edward M. Green
Hospital Superintedent
1919-1934

Aerial view of hospital in winter, about 1930. Shows clearly the Italianate "window" design of the grounds. Ravine is to the left, morgue is in the lower right, and the Sun Parlour is in the center. The airing courts on the building for the Chronic Insane are clearly visible, as are the covered undergrounds connecting the buildings.

Physical therapy on the female side of the hospital, 1930's.

Patients shoveling snow off the hospital underground walkways, 1950s.

Howard K. Petry
Hospital Superintendent
1934-1954

Hamblen C. Eaton
Hospital Superintendent
1954-1969

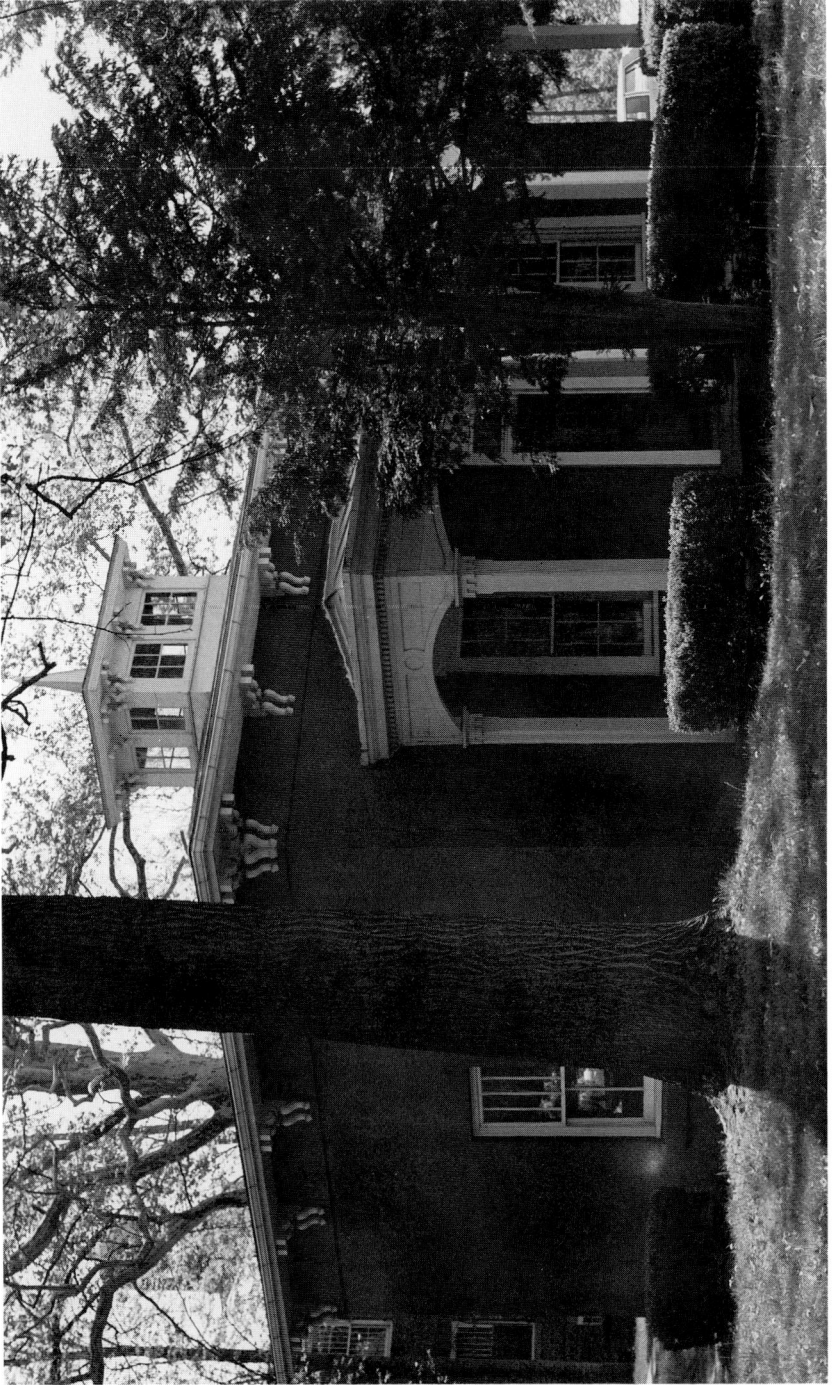

Dix Museum, erected in 1853. One of the two remaining buildings from the original hospital.

Hospital ravine with stone bridge.

190

Chapel, built in 1913 by John A. Dempwolf.

Poplar Drive, approaching the site of the old ice house.

XIV

THE LAST FIEFDOM

During the years between World War I and World War II life for the hospital staff and their families was not unlike that on a college campus. While the patients, especially those in the "Violent and Destructive" buildings, were locked in at all times, typical family living continued among those who ministered to their needs.

Early each morning the steward and the physicians who lived in the houses near the gate at Cameron and Maclay Streets would start out—some by automobile, some on foot—along the road as it wound up around the hill towards the Administration Building. In summer the bright northern sun would be filtering down from high in the broad-leaved sycamores which lined the roadway. Each spring long-stemmed violets would bloom in profusion in the hollow that curved away to their right. In winter the snow would squinch underfoot. As the days changed from spring to summer to fall, so would the leaves on the trees; and so too, in turn, would the blooms of the many kinds of wildflowers that lived on the hillsides and along the creek. Known by then as "Asylum Run" the stream's water came down through the ravine from the rolling farmland behind the hospital buildings; meandering past the powerhouse, which generated the life-sustaining electricity on which the community depended, past the old ice house, past the abandoned filter beds, past the red brick morgue. As they rounded the turn at Azalea and North Circle Drives, the group might be joined by other staffers coming from their homes on the northern part of the hospital grounds.

When this little procession reached the Administration Building, and entered through Hutton's Italianate doorway, they were confronted by an impressively wide staircase that rose from across the tile-floored lobby to the upper levels. Wood paneling was in evidence up and down the spacious hallways which led away to the left and the right. In the baronial room at the end of the hall to their left, the families and the physicians that lived on the second floor of the Administration Building were finishing breakfast. They were all seated together at the huge banquet table which filled the center of the room. There they had been waited on individually with a breakfast of plenty: eggs, bacon, sausage, pancakes, toast, juice and coffee.[1] In the room above them, on the third floor, the superintendent and his family also were eating their morning meal. The food, which had been brought in through the underground to the main building was prepared, however, by the cooks assigned to the administration building. Grace was never said at these meals; religion like politics was a forbidden subject.

While the superintendent and the residents of the Administration Building were breakfasting, the single men and women, the professionals and staff people who stayed in the Vista Dome,[2] were eating their morning meal on the first floor of the Nurses Dining Room (officially known as the "Steward's Dining Room"). The laborers and farm hands, who came dressed for work, took their meals in a dining room on the second floor of this building. Similar rituals were performed at dinner time each evening. The last meal of the day might consist of beef or pork roasts, poultry, steaks, or perhaps a shellfish dish and a plentiful selection of vegetables and breads. If late shifts were working, the Steward's Dining Room, which was adjacent to the itchen in the center of the hospital grounds, would be open all night to serve the physicians and nurses who were on duty.

The one feature that the City on the Hill lacked was a school system. The children had to descend the hill, exit the hospital grounds through the stone-posted gate, cross Cameron, or Eleventh Street as it had been called in Curwen's day, and wait for the school bus to take them to their classes in Susquehanna Township schools. When they were at home the younger children, especially those who lived on the second floor of the Administration Building, generally stayed within their own immediate areas. Brothers and sisters or perhaps the children of the immediate neighboring physician were their principal playmates.

There was a small playground behind the Administration Building. It contained a sliding board and a sand lot. An informal ball field also stood behind the Dixmont cottage, which was off to the right of the Administration Building. It was there that the Dennison family lived.[3] The older boys and girls, of course, would play ball, ride their bicycles all over the grounds, and in winter toboggan from under the portico outside the main entrance—down the hill, over the ravine, all the way to the front gate.

The younger children would stay closer to their quarters than their older brothers and sisters, often under the informal supervision of Dorothy Anderson. From the first they called her "Dorothy." They took to calling her "DA" after they were admonished by the new superintendent, who directed that they call her Mrs. Anderson. This they refused to do and shortly thereafter she became known to everyone, including H. K. Petry, by those initials.

It was a protected, sheltered environment in which the children grew up. There were servants to wait on them at mealtime and maids to make up their rooms each day. No matter where they went on the grounds there was a member of the "hospital family" to help them, if they were in need, or to watch and report on them, if they got into trouble. On those occasions when they had to go off the grounds, it often was with a sense of relief that they would return. And the most difficult transition many of them had to make was the one out into the community when they finally left.[4]

*   *   *   *

Howard K. Petry, who in 1934 had been selected to replace the retiring Edward Green, maintained his office to the right of the entrance door of the Administration Building. In this way he was able to keep track of all the hospital goings-on. He seldom went out onto the grounds or to the other buildings during the course of the day. His staff came to him.

Visitors to the institution all had to come past Petry's doorway. None, whether professionals, politicians, or service people, got by without enduring his scrutiny. Those individuals who arrived on the trolley car would be driven up to the Administration Building by the attendant who was on duty outside the steward's house. People could drive onto the grounds without being stopped at the gate, but they could not get into any of the buildings without a pass from the superintendent's office. Even the chaplain was escorted to the Chapel each Sunday by the resident physician on duty that day.

Petry had been born at Springfield, Missouri, on February 16, 1895. At an early age the boy's family moved to Wilkes-Barre, Pennsylvania, where Howard was educated in the local schools. He graduated from Wilkes-Barre High School in 1911, after which he went to Wesleyan University. He received his BA degree there in 1915 and then entered the Medical School of the University of Pennsylvania from which he received a Doctor of Medicine degree in 1920.[5]

After serving his internship in psychiatry, he accepted an appointment to the staff at Warren State Hospital in Warren, Pennsylvania. There he became a favorite of superintendent H. W. Mitchell. In 1932 he left Warren to become the clinical director of Torrance State Hospital. While he was at Torrance he was also a consultant in neuropsychiatry at the Connellsville State Hospital. He came to Harrisburg two years later and remained there until his retirement.

*　　*　　*　　*

Although Howard K. Petry only held staff meetings with the steward and the other department heads once a month, he continued Green's practice of holding meetings with his medical staff three times a week. At these morning meetings each new case was discussed and a disposition made. Physicians were assigned to new admissions on a rotating basis, case by case as they arrived at the hospital. There was no assignment to individual doctors based on the type or severity of a patient's illness. Thus each physician would have to evaluate and present recomendations before his peers for whatever patient problems came before him or her. One of the weekly medical meetings was always devoted to parole discussions.[6]

After these morning meetings, the doctors would then go

out to the wards and make their rounds. Each Wednesday afternoon was set aside to answer questions from visiting family members. Parents, wives or husbands and friends would gather in long lines outside each doctor's office waiting to see the physician assigned to care for their loved one. Most of the hospital's medical staff dreaded Wednesday afternoons more than treating their patients. Almost as onerous, Friday afternoons were devoted to catching up on paperwork.

The superintendent, who read all incoming as well as signed all outgoing correspondence, was a stickler on the written word. "He stressed perfection in writing—letters, reports, all were expected to be short and to the point with nothing ambiguous." Although there were arguments over patient diagnoses or treatments, especially with his clinical director, Hamblen Eaton, H. K. Petry "conducted the hospital's administration without advice."[7]

The medical residents were given room and board, but individual salaries were modest. Single physicians were preferred and once hired they were not encouraged to marry. When he had been at Warren, Petry felt obliged to check with the superintendent, Harry W. Mitchell, before marrying Marion Hughes.[8] Petry's subordinates at Harrisburg also felt obliged to check with him before they did likewise. The concern, of course, was over the lack of adequate housing for families.

*   *   *   *

Not too long after Petry took over in Harrisburg, several new, radical therapies were introduced in psychiatry. These included several modes of shock treatment as well as a surgical procedure.[9] At the time of their introduction they were considered by many physicians in Europe and America as breakthroughs in the treatment of mental illness. Among the new treatment methods that Petry's physicians could employ were Insulin-coma, metrazol-convulsion and then later electroshock. Belief in their curative value was based on the idea that convulsions are therapeutic. Just as earlier patients had been inoculated with the blood of individuals affected with malaria to induce a fever, which was considered to be therapeutic, so too by the mid-1930s the inducing of convulsions was considered as therapeutic—only discussion of the merits of the various means of causing a convulsion was an issue among physicians.

In 1933 a Viennese physician, Manfred Sakel, had accidentally induced a deep coma in a patient, by injecting a high dose of insulin. The mental state of the patient, who was psychotic as well as a drug addict, appeared to improve after his recovery from the coma, so Sakel began to experiment on animals with insulin. Not too long afterward favorable results were being reported all over Europe. In 1936 insulin therapy was introduced in New York State and shortly thereafter spread rapidly throughout the United States.[10]

About this same time a young Hungarian, Ladislas von Meduna had begun examining the brains of former epileptic and schizophrenic patients and concluded on the basis of his observations that there was a mutual antagonism between epilepsy and schizophrenia.[11] This led him to the idea that inducing convulsion in schizophrenics would lead to a cure and thus he started injecting first camphor and then later metrazol into his patients. Meduna claimed recovery in ten of his patients, good results in three and no change in thirteen. Within a year after he published his paper, interest in the method had spread widely.

The invention of electroconvulsive therapy, or ECT, on the other hand, is attributed to two Italian doctors, Lucio Bini and Ugo Cerletti. Their work, which was reported in 1938, was introduced into the United States two years later. Its use spread rapidly as it was much more convenient to administer to patients than either insulin or metrazol. While insulin and metrazol treatments took hours of preparation and recovery time for each patient, ECT could be administered in a few minutes. The patient was simply stretched out on a table, his or her arms and legs held to prevent injury when the convulsion occurred, and the two electrodes applied to each temple.[12]

In truth electrotherapy had been practiced long before the two Italians began their experiments. The cleric John Wesley had described an electrical treatment machine in his *Desideratum or Electricity Made Plain and Useful* as early as 1760 and Freud had considered it as part of his therapeutic arsenal during the late 1880s but soon discarded it.[13]

Although these early efforts are some times described as "non-convulsive" electrotherapy, in truth shocks were actually administered to patients by the machines that were used.

As early as 1879, for example, John Curwen was interested in buying one of these electrical machines. That year he received detailed specifications from the Philadelphia firm of James W. Queen concerning just such an instrument.[14] The device, which could produce variable as well as intermittent shocks, was designed so that the treatment was administered to a sitting patient. Since he wrote later to the same firm about purchasing batteries, in all probability he did buy one of the devices for the hospital. There is no record, however, of its use.

Bini's and Cerletti's ECT was introduced in Harrisburg in March of 1941 and was used for the next several years in a research mode. Attempting to administer the treatment to a random group, 566 patients of both sexes and across all age groups were selected without regard to their disorder or the duration of their illness. Of those treated 67 percent were reported as greatly improved, a little more than half of this number sufficiently so as to be returned to their homes. According to Petry, "the best results were in the involutional melancholia, the manic-depressive, and the psychoneurotic depressed types." He concluded, moreover, that "the earlier the treatment is received, the more apt improvement is to occur." By the end of the decade he reported that about 600 patients were receiving an average of 17 treatments each year.[15]

Petry took great pride in the fact that the Harrisburg State Hospital was among the first to investigate and then use these new techniques. He wrote: "We are pleased to note in retrospect the enviable record which this hospital has for the aggressive acceptance of newer therapies." He claimed that the hospital had been the first in the commonwealth to adopt the malarial treatment of neurosyphilis[16] introduced by Wagner von Jauregg in the first quarter of the century and that "when Manfred Sakel came to New York State and began demonstrating the use of insulin therapy ... we sent a representative from this hospital to take an intensive course of instruction and became the first State Hospital in Pennsylvania to use insulin shock therapy."[17]

He also claimed that the hospital was among the first to employ electroshock in the treatment of depressed patients and had in fact begun this treatment with a custom-made machine in 1941 before such equipment was commercially available. He went on to state that:

The benefits derived from these various therapeutic approaches are just short of miraculous and we are proud to feel that we had the foresight to adopt these procedures at an early date, even before the therapeutic value had been completely established. (18)

In 1952 Petry wrote that "we have now given over one hundred thousand electroshock treatments here and the experience which we have gained has made our work much more effective." Although the superintendent made it clear that he did not consider shock treatments as completely "curative," he did claim that "they have given us a measure of control of the affective disorders and have made it possible for us to dissipate them." One of the physicians who became active in administering electroshock treatment was a young physician, John B. Logan.[19]

At the same time, however, that these "advanced" treatments were being used, the woodworking shop of the hospital was still turning out "floor blocks." These consisted of large, heavy two-inch-thick blocks of wood which were covered with a piece of indestructible blanket. The blocks were affixed to the end of a long handle. Patients were assigned to push these blocks back and forth the length of the long halls in the ward buildings. It was hard work and took up much time. The method was designed to polish the floor but more important to tire out the user and thus reduce night-time problems for the staff.

*　　*　　*　　*

"Pennsylvania is a mud hole of politics," Harlan Smith's boss in Chicago warned him. But the young World War II navy veteran decided to take the job of steward, after coming to Harrisburg to see Petry. During his day-long interview, the superintendent had made it clear to Smith that being apolitical was a prerequisite for each member of his staff. At the Harrisburg State Hospital, Petry alone dabbled in politics or even spoke with politicians. No one ever knew whether a coworker was a Republican or Democrat let alone how he or she voted or thought on a political issue. It was H. K. Petry who dealt with the "people downtown."[20]

Smith had come to the attention of Petry through Edward Green, the son of the previous superintendent. Smith and the younger Green had served in the navy together in Washington state, where they ran the commissaries and the officers' club at Whidbey Island. Green, a Harrisburg banker, helped Harlan Smith with the bookkeeping part of their navy work. Smith, a manager for a restaurant company in Chicago, helped Green with the food service aspects of the job.

One of the first things that Petry wanted his new steward to do was to provide better meals for the patients. "I want you to get familiar with the dietary area and improve it!" he told Smith.[21] After a modest breakfast of cold cereal, toast, juice and coffee, the patients received their main meal at noon. It invariably consisted of meat and potatoes along with a dessert, usually pie or a pudding. In the evening the residents would be served a light meal—perhaps bologna, but again with potatoes. They ate "family style"; there were no seconds.

Harlan Smith was, as L. B. Harper had been before him, responsible for all of the non-medical aspects of the institution. He would review construction and maintenance projects before contract award as well as during the actual work. He would prepare the hospital's annual budget. Each morning the several department heads—the grounds chief, the laundry manager, the dietitian, the personnel director, the head of farming, the engineer—would come one after another into Smith's office to review the previous day's progress and to receive instructions.

Later in the day the steward would go out to visit the various areas, especially those where maintenance work was being done. He also would inspect the hospital's pantry. Although on occasion he would have to order the disposal of food that had been kept in storage too long, the major problem that Smith saw with the food service was that the less aggressive patients often got little to eat in the family-style dining that had been hospital practice since the beginning of the century. He, therefore, introduced a cafeteria approach to meal service. The food was still basically the same but the cafeteria arrangement meant that everyone got essentially the same portions. One problem that Smith was able to overcome only partially was the absence of fresh fruit. Vegetables from the farm and garden were plentiful; fresh fruits were available for the patients only on special occasions such as Christmas.[22]

* * * *

Howard K. Petry's staff considered him to be a most professional superintendent; one, however, with strong political ties. A good friend of state senator Harvey Taylor (with whom he served on the Board of Directors of the Harrisburg National Bank and Trust Company) and a leader who adroitly kept the people downtown at bay, in truth he was interested in broader horizons than those that could be seen from windows of the hospital's Administration Building. He believed strongly in medical education, not only improved standards of training for the professional staff, but also education of the public on the value of the state hospital system.

In June of 1939, for example, the hospital hosted the Pennsylvania Medical Society in a visit to the facilities at Harrisburg. Petry had gone to great lengths to set up in the Chapel exhibits and demonstrations for the visiting physicians from around the state. After explaining a little about the exhibits, the superintendent gave a historical overview of the hospital and then had several of his staff physicians present representative cases from among the hospital patients.

Fred B. Hooper described the case of a young white female, who had always been a poor eater and soon after becoming pregnant developed emesis. Within a month her vomiting became pernicious and she developed a psychosis, which was accompanied by muscle atrophy. She was treated with vitamin B complex and nicotinic acid and after several weeks began to respond to the treatment. After the birth of a normal child, the woman's palsy began to improve even more rapidly, although she still showed evidence of "foot drop."[23]

Hamblen C. Eaton presented three cases of general paresis with "diverse symptoms and manifestations." He went to great pains to point out that "general paresis seldom shows itself as any one typical or classical picture, and that the disgnosis depends in large part on the blood and spinal fluid Wassermann, the globulin content of the spinal fluid, and the reading of the colloidal gold curve." Herbert E. Heim presented a paper on "The Results of Insulin Therapy" and Fred Hooper read one that he and Julius H. Anderson had prepared on their "Observation on Sulfanilamide Therapy." One of the advantages that Hooper and Anderson described was that sulfanilamide treatment was ideal for patients who refused to keep dressings on their lesions.[24]

Eaton, the clinical director, closed the session with a summary of the outpatient services that were available. He stressed that this was a consultant service, which was available to a local physician. No charge was made for the service and no treatmcnt was givcn. Only a report of the examination, along with a suggested treatment, was sent back to the referring physician.

Howard K. Petry was a Fellow of the American College of Physicians, the American Medical Association and the American Psychiatric Association as well as President of the Pennsylvania State Medical Society in 1946.[25] In his Presidential address that year, he pointed out that "only seven percent of all neuro-psychiatric rejectees were psychotic or showed evidence of purely psychiatric disturbances." From this he suggested to the delegates assembled at the Bellevue-Stratford Hotel in Philadelphia that "society must learn to use to the limit the potentialities of the great majority of the handicapped individuals such as the five million draftees rejected for physical reasons. Only then will we have an efficient and truly democratic society and be able to decrease the growing long-time population of our mental institutions."[26]

He also issued two warnings to his fellow physicians. The first was of "the injection into the problem of hospital care of an extensive development of desirable prepaid hospital service plans but [which] placed in the hands of a group outside of the hospital a definite controlling financial interest." The other was that "if doctors do not take more interest in the management of the hospitals in which they work they will gradually find themselves working not in, but for, these hospitals."[27]

After he left the Presidency of the Pennsylvania Medical Society, Petry continued to serve as chairman of the organization's Committee on Public Relations as well as a member of its Advisory Committee on Vocational Rehabilitation. He lectured widely on the radio and across the state on such subjects as "Facing the Facts of Mental Disease," "Increasing the Span of Human Life," "Sleep" and "Medicine Faces the Future." Governor Duff appointed him to the state's Advisory Hospital Council, which conducted a survey of all the state's hospitals with a view to applying for federal aid under the Hill-Burton bill.[28] And in 1951 Governor Fine sent him to Mexico City to represent Pennsylvania at an International Mental Hygiene Conference. (31) He also appeared frequently for the state as an expert witness in criminal cases.

Howard Petry believed not only in education but also in the importance of knowing the past as a way to gain a better appreciation of the present. The lives of Dorothea Dix and John Curwen were frequently mentioned in his talks and in 1948 he wrote *A Century of Medicine*, the one-hundred-year history of the Medical Society of the State of Pennsylvania. With characteristic modesty the title page of the book states it was "edited" by him. Interestingly he cited the "discovery of the germ theory of the origin of disease by Pasteur, antisepsis by Lister, and anesthesia by Crawford Long" as the three causes of the "tremendous changes in the pattern of society" during the previous one hundred years, To these three he attributed the "spectacular conquests of many diseases."[30] Although there was no hint of prophecy in his observation, within a few years it would be possible to add the discovery of the psychotropic drugs to his list.

When he retired in December of 1954, Petry recommended to the hospital's board of trustees that he be replaced by his long-time assistant. They agreed and Hamblen Eaton became the sixth superintendent of the Harrisburg State Hospital. Petry continued to do consulting work and to see private patients from the front porch office of his Second Street, Harrisburg home until his death in April 1962.

*   *   *   *

If Petry ran the hospital from his first floor office in the Administration Building, Eaton ran it from everywhere but the office. A tinkerer by nature, he was likely to pop up anywhere on the grounds at any time of the day or night. If a piece of equipment in the powerhouse was inoperable, he would be there to see what it needed and that it got fixed promptly. If there was an instrument in the lab that was broken, back it would go to his quarters to be repaired by him that night. A patient's radio or a water leak in the Admission Building were typical of things set in order by his hand, especially on weekends when laborers were unavailable.[31] This was not simply a matter of personal interest or lack of concern for the larger issues of hospital management; it was a conscious part of his management philosophy. He believed that to have a good hospital it was necessary to have things run properly.[32]

John Curwen had wanted pleasant surroundings for his patients; Hamblen Eaton wanted a smoothly operating facility for his. Eaton's interest in moral management-like issues was more than a coincidence. When the area behind the Orth-Hutton administration building had been excavated in 1950 for a new Admission Center, the "Petry Building," Eaton, for example, showed great interest in inspecting the debris that was uncovered from the earth on which the old "Kirkbride" building stood. In 1956, soon after he became superintendent, moreover, he wrote that:

> The Harrisburg State Hospital is attuned to the use of psychotherapy in its broadest sense. This includes wholesome environment, good buildings, appropriately furnished and appropriately landscaped surroundings. ... It is the total push that results in the improvement of the patient.[33]

The total push that he had in mind included not only psychiatrists, well trained nurses, aides, psychologists, social workers, occupational therapists and physical therapists but also the new psychotropic or tranquilizing drugs. The value of using these drugs on mental patients had been discovered in France by accident, while testing antihistamines to reduce the occurrence of surgical shock. General anesthetics rendered patients unconscious and immobile but did nothing to prevent a state of shock from occurring, which often was fatal. A Paris physician, Henri Laborit, who was conducting the tests, observed that his patients became sleepy and less apprehensive with the antihistamines. Seeing other possibilities, Laborit got the drug into the hands of several Paris psychiatrists, who soon confirmed his thoughts. Although the results were unimpressive with some patients, those who responded dramatically had one thing in common; they were schizophrenics.[34]

Eaton made no claim of miracles in the first years the drugs were used at Harrisburg. He described their use rather as "encouraging." He reported that many patients did go home, some of whom had been in the hospital for years. He was cautious, however, as some of them returned to the hospital in a relatively short time. He asserted that this:

> ... points up the need for closer cooperation between the hospital and the community to see that these drugs are continued. In instances the families have been unable to purchase the drugs, or felt that they could not afford the cost or did not see the need of continuing their use. (35)

The superintendent went on to explain that there even "was a hesitancy on the part of some family physicians to continue treatment for which they were not yet fully prepared to ccept responsibility." After pointing out that it might be cheaper for the hospital to supply the drug than to maintain the patient in the hospital, he called for a "closer relationship between the family physician, social worker, community hospitals and mental health clinics" which he stated "may eventually solve this problem." His call for cooperation closed with what now appears to have been a prescription for the future of mental health care.

The mental health program should be broad in its

aspects and endeavors. It should operate in a somewhat similar manner to the Public Health program.[36]

By the end of the decade, however, the verdict was in. Late in 1958 Eaton had John Logan prepare a special report on the hospital's work in using the ataractic or tranquilizing drugs as they were to become more popularly known. Logan claimed that each of the drugs that had been tested had "produced some degree of change in our total hospitalized population, and that some had produced changes to a marked degree, assisting in 'reclaiming' heretofore inaccessible 'back-hall patients,' at least to a working status, and a few even to a parole status."[37]

John Logan made it clear that success in the use of the drugs required that "treatment must be individualized to a high degree, there being no standardized procedure as with insulin therapy." He also reported that "they appear to have such a minimal effect in depressions that electroconvulsive therapy still remains the treatment of choice when these symptoms are primary." After admitting that "our knowledge concerning their mechanism of action is embarrassingly limited," Logan asserted that "they have proven a valuable addition to our therapeutic efforts." Julius Anderson, who by that time had supervision of a large portion of the male side of the house, agreed with Logan's assessment.[38]

In addition to opening up new approaches to the treatment of mental illness, these drugs and new Federal laws concerning supervision of narcotics and tax-free alcohol, placed an increasing strain on the pharmacy. In two years, from 1956 to 1958, the hospital demand for drugs and medical supplies increased fifty percent while the costs more than doubled. The laboratory under the direction of the pathologist Thelma Boughton also was busy conducting 30,000 tests a year. For each of the three technologists whom Boughton had in the lab, this meant 10,000 tests a year. They were so involved in conducting chemistries, urinalyses, and bacteriological examinations that it was necessary to set aside much of the hematology and tissue work that might have been done.[39]

*   *   *   *

Knowledge of Eaton's strong interest in machinery should not obscure our understanding of his concern for his patients. His strong clinical background and his interest in the hospital's outpatient clinics, which he had overseen for years, led him to focus on the patient from a new direction. He felt that "the community is the locality where the patient's mental illness began and that the community must play a very mportant role in the prevention ... and the rehabilitation of the mental patient."[40]

He felt that the stumbling blocks that the community placed before the paroled or released patient caused many of them "to become despondent and return to the hospital out of self-protection." Neighbors and friends would shun them, industry refused to re-employ them or else gave them inferior positions, even the state revoked their driver's licenses. The superintendent hoped that by enlarging the hospital's out-patient clinic and its social service department, which now included seven workers, greater contact with the communities would "promote better mental hygiene in the community as well as lead to better treatment both within and outside the hospital.[41]

Part of the overall program that Eaton had in mind included the establishment in November 1955 of a hospital chaplaincy program. Not only were Jewish services inaugurated but the number of Roman Catholic services was increased. Beginning in 1958 both Catholic and Protestant services were conducted every Sunday of the year. The Chaplian, moreover, began to conduct Bible classes in the wards and to distribute devotional booklets to the patients. The hospital even began training ministers with an intensive six week course in the role of chaplaincy in state institutions and in an understanding of mental illness. By the end of 1958, a total of twenty-three ministers had completed the course.

*   *   *   *

Hamblen C. Eaton was born in Warren, Pennsylvania on March 1, 1901. He was the eldest of three sons and a daughter of Frederick C. and Maygwin H. Eaton. Frederick Eaton was the manager of the Valvoline Oil Plant in Warren. It was there among all the plant equipment that Hamblen first developed his love for mechanical and electrical things. The boy graduated from Warren High School in 1918 and from Allegheny College in 1922. He completed his medical studies at Western Reserve University School of Medicine in 1926.[42]

After an internship at the Allegheny General Hospital in Pittsburgh he served successively at the Warren State Hospital as a staff physician, pathologist and then as clinical director. In 1936 he became the clinical director of the Polk State School in Venango County. The following year Petry, whose career had paralleled Eaton's at Warren, invited him to come to Harrisburg as his clinical director. He remained with Petry in that capacity until becoming superintendent.[43]

In 1928 Hamblen married Zelma Bowman of Warren, Pennsylvania. They had two sons, David and Robert, both of whom grew up on the grounds of the hospital at Harrisburg. As a member of the Naval Reserve, Eaton was called to active duty from December 1941 to the end of World War II in 1945. In 1957 he became President of the Dauphin County Medical Society. He also served for several years as Chairman of the Mental Hygiene Commission of the Medical Society of the State of Pennsylvania.[44]

*   *   *   *

H. K. Petry was able somehow to keep the forces for change away from the hospital's gate. Eaton, unfortunately, had to accept the inevitability of their arrival. Gradually, the power of the Board of Trustees and the superintendent were being transferred downtown to the Pennsylvania Department of Welfare. Vacancies in the board went unfilled by the Governor. During Petry's final year there had been one. By the end of Eaton's first year there were four. In the following two years there were three more resignations including that of the board president, William C. Freeman. A former state senator, Freeman's long involvement with the hospital represented the power that board membership had formerly signified.

One of the three new board vacancies in 1954 was created by the death of George Wolf Reily, Jr, the grandson of Luther Reily, who had been the first president of the hospital's board of trustees. The younger Reily had served as a trustee more than fifty years and as Vice-President of the board for his last twenty-three. This break in the board's link with the hospital's beginnings in 1851 almost symbolically signaled the significant changes which were to come.[45]

Not only did the incoming governor, George M. Leader, (governor from January 1955 to January 1959) fail to fill vacancies on the board of trustees, but he also appointed Harry Shapiro as the state's Secretary of Welfare. With Shapiro's arrival the process of change accelerated. The new Secretary, a forceful man in his own right, had an agenda that he wanted to put into effect. He and the governor were appalled at what they had seen in many of the state hospitals.[46]

They attempted at first to clean up several of the worst cases. Shapiro sent Hamblen Eaton to Allentown to make recommendations for better management at the facility.[47] Apparently sensing the futility of this approach, the Governor and the Secretary of Welfare began to solicit the help of several growing mental health advocacy groups—ones such as the Pennsylvania Citizens Association and Pennsylvania Mental Health, Incorporated. Together they pushed House Bill 670 through the legislature. Governor Leader signed the bill into law in December 1955. Public Law 255, as it became known, not only placed mental health personnel under the merit system but also transferred the administrative powers of the boards of trustees of the state hospitals to the Department of Welfare.[48]

Harry Shapiro was a Philadelphia lawyer and a former member of the Pennsylvania Senate. While in the Senate, he had been chairman of the committee which investigated conditions at the Philadelphia State Hospital. He also had been a member of the board of trustees at Mount Sinai Hospital for thirty years. Like most dedicated men, he exasperated many people including those in the state hospitals as well as those in the legislature. He was a newsmaker, however, and reporters loved him. Those who were assigned to the capitol press room called the wildest game of poker that they played "crazy Harry" in his honor.[49]

While the changes that Shapiro implemented were largely administrative rather than medical, any intrusion into the running of the hospital tended to be seen by the superintendent and the medical staff as interference in decisions over the care of the mentally ill by a non-medical individual. But it was what they perceived as Shapiro's "political" behavior that was especially annoying to them. As a previously insulated professional staff they never had been exposed to that sort of thing. Each time he came to the hospital the Secretary of Welfare arrived with a large retinue of department employees as well as with a personal photographer; picture taking always seemed to be a significant part of his travels.[50] While he was attempting to force change from the outside by raising the public's awareness through publicity, internally he was seen as using the publicity as an opportunity for personal purposes.

In May 1958, the crisis between the Secretary and the hospital superintendent at Harrisburg flared into the open. Shapiro had ordered all of the state hospitals to move those employees who were living on hospital property out of their quarters. [51] Eaton first interpreted the Secretary's memo as leaving the decision to a superintendent's discretion and thus advised the board of trustees that, to provide proper patient care, his staff was needed on the grounds at all times. When Shapiro insisted, Eaton directed his staff to remain. Shapiro then threatened to hold up paychecks for those who did not leave, and when the superintendent indicated that he would pay their salaries out of his own funds,[52] Shapiro carried out his threat. Shortly thereafter, all but the most essential employees left the premises.

The Department of Welfare was now in charge. The responsibility for the care of Pennsylvania's mentally ill finally, fully lay at the state level.

END NOTES

1. The ward nurses and male attendants, however, ate whatever the patients had for meals.
2. The Solarium was remodeled into living quarters and renamed Medical Center in 1938. A third floor sleeping area was added and the interior of the dome was no longer visible. Since 1969 the structure, which is now attached to the Petry Admissions Building, has been known as the Vista Dome. Arnold Bowman, therapist, who ran the hospital's music program, was one of the individuals who lived in the Vista Dome.
3. In recent years this small building has been used by the Community Living Outreach Program (CLOP).
4. Petry, Robert, Interview, January 14, 1991. Young Petry spent his college summer vacations working at the hospital in various maintenance positions.
5. Godcharles, Frederic A., *Chronicles of Central Pennsylvania*, Lewis Historical Publishing Company, Inc., New York, 1944, Vol. IV, page 387.
6. Logan, John B., Harrisburg State Hospital Oral History, September 9, 1990.
7. Logan, John B., Interview, October 17, 1990.
8. Hartz, Fred R. and Hoshino, Arthur Y., op. cit., page 119.
9. Although in 1950 Petry stated: "We are now prepared to undertake lobotomies in this hospital," four years later the hospital had performed few if any such procedures. The superintendent claimed that this was "because of our concern regarding the permanent structural damage which such treatment involves." A few patients, however, were sent to Philadelphia and Washington for the operation. Petry, Howard K., *Harrisburg State Hospital Biennial Report*, 1952-1954, page 12.
10. Valenstein, Elliot S., *Great and Desperate Cures*, Basic Books, Inc., New York, page 48.
11. Ibid., pages 48-50.
12. Although a patient is able to "function" soon after an ECT treatment is administered, there is a loss of memory. The extent and the length of an individual's memory loss increases as the number of treatments are given.
13. Gay, Peter, *Freud, A Life for Our Time*, Doubleday, New York, 1988. page 62.
14. Queen, James, letter October 27, 1879.
15. Petry, Howard K., *Harrisburg State Hospital Biennial Report*, 1948-1950, page 39. Petry's statement that the average number of treatments per patient was 17 is, however, misleading. Based on a review of the detailed ECT records which were kept by the hospital during these years, some individuals received as many as twenty-five or thirty treatments in the course of a two-month period. Continuation of electroconvulsive treatment seems to have depended on whether or not the physician believed the patient was getting better. Treatment of some individuals, for example, was discontinued after six or seven treatments when there was no indication of improvement.
16. Patients suffering from syphilis-induced paresis were inoculated with the blood of patients suffering from malaria. The malaria, which was controlled by quinine, caused the fever which arrested the paresis.
17. Petry, Howard K., *Harrisburg State Hospital Biennial Report*, 1952-1954, pages 11-13.
18. Ibid.
19. Petry, Howard K., *Harrisburg State Hospital Biennial Report*, 1950-1952, page 7.
20. Smith, Harlan, Interview November 12, 1990. By Petry's time the Department of Welfare had become a bastion of patronage. Only 300 of 14,000 jobs were non-political appointments. [Cooper, Richard and Crary, Ryland W., *The Politics of Progress*, Penns Valley Publishers, Harrisburg, Pennsylvania, 1982, page 54.] That Petry was able to maintain a non-political environment at the Harrisburg State Hospital was a remarkable accomplishment. The staffs at many state hospitals were filled with political appointees.

21. Concern for his patients' diet and the fact that Harlan Smith was working for a restaurant company in Chicago may have had something to do with Petry's interest in hiring Smith.
22. Smith, Harlan, Interview, November 12, 1990.
23. Brewen, Stewart F., article in *The Pennsylvania Medical Journal*, Vol. 42, No. 11, August 1939, published by the Medical Society of the State of Pennsylvania, pages 1394-1395.
24. Ibid.
25. One measure of the stature of the hospital at Harrisburg can be found in the fact that in its first 100 years there were only five superintendents. And of these five, three were elected President of the Pennsylvania State Medical Society: John Curwen in 1868, Henry Orth in 1892 and Howard Petry in 1946. Five members, moreover, of the Board of Trustees of the hospital: Hiram Corson (1852), John L. Atlee (1857), Traill Green (1867), Stephen B. Keefer (1873) and Alexander Craig (1890) also were Presidents of the State Medical Society.
26. Petry, Howard K., *A Century of Medicine*, printed privately for the Medical Society of the State of Pennsylvania, 1952, pages 178-179.
27. Ibid.
28. Petry, Howard K., *Harrisburg State Hospital Biennial Report, 1946-1948*, page 26.
29. Petry, Howard K., *Harrisburg State Hospital Biennial Report, 1950-1952*, page 31.
30. Petry, Howard K., *A Century of Medicine*, printed privately for the Medical Society of the State of Pennsylvania, 1952, page v.
31. Slothower, Martha, Oral History, 1988, page 23.
32. Eaton, Robert, Oral History, September 26, 1990.
33. Eaton, Hamblen C., *Harrisburg State Hospital Biennial Report, 1954-1956*, pages 9-10.
34. Snyder, Solomon H., *Madness and the Brain*, McGraw-Hill Book Co., New York, 1938, pages 13-16.
35. Eaton, Hamblen C., *Harrisburg State Hospital Biennial Report, 1954-1956*, page 10. The psychotropic drugs are not curative in the sense that they do not modify the patient's condition; they only relieve schizophrenia's symptoms. Thus patients must continue to take them.
36. Eaton, Hamblen C., *Harrisburg State Hospital Biennial Report, 1954-1956*, page 11.
37. Eaton, Hamblen C., *Harrisburg State Hospital Biennial Report, 1956-1958*, pages 27-28.
38. Ibid.
39. Eaton, Hamblen C., *Harrisburg State Hospital Biennial Report, 1956-1958*, page 28.
40. Eaton, Hamblen C., *Harrisburg State Hospital Biennial Report, 1954-1956*, pages 11-13.
41. Ibid.
42. Eaton, Robert, Oral History, September 26, 1990.
43. Ibid.
44. Eaton, Hamblen C., *Harrisburg State Hospital Biennial Report, 1956-1958*, pages 23-24.
45. George Wolf Reily, Jr. was, as his father and grandfather before him, a physician. He also was a prominent enough state banker that three presidents (Cleveland, McKinley and Theodore Roosevelt) appointed him a national bank examiner.
46. Silverstein, Max, *Vital Connections*, Lexington Books, Lexington, Massachusetts, 1990, page 50.
47. Eaton, Robert, Interview, January 29, 1991.
48. Silverstein, op. cit., pages 51-52.
49. McGreary, M. Nelson, *Pennsylvania Government In Action: Governor Leader's*

Administration, Penns Valley Publishers, State College, Pennsylvania, 1972, pages 109-110. Also Smith, Reed M., State *Government in Transition*, University of Pennsylvania Press, Philadelphia, 1963, pages 94-95.

50. Smith, Harlan, Interview, November 12, 1990.
51. The move was designed to make additional space available for patients. Although desperately needed, much of the staff living space would have been inappropriate as wards for patients.
52. Eaton, Hamblen, letter to the Board of Trustees, May 2, 1958.

XV

RETURN TO THE COMMUNITY

The decade from 1962 to 1972 was as momentous in the nation's and the state's history of mental health care as were the years between Dorothea Dix's survey of the counties of rural Pennsylvania in 1845 and the founding of the first state hospital at Harrisburg in 1851. Curiously, the issue was the same both times: whether local or state care of the indigent insane was the more appropriate. For the first time, however, in the 1960s, the issue was joined at the federal level—initially in a legislative act, and then in a court case.

Based on the report, *Action for Mental Health*, which was the work of a commission (established in 1955) to look into mental illness and mental health issues, President John F. Kennedy issued the first executive message ever devoted to the proposition that the U.S. government should provide for mental illness.[1] From his 1963 speech came the idea of community mental health centers.[2] As Kennedy put it, "the cold mercy of custodial isolation will be supplanted by the open warmth of community concern..." Thus the drive to create mental health centers in communities throughout the nation began. Each center receiving federal money was required to provide five basic services: inpatient, outpatient, partial hospitalization, emergency care, consultation and education.[3]

The state of Pennsylvania followed suit in 1966 with a similar but even more comprehensive law. It directed that "each county shall ... establish a county mental health and mental retardation program." This act, which Governor Scranton signed into law in October of that year, gave the Department of Welfare the right to review all non-criminal commitments that were made. The state's Secretary of Welfare would no longer be forced to "climb the fence" to find out what was going on in a state facility.[4] The new law also placed, in habeas corpus cases, the burden of proof for a person's continued detention upon the administrative head of the facility.

* * * *

Although Hamblen Eaton had felt that the community should play an important role in the prevention and the rehabilitation of the mental patient and did continue to encourage community participation through support of local clinics, it was not until S. Philip Laucks became the hospital's seventh superintendent in 1969 that a truly new, bold plan was introduced at Harrisburg in support of the community mental health center idea.[5]

Eaton, wearied perhaps by his struggles with the Department of Welfare, had retired that year.[6] Before he left, however, he was able to make arrangements with the Pennsylvania Historical and Museum Commission to preserve Henry Orth's magnificient collection of French furniture and silverware. Today the bulk of the nearly 1,600 items are housed in the Pennsylvania State Museum and the Pennsylvania Governor's Mansion.

After his retirement, Eaton continued his favorite pastime of building Heath kits and fixing electronic gear. He also appeared from time to time as a "friend of the court" —in cases in which the judge needed sound, unbiased professional advice to sort through the prosecution and defense arguments and the claims of their psychiatric witnesses. He died in September 1983. Ron Sider, the organist at Grace United Methodist Church on State Street, where Hamblen Eaton was once President of the Administrative Board, played two of the former superintendent's favorite hymns: "God of our fathers" and "For the beauty of the earth."

* * * *

Stanley Philip Laucks was descended from a York county family of long standing. He had graduated from the University of Pennsylvania's School of Medicine in 1946 and did his psychiatric residency at Harrisburg from 1947-1949. The

Harrisburg State Hospital was one of the few state facilities to provide such residencies in psychiatry. After spending two years at the Friends Hospital in Philadelphia, he returned to Harrisburg as a staff physician. He left again in 1952. He spent several years in private practice and in military service and then came back to the hospital in 1962 as the Director of Residency Training. The hospital's residency program had been decertified and Eaton wanted the returning physician to correct the deficiencies. Laucks did and the following year he was made Clinical Director. He held this position until he was appointed superintendent.[7]

As the new superintendent, he completely restructured the Harrisburg State Hospital—the physical plant as well as the staff.[8] He put together multidisciplinary teams, consisting of a psychiatrist, a psychologist, rehabilitation counselors, nurses, social workers and aides; gathered all the patients from the same county into one building and had them function as if they were a separate hospital. (The men and the women, however, were still housed on separate floors.) Each of the medical teams was more closely allied with the community mental health unit in the county which they served, than with their fellow professionals in the other "units" of the hospital. The plan was called simply the "Unit" System.

By 1971 there were four such county units functioning at the hospital: Dauphin, Cumberland/Perry, York/Adams and Lancaster.[9] There was also a geriatric, an adolescent, and an alcoholic rehabilitation unit. These latter functions had been added to the federal law, which provided money for the community mental health centers. Thus those counties which received grants had to provide the services, with the state hospital following suit.

Attempts were made to eliminate the staff "caste" system at the state hospital by placing an individual other than a psychiatrist in charge of some of the units. It was hoped, by focusing on each member's function within the team rather than on their traditional disciplines, that greater cohesiveness and more active treatment of patients would result. Patients, moreover, were not segregated into acute and chronic. All lived and worked together in the same building. The ultimate objective was to develop "clear, intense ties" with the community mental health center. In this way it was hoped that fewer cases would come to the state hospital, and that the cases which did could be returned more quickly as outpatients to the center from which they had come. The objective as expressed in one Dauphin County Unit report was that mental hospitals should be "schools for living,"[10] not dormitories for dying.

By most accounts the system was a success. Its implementation, however, was not without difficulties. The loss of previous lines of reporting and responsibility, and the working out of new ones were hard for some to adjust to. The members of the nursing staff, for example, who in the past had reported to the Director of Nursing, now were responsible to the head of the team (a physician) in each unit. This not only changed the relationships for individual nurses, but also meant that the duties of the Director of Nursing, Betty S. Hummel, had to be revised. It was only after months of difficult debate that issues such as these were resolved.

Under the unit system not only the staff but also the residents and private volunteers from the community were involved in treatment decisions. The idea was one of doing something "with" the patient rather than "to" him or her. This approach also repudiated the concept of the patient as "sick" and thus not accountable for his or her behavior. Through the use of a patient governing body, social interaction was stimulated and improvements in personal hygiene were encouraged. Education and cooperation with the community improved markedly.[11]

The alcoholic rehabilitation unit, for example, worked closely with the Dauphin County Mental Health Clinics. With a twelve-bed patient capacity and a staff of seven, the unit was able to relieve the heavy case load of local and transient alcoholics that the county units were handling. The hospital group became involved, moreover, with the community rehabilitation and treatment programs.

An additional outgrowth of this effort of focusing more on the individual patient was the gathering and analysis of a much wider range of data about each of the residents. This data was used, moreover, in attempts "to answer theoretical questions about mental health rather than simply being focused on the services to the population in the hospital."[12] Studies in color perception, for example, were conducted using patients in the geriatric unit. Computer processed behavioral ratings and a patient Rehabilitation Progress Profile, which including 59 items of measurement, were developed. The RPP, as the profile became known, consisted of tracking patients on their individual Social and Living Skills, their Communication Skills, their Awareness and Adjustment progress, and the improvement shown in their Personal Care. By 1970 the hospital's research department had a staff of 14 and a budget of 130,000.[13]

While the rate of change at the hospital accelerated dramatically during this period, the staff continued to carry forward traditions from the hospital's earliest years. When John H. Mentzer the assistant superintendent of the hospital died in 1971 at age 67, they planted 150 cherry trees on the grounds in his memory. Mentzer, a native of Denver, Pennsylvania, who started out as a public school teacher, returned to the University of Pennsylvania to earn a medical degree in 1930. He came to the hospital in 1947 and soon came to be regarded for his "impeccable integrity, uncompromising fairness, and devotion to duty."[14]

* * * *

In April, 1972, the "other shoe" was dropped on state mental hospitals across the nation. The U. S. Middle Court in Alabama issued its decree in the case of Wyatt versus Stickney. In what became a class action suit, Ricky Wyatt, through his aunt, had sued the state of Alabama over the quality of care he was receiving at Bryce Hospital, Tuscaloosa. The court agreed that the hospital's treatment program was "deficient in that it failed to provide a humane psychological and physical environment," that there were insufficent doctors to "administer adequate treatment," and that "non-therapeutic, uncompensated work assignments and the absence of any semblance of privacy, constituted dehumanizing factors."[15] The court's decision was no less than a patient's "bill of rights." It provided among other things that:

Patients have a right to privacy and dignity.

Patients have a right to the least restrictive conditions necessary.

Patients have an unrestricted right to send sealed mail.

Patients have a right to be free from unnecessary or excessive medication.

Patients have a right to be free from physical restraint and isolation.

Patients have a right not to be subjected to treatment procedures such as lobotomy, electroconvulsive treatment or other unusual or hazardous treatment procedures without their consent.

Patients are not deemed incompetent to manage their affairs, to contract, to marry, to register and vote or to hold professional or occupational or vehicle operator's licenses by reason of their commitment to a mental hospital.

The greatest blow, however, to the historic method of managing state mental hospitals was the court's decision that "no patient shall be required to perform labor which involves the operation and maintenance of the hospital." Patients would be permitted to work voluntarily, but all such labor had to be compensated in accordance with the minimum wage laws.[16]

No longer would armies of patients march each summer across the lawn at Harrisburg pushing hand mowers, no longer would platoons of men shovel the winter snows from the roadways and sidewalks of the hospital, no longer would squads of women sew together "indestructible" blankets or make underwear for new patients, no longer would individuals push the polishing block up and down the long ward halls, no longer would any resident milk the cows, or plow the farm land or plant the garden crops or dig that staple of the hospital's dining room, potatoes. The organization of the Harrisburg State Hospital had changed drastically under the community mental health act and the unit system, but changes to the life of the patients had been more subtle. After Wyatt versus Stickney almost all aspects of daily existence at the institution were completely reordered for everyone.

The heart of the court's decision was that each patient's treatment (including all therapeutic tasks and any labor) must be tailored to his or her individual condition and needs. After Wyatt a separate "treatment plan" was required for each patient. The U.S. Middle Court, moreover, established precise staffing ratios, the minimum acceptable number for each position in a state hospital. It specified, for example, that 2 psychiatrists, 4 physicians, 3 psychologists, 12 nurses and 70 aides were required for each 250 patients. It even set standards for the number of toilets and showers, the frequency of linen service, the size of the physical plant, and the patient's nutritional requirements.[17]

* * * *

In spite of the therapeutic success of the unit system, 1972 also saw a return to a "needs" organizational approach at the Harrisburg State Hospital. The patients seemed to benefit by the unit organization, but the resources required to support the system outstripped those available to Laucks. Dedicating staff members in large numbers to each unit improved patient care and eased their transition to and from the community mental heath centers, but meant a drain on hospital resources. Many economies of scale were lost even in such mundane areas as ordering and maintaining supplies and equipment. These had become a unit responsibility and necessitated management time as well as money.

The hospital, moreover, by this time was completely under the budgetary control of the Department of Welfare. There were no more paying patients, there were no private fundraisings by the Board of Trustees, there were no sales of goods from the farm or the garden or the various "manufacturing" activities of the hospital, there was only the state's annual appropriation—fixed and always less than was requested.

S. Philips Laucks resigned as the hospital's superintendent in 1972, just as the dismantling of the unit system and the transition back to a needs system was being carried out. He left the completion of this job to John Logan, who by then was the hospital's chief psychiatrist. Filled with the executive restlessness typical of twentieth-century men of position, Laucks seldom stayed in one job more than three or four years. His management of the Harrisburg State Hospital also exhibited modern executive tendencies.

Unlike Petry, he had not been interested in closely watching visitors or even employees. Unlike Eaton, he had not been on a first-name basis with the staff—his immediate predecessor had known and would greet even the lowliest members of the maintenance crews on his trips around the grounds. Although Philip Laucks was a man of compassion equal to that of his former bosses, he had preferred to run the hospital through his subordinates. During his administration there was no more open-door policy, even for members of the senior medical staff. An unannounced visit to his office would usually draw a suggestion from a secretary to see some other senior staff member or some committee head, rather than to "go right in."[18]

After his return to York County, Laucks became first a Psychiatric Coordinator and then in 1984 the Director of Medical Education at the York Hospital. In 1987 he retired to his farm where he continued to raise prize sheep.[19] At the Harrisburg State Hospital he was followed by a succession of short-term superintendents and acting superintendents.

The first of these was David Lasky. Lasky, a Ph.D. rather than a physician, had been the Director of the Research Department for a number of years. He was head of the hospital, however, less than six months. When he returned to staff duties, Lasky was followed by Frank Herzel. Although Herzel was a physician, he was not a psychiatrist. He came to the position of acting superintendent from the directorship of the hospital's Geriatric Unit. A soft-spoken family practitioner type, he seemed to lack interest in the active management of a large institution such as the Harrisburg State Hospital. Within a year he too resigned and was replaced by James C. Powell.

Powell, a social worker, was a native of California. He and Lasky were the first non-medical superintendents to run the hospital. The 1966 state law that reorganized Pennsylvania mental health care permitted the director of a mental hospital to be other than a physician as long as a physician was in charge of all medical diagnosis, treatment and care.[20] Powell, a large genial man, was actually a political appointee. He reportedly was assigned to the hospital with the idea of closing it, but he also resigned after less than a year as superin-tendent.[21]

By this time morale of the medical staff had reached such a low point that several of John Logan's co-workers got together a petition requesting him to apply for the position. Reluctantly he did. He was appointed by the Department of Welfare in September, 1974, and left his beloved clinical work to take over the superintendency. The hospital, which in 1955 had 2,739 residents and 802 individuals on approved leave, was now down to a total of 750 patients.[22]

John Flatley, a psychologist, became Logan's chief of staff. He did much of the administrative work for the new superintendent. This enabled Logan to continue concentrating on the clinical aspects of the hospital. The superintendent kept his patient load as well as his long hair, and continued to wear jeans and boots to work.[23]

On the occasion of the one hundred twenty-fifth anniversary of the founding of the hospital on October 19, 1976, John Logan described the hospital as "an integral component of a dynamic mental health/mental retardation delivery system..." He went on to state that "perhaps in yet-to-be exposed arenas of public indifference the myths of mental illness and state institutionalization still remain. But the important note to be played and repeated as we continue to search for and find answers to the dominating question of delivering the best quality of service ... is one of hope and optimism."

John Logan closed his speech by saying, "It is my feeling ... that what is really being praised today is not the establishment of the Harrisburg State Hospital but the existence of the enlightened and humane concern for fellow human beings that gave us Dorothea Dix, Dr. Curwen, and each of you who are present today."[24] Although he stayed as superintendent until 1979, Logan's heart was in the hospital's wards, not its administrative offices. Twelve years later he continues to minister to his patients as the hospital's chief psychiatric physician.

Ford S. Thompson, Jr. from the Department of Welfare followed Logan in 1979, first as the acting superintendent and then two years later as the superintendent.[25] When Thompson arrived the hospital was no longer accredited as a mental health care facility. While the exodus of patients continued, Thompson and the medical staff worked to restore the hospital to its former position. In 1981 the Joint Committee on Accreditation of Hospital Organizations, a nationally recognized independent review agency from Chicago, returned the Harrisburg State Hospital to its list of accredited institutions.

In 1988 John Flatley was made acting superintendent, while Thompson took over responsibility for the Bureau of the Central Region. The Department of Welfare by that time had divided the state into four regions. The Central Region comprises 24 counties and four state hospitals. Three years later Flatley is still running the Harrisburg State Hospital as the Acting Superintendent.

END NOTES

1. In 1854 Congress had passed a Dix-sponsored bill which would have brought the Federal government into the fight for the mentally ill. The law provided for an endowment of ten million acres of public land, which was to be distributed among the states based on their geographical size and their representation in the House. President Pierce vetoed the bill on the grounds that Congress did not have the power to make provision for the insane. It was one of the few defeats that Miss Dix ever suffered.

2. Silverstein, Max, *Vital Connections*, Lexington Books, Lexington, Massachusetts, 1990, page 11.

3. The money was provided through the Mental Health Centers and Mental Retardation Act of 1963.

4. In what may be an apocryphal story, Harry Shapiro had to climb the fence and crawl through a cellar window one night to get into Philadelphia's Byberry Hospital because the superintendent refused to let him inspect the facility. (Edith Krohn, Interview, January 30, 1991)

5. The idea of organizing state hospitals along "unit" lines was not original with Laucks. By 1969 it was sweeping the state and the nation as more and more community mental health centers were set up.

6. Shapiro frequently sent Eaton notes on Friday afternoons, thus reportedly spoiling his weekends. (Harlan Smith, Interview, November 12, 1990)

7. Laucks, S. Philip, Interview, July, 1990.

8. The change over to the unit system was begun in the final year that Laucks was Clinical Director.

9. Due to the lack of local resources many counties joined with others to form single community mental health centers. The Cumberland/Perry unit actually comprised seven central Pennsylvania counties: Cumberland, Perry, Franklin,

Juniata, Mifflin, Fulton and Huntington.

10. Dauphin County Unit report, "Organizational Description, Goals, and Programs—July, 1969."
11. Ibid.
12. Sayers, Calvin, editor, *Harrisburg State Hospital Research and Projects Monthly Bulletin*, Vol. II, No. 11, November 1971, page 10. Animals, especially a wide array of dogs, were housed as pets in the administration building when the physicians' children were still living there.
13. Ibid, pages 9 and 16.
14. The Harrisburg *Evening News*, June 7, 1971, page 5.
15. Ricky Wyatt versus Dr. Stonewall B. Stickney, U. S. District Court, Middle District, Alabama, April 13, 1972. Federal Supplement No. 344, pages 373-387. The effect of the decision of the court, of course, was applicable nationwide.
16. Ibid., page 381.
17. Ibid., pages 382-384.
18. Logan, John, Oral History, September 1990.
19. Laucks, S. Philip, Interview, July 1990.
20. The law's provisions for a non-medical director were revised by the legislature in 1975 to read: "he shall also be a physician where possible or demonstrate ... knowledge and competencies in the field of mental health... The director of the clinical program of the hospital shall be a physician ..."
21. Flatley, John, Oral History, August 28, 1990.
22. Unattributed remarks on the occasion of the presentation of historic documents marking the one hundred twenty-fifth anniversary of the Harrisburg State Hospital, October 19, 1976.
23. Flatley, John, Oral History, August 28, 1990. Flatley, a graduate of Gannon College, did his graduate work in counseling at Pennsylvania State University. He came to the Harrisburg State Hospital in 1972, fully expecting to leave eventually for a job in physical rehabilitation.
24. Logan, John, "Introductory Remarks" on the occasion of the presentation of historic documents marking the one hundred twenty-fifth anniversary of the Harrisburg State Hospital, October 19, 1976.
25. Thompson, who holds degrees in Public Administration from Lebanon Valley College and the George Washington University, had been the Regional Deputy Secretary of Public Welfare before he came to the hospital. In that position he had been responsible for all of the human services programs of the department.

XVI

THE PRESENT AND
THE FUTURE

Three decades after the inception of the community mental health center idea it is, as was the state hospital system which it replaced, beset with problems. Charges of inadequate or inappropriate treatment, of too broad a mandate, of internal professional bickering, of class favoritism, even of outright fraud regularly surface. It now appears that the change to a community-based system was more of a political and social adjustment designed to satisfy the nation's attitudes about treatment of the mentally ill, rather than a substantive improvement in their care. As John Talbot, a past president of the American Psychiatric Association, put it, in many cases "the chronically ill mental patient has had his place of living and care transferred from a single lousy institution to multiple wretched ones."[1]

While the community concept still appears to be a feasible one, its implementation has gone awry. Initially it was intended that local mental health facilities would be available to provide outpatient and short-term inpatient care for the people being "deinstitutionalized" by state hospitals. To this end, it was projected that 2,000 centers would be needed nationally. The actual number that have been built is about 870.[2] Most of these serve, moreover, a middle-class clientele. Dorothea Dix's "indigent insane" have simply been returned to the streets—in the words of one judge, from the nation's "back wards" to its "back alleys."[3] It is estimated that today there are about 250,000 individuals who are seriously ill with schizophrenia or manic-depressive illness. Only about 68,000 of these people are receiving any hospital care.[4]

Since 1970, moreover, a succession of national administrations has attempted to get the federal government out of the business of social and mental health services. Where a direct reversal of the 1960s policy was not politically sound, other techniques were used: Under Richard Nixon it was the policy of impoundment of legislated monies; under Gerald Ford it was the vetoing of legislation to provide funds for new mental health centers; and under Ronald Reagan it was first budget reconcilation and then block grants, which sharply reduced even further the federal funds available for mental health.[5]

Although there are debates about issues such as commitment policy and community versus state facilities, the primary struggle within Pennsylvania is still over who gets the money. Claims are made that there is "a funding imbalance that ties up too many dollars in inpatient institutional care... "[6] After 150 years, we still look for the answer to our mental health problems first in technology and then in methods of organization or reorganization. Meanwhile individuals on all sides of the debate (and there are as many sides to the question as their were to Haviland's building for the chronically ill) claim that given enough money their solution would prove to be best. The truth probably lies elsewere. Perhaps, as Earl Bond suggested, more "within us."

The *Philadelphia Inquirer* stated when the Philadelphia State Hospital (Byberry) finally was closed in 1990: "We're not completely sure what the message is, but the fact is that just a few miles from Byberry... there is another mental-health facility. It is thriving after more than 175 years of service. It has a reputation for caring—and succeeding. It is Friends Hospital... " The editorial went on to claim that "mental-health facilities can work, given proper funding, attention and a respect for the worthiness of every individual."[7] On all three items we seem, however, to always come up short. While the solution to funding problems is within human grasp, unlikely as that is to happen, no amount of money or organizational rearrangement will guarantee the presence of the other two.[8]

*　　*　　*　　*

Today the Harrisburg State Hospital maintains a patient level of about 450 individuals. Only those who have repeated admissions to a community mental health center are referred to the state facility. This is a matter of convenience rather than law. The Community Mental Health Centers Act of 1963 made no provision for long-term custodial care and no allocation of resources for such treatment has been provided. The centers, therefore, do not view such patients or their care as a suitable responsibility. Thus they are referred to state facilities.[9] The average stay at the Harrisburg State Hospital now is six months. There are, however, chronic long-term patients at the facility—some for as many as twenty years.

The relationship between a patient's ability to pay and the state's responsibility also has become blurred. The Harrisburg State Hospital is now run just as any private facility. The first thing that is done when a new patient is admitted is to determine the individual's ability to pay for his or her care, whether or not the patient has appropriate insurance or the hospital has to find a source of money (usually the state) for him or her. For many types of treatment, moreover, the hospital contracts out for the service. Those few patients for whom electric shock is prescribed, for example, are sent to the Polyclinic Hospital for the procedure.

The hospital does engage in an active research program, one of perhaps more importance than at any other time in its long history. Working closely with the Mental Health Clinical Research Center at the University of Pennsylvania in Philadelphia, the Harrisburg facility has helped to establish an "autopsy section"—one that is helping to investigate brain-behavior relationships in schizophrenia. And on a more immediate level the hospital has been using pet therapy in working with violent and aggressive psychotic patients who have not been able to establish satisfactory relationships. After 140 years, John Flatley has taken down the "No Pets Allowed" sign at the hospital gate.

One other program that the hospital at Harrisburg has been running for schizophrenics since 1983 is a "relationship" program. In 1908 Clifford W. Beers, a former mental patient in New York State, wrote his now famous *A Mind That Found Itself*. In this book, which marks the beginnings of the citizen organization movement on behalf of mental health, Beers claimed that what the insane want most is a friend. The expectation of the Harrisburg program is that once "a patient relates to others in friendship, it can make for more consistent attachments."[10] Volunteers for the program must agree to commit to a long-term friendship with the patient. More than 42 such relationships are now in existence.

Continuing a seventeen-year-old tradition the Harrisburg State Hospital also runs a continuing education program each year. This program, which was started by Edith Krohn, the Coordinator of Consultative Services, and Spencer S. Lebengood in 1974, is designed to provide participants with the latest techniques in medical and psychiatric treatment.[11] Topics such as "post-traumatic stress disorder" or "neurochemistry and neuroimaging in bipolar disorders" or discussions on the most up-to-date research into the broad range of medications being used in the treatment of mental illness are among the many subjects covered. Physicians from around the state attend these sessions.

Patient training, especially after Wyatt, is even more important. Six teachers, under the direction of Joan Leopold, work throughout the institution, even the back wards, instructing patients whose educational levels range from grades 0 to 12. They teach not only language and mathematics fundamentals but also very basic skills such as how to use the telephone and perform general housekeeping duties. The GED (high school equivalency examination) is given four times a year. Among the unique curricula the hospital has developed is a six-week one on how to vote. This course includes hands-on use of voting machines. About forty percent of the patient population is involved in some portion of the hospital's training program.[12]

The hospital still serves a seven-county area composed of Adams, York, Perry, Cumberland, Dauphin, Franklin and Fulton counties. And each year John Flatley and his staff now prepare a "Program Plan and Budget" document. Utilizing modern management techniques, it follows a management by objectives approach. Reports are made on completed goals—ones such as: "increasing patient awareness concerning their individual medication regimen"—and in identifying additional ones. Prominent among the new goals and objectives in the 1990-1991 plan is one for "increasing the participation of patients in the development of their Individual Treatment Plan."

*   *   *   *

In 1953, Howard Petry started the practice of holding annual "old-timers" dinners. A decade later the hospital also published a retirees booklet, in which appeared photographs of many of the former employees who were still living. The pictures of plumbers, social workers, nurses, steam fitters, bakers, electricians, tinners, shoemakers, accountants, poultrymen, auto mechanics, masons, plasterers, refrigeration experts, upholsterers, sign painters, beauticians, firemen, and seamstresses parade across its pages—many of these holders of jobs which no longer exist or are performed by contractors or volunteers.

Holsteins still graze on the hills that roll outward behind the brick structures that Henry Orth built at the beginning of the century. The cows produce their milk, however, not for the hospital staff or its patients, but for a tenant who leases the farm from the state. The piggery and the hennery are gone. Hutton's building for the chronically ill has been added to so haphazardly through the years that its architectural integrity has been destroyed. It is now a misshapen hybrid used as a Department of Welfare office. Trees and plants, the remnants or descendants of those that earlier populated John Curwen's and Jerome Gerhard's pleasure grounds, still cover the hillsides around the main complex while Dorothea Dix's brick cottage still stands nearby—transformed into a museum. The trolley car no longer drops off friends and family members at the front gate on visiting days. In the winding hollow the powerhouse along Poplar Road no longer generates electricity. Nearby the morgue sits silent, not out of respect for the dead lying within, but with a lack of the living.[13]

The legislature and the governor of Pennsylvania continue to struggle with budget problems—where to get the money and how to slice up the pie.[14] The trend of federally mandated programs being levied on the states, often without matching monies, which started with Wyatt, continues as a legacy of the Reagan years. The trend today in mental health care in Pennsylvania appears to be directed toward a "unified system,"[15] one in which the "consumer" or "client" (words which are now preferred to even that of patient) will have an even greater say in his or her choice of treatment. This unified system would "allow the funds to follow the client," as a Mental Health Association in Pennsylvania flyer states. Suggestions are also being made to permit individuals "to pick the least expensive alternative from among several choices."[16] One of these will still probably be a state hospital.

The state hospital, of course, will continue as the most restrictive of the available alternatives. While the number of these hospitals in Pennsylvania will continue to shrink—it is now at fourteen—the central location and the importance of the area which the Harrisburg State Hospital serves probably will ensure its continued existence for some time.[17] The number of chronically ill homeless, meanwhile, continues to grow.[18] In words that sound strikingly similar to those of Dorothea Dix a century and a half ago, The New York Times reported in September 1990 that: "the largest 'de facto mental hospital' in the United States is the Los Angeles County jail."[19]

Since the days of Dorothea Dix and Thomas Kirkbride their name has been changed from lunatic, to inmate, to insane, to patient, to consumer, and now to client; the name of their place of treatment, moreover, has been changed from asylum, to hospital to mental health center. Each of these shifts was designed to eliminate the opprobrium that quickly developed during the use of the previous term, as well as to soften the public's image of the mentally ill. If there is, however, a promise of a future for them, bright or even just less dismal, no one seems to know when or how it will be achieved. We are able to fill our armories with weapons of destruction, to explore deepest space, but the best that we have done in 150 years for those who are seriously ill with dementia praecox is to give their disease a new name, schizophrenia.

END NOTES

1. Cohen, Neal L., editor, *Psychiatry Takes to the Streets*, The Guilford Press, New York, 1990, page 274.
2. Silverstein, Max, *Vital Connections*, Lexington Books, Lexington, Massachusetts, 1990, page 105.
3. Ibid, page 75.
4. Hilts, Philip J., "U.S. Returns to 1820's in Care of Mentally Ill," *The New York Times*, September 12, 1990, page A28. Estimates of the total number of people in the U. S. with some form of mental illness range from 15 to 20 percent of the population, approximately 80 million individuals.
5. Silverstein, op. cit., pages 71-72 & 101. In 1981 alone the total federal package was cut by 25 percent. Silverstein, op. cit., page 105.
6. Kukovich, Allen, (Democrat from Westmoreland County), quoted in the Altoona *Tribune-Review*, June 15, 1989. The Republican side of the legislature, meanwhile, is concerned with easing the commitment procedures. In this way it is hoped that "a system in extreme disorder" can be changed from one that provides "protection orders rather than access to facilities." Loeper, F. Joseph, quoted in the *Philadelphia Inquirer*, September 29, 1989.
7. *Philadelphia Inquirer*, June 24, 1990.
8. The state now gives the money to Philadelphia instead of putting it into Byberry. The city is responsible for developing community programs with it. These are being established though contracts with private agencies. The programs include development of "crisis teams, care for substance abusers, group homes and training and extra help for families of mental health patients." *Philadelphia Inquirer*, January 29, 1991.
9. Silverstein, op. cit., page 33.
10. Harrisburg *Patriot News*, May 28, 1990, page C1.
11. Krohn, a psychologist, was one of the individuals that Governor Leader and Harry Shapiro recruited during their many campaigns for the mentally ill around the state. Lebengood, a 1938 graduate along with his wife from the Philadelphia College of Osteopathy, came to the hospital in 1964 from York, Pennsylvania where he was in private practice.
12. Joan Y. Leopold, a 1961 graduate of Dickinson College, runs the hospital's Education Department. She and Edith Krohn have been instrumental in fostering the historical awarness of the hospital and in establishing the Dix Museum.
13. In January 1986 the hospital site was added to the National Register of Historic Places.
14. In 1990 "the community mental health system in Pennsylvania was receiving state allocations of approximately $305 million a year and serving 225,000 patients. The state hospital system was spending $455 million a year on 9,500 patients." (Silverstein, op. cit., pages 142-143.) While these figures appear to be weighted heavily in favor of the state hospital system, a comparison of the number of patient days of service for the two systems shows, however, that the dollars invested are fairly evenly distributed—1.6 million patient days for the community systems versus 3.4 million patient days for the state hospitals.
15. Thompson, Ford S. Jr., Interview, March 11, 1991.
16. Organizations such as the Mental Health Association in Pennsylvania and The Alliance for the Mentally Ill in Pennsylvania are active in pushing for increased decision making by the "consumer."
17. Thompson, Ford S. Jr., Interview, March 11, 1991.
18. Estimates of the homeless who have some form of mental illness range between thirty and fifty percent.
19. Hilts, Philip J., op. cit.

APPENDICES

CHRONOLOGY

1845 Dorothea Dix's Memorial presented to the Pennsylvania Legislature—Feb 3rd.

1845 Act establishing the Pennsylvania State Lunatic Hospital signed into law—April 14th.

1848 John Haviland hired as architect; construction started.

1849 Cornerstone laid April 7th by Governor William F. Johnston.

1851 First meeting of the hospital trustees. John Curwen elected Superintendent, February 14th.

1851 Hospital opens October 1st for patients.

1851 First patient admitted October 13th.

1853 Dixmont and Dorothea Dix Library buildings erected.

1856 Dam and Water Works erected in ravine.

1859 Barn burned by an irate ex-patient.

1865 Smallpox epidemic.

1871 First use of hypodermic injections and of anti-convulsant drugs and drugs for sleeplessness.

1873 Wash house destroyed by fire.

1874 Gas works erected.

1875 Steward's residence built—later used as gatehouse.

1880 Margaret A. Cleaves elected July 8th as the first female physican in complete charge of the female side of the house.

1881 Jerome Z. Gerhard appointed new Superintendent February 14th.

1883 Jane Kimmel Garver appointed September 1st as "physician in medical control of female patients."

1887 Laundry, carpenter's and paint shops built.

1891 H. L. Orth appointed new Superintendent, November 1st. Hospital passes the 1,000-patient mark.

1893 Addison Hutton hired to rebuild hospital around the "cottage" plan.

1895 New Administration building completed in May.

1900 Building for the Chronic-Ill, the "Helpless and Harmless" patients is built. (Later known as Geriatrics −1)

1906 Buildings for the Acute and Recent Cases and for the Dangerous and Destructive patients were completed on the male side.

APPENDIX A

1907 Pifer Building erected as a nurses' dining room.
1910 Dairy herd destroyed as a result of test for tuberculosis.
1912 Sun Parlor finished.
1913 Nurses Home and new Chapel erected. Nurses Home left unfurnished for a year awaiting legislative appropriation.
1914 Chapel formally opened February 15th.
1916 One of barns struck by lightning and destroyed.
1917 Edward M. Green appointed Superintendent, December 1st.
1919 Flu epidemic—342 cases reported.
1921 Act of General Assembly provides for commitment of drug addicts to state hospitals . . . name of institution changed to Harrisburg State Hospital, May 31st.
1922 School for licensed attendants established.
1930 Second floor added to Geriatrics –1 building.
1934 Howard K. Petry appointed Superintendent.
193? Insulin shock treatment introduced.
1938 Tubercular Building and a new power plant erected.
1941 Electroshock treatment introduced in March.
1947 Hospital population passes the 3,000 mark.
1951 Petry Admissions and a separate building for the Acutely Disturbed Women constructed.
1952 Psychotropic drugs introduced.
1954 Hamblen C. Eaton appointed Superintendent, December 16th.
1957 Eaton Building constructed.
1958 Staff residence on hospital grounds discontinued.
1966 Outpatient services discontinued with passage of the Mental Health Act of 1966.
1969 S. Philip Laucks appointed Superintendent.
1970 County "Unit" System adopted.
1972 U. S. Middle Court Decision—peonage and farming discontinued.
1974 John B. Logan appointed Superintendent.
1979 Ford S. Thompson, Jr. appointed Superintendent.
1988 John Flatley appointed Superintendent.

PENNSYLVANIA STATE HOSPITAL OFFICERS

APPT. DATE	PRESIDENT BOARD of TRUSTEES	SUPERINTENDENT	STEWARD	MATRON
1851	Luther Reily	John Curwen	William D. Slaymaker	Mary Ann Wilt
1853	Thomas Kirkbride		David Smith	
1954	F. A. Muhlenberg			
1855	Thomas Kirkbride		Joel Hinckley	
1860			William S. Rutherford	
1862	George Dock			
1866				Ellen Cole
1867	John L. Atlee			
1879			Benjamin F. Kendig	Sarah H. Pollock
1881		Jerome Z. Gerhard		
1886	Traill Green			
1892	*Louis W. Hall	Henry L. Orth	J. B. Livingston	A. C. Sprecher
1893				M. M. Candlish
1895				Isabella Cruikshank
1896	*Charles L. Bailey			
1899	Spencer C. Gilbert			
1901				R. C. Southard
1903				C. G. Hough
1905				B. H. Griffiths
1907				Eleanor Curtis

APPENDIX B

PENNSYLVANIA STATE HOSPITAL OFFICERS

APPT. DATE	PRESIDENT BOARD of TRUSTEES	SUPERINTENDENT	STEWARD	MATRON
1979		Ford S. Thompson		
1988		John Flatley		

NOTES:

1. Between the years of 1852 and 1861 the President of the Board of Trustees was not identified separately in the hospital's annual reports, therefore, the years of appointment are not conclusive as the first named individual is assumed to have been the President. The names, however, are not.

2. Appointment dates followed by an asterisk may have occurred earlier than indicated. Date given is the earliest known based on the available annual reports for the hospital.

3. By 1946 the job of matron had been placed under that of the steward. Hostetter remained as "housekeeper" until 1953 but reported to Harper. A new position of dietitian also was established at that time.

4. Title of position was changed from steward to Assistant Director for Administration.

HARRISBURG STATE HOSPITAL CONSTRUCTION JOURNAL

DATE BUILT	BUILDING NAME	CURRENT TYPE OF PATIENTS	NAME/USE	PLOT PLAN	GROUNDS SCHEMATIC
1851	"Kirkbride"	All eight wards	torn down	—	—
1853	Physicians' Res.	—	Community Living	M	7
1853	Occupational Cottage	—	Dix Museum	N	9
1880	Residence	—	private home	I	—
1887	Male Wards[1]	Moderately Disturbed		9	
	Female Wards[1]	Moderately Disturbed	torn down	10	—
	Blacksmith Shop	—		Q	37
	Pumping Station	—		T	38
	Filter Beds	—		U	(not shown)
	Power Plant[2]	—		V	34
	Carpenter and Paint Shop	—	Laundry	W	18
1895	Administration	—		A	11
	Garage	—		L	—

APPENDIX C

HARRISBURG STATE HOSPITAL CONSTRUCTION JOURNAL

DATE BUILT	BUILDING NAME	CURRENT TYPE OF PATIENTS	NAME/USE	TOPO PLOT PLAN	GROUNDS SCHEMATIC
1900	Male Wards 1 & 2 (second floor added 1930)	Chronic-Helpless & Harmless		1	43
1900	Female Wards 1 & 2 (second floor added 1930)	Chronic-Helpless & Harmless		2	43
1902	Kitchen & Bakery	—		C	14
1903	Morgue	—	not in use	O	33
1904	Cold Storage Plant	—			
1905	Male Wards 3 & 4	Admission		3	21
	Male Wards 5 & 6	Quiet		5	22
	Male Wards 7 & 8 (second floor added 1927)	Violent & Destructive	torn down	7	23
1906	Female Nurses Home	—	torn down	G	—
1908	Female Wards 3 & 4	Admission		4	31
	Female Wards 5 & 6	Quiet		6	32
	Female Wards 7 & 8 (second floor added 1927)	Violent & Destructive	torn down	8	35
1910	Sewerage Plant	—		R	—
1910	Commissary	—	torn down		
	Sewing Room	—	Clothes Tree	S	36

DATE BUILT	BUILDING NAME	CURRENT TYPE OF PATIENTS	NAME/USE	TOPO PLOT PLAN	GROUNDS SCHEMATIC
1911	Solarium (converted to "Med Center" in 1937)	—	Vista Dome	B	12
	Male Nurses Home	—		F	25
1913	Chapel	—		D	15
1928	Married Employees' Bldg.	—		Z	26
1930	Dairy Barn	—		AA	3
	Dairyman's Cottage	—		BB	56
	Horse Stable	—		CC	28
	Physician Residence	—		K	5
1934	Hospital for Physically Ill	any	Slothower	E	16
	Blacksmith's Shop	—	4		
1935	Chicken Barn			DD	29
				J	
1938	Power Plant (new)		5		44
	Tubercular Building (new)	any	Geriatric		52
	Kitchen (new)				
	Garage				
1951	Separate Admissions	any	Petry		17
	Separate Building for Acutely Disturbed Women				

HARRISBURG STATE HOSPITAL CONSTRUCTION JOURNAL

DATE BUILT	BUILDING NAME	CURRENT TYPE OF PATIENTS	NAME/USE	TOPO PLOT PLAN	GROUNDS SCHEMATIC
1957	Patients' Building & Dietary Service Unit	Chronic	Eaton		54
1966	Work Advancement Center				

Notes:

1. Male and Female ward buildings built in 1887 were also referred to as "Branch Buildings."
2. The boilers for the generation of power were in the west end of this building, which contains the distinctive Lombardic tower.
3. Shown as "old dairy barn."
4. Named, after her retirement in 1969, for Martha B. Slothower, a psychiatric nurse. Slothower a most capable nurse never aspired to the position of Director of Nursing. She preferred to spend almost all of her 37 years working in one building, the Hospital for the Physically Ill.
5. Power plant is now used only to generate steam.

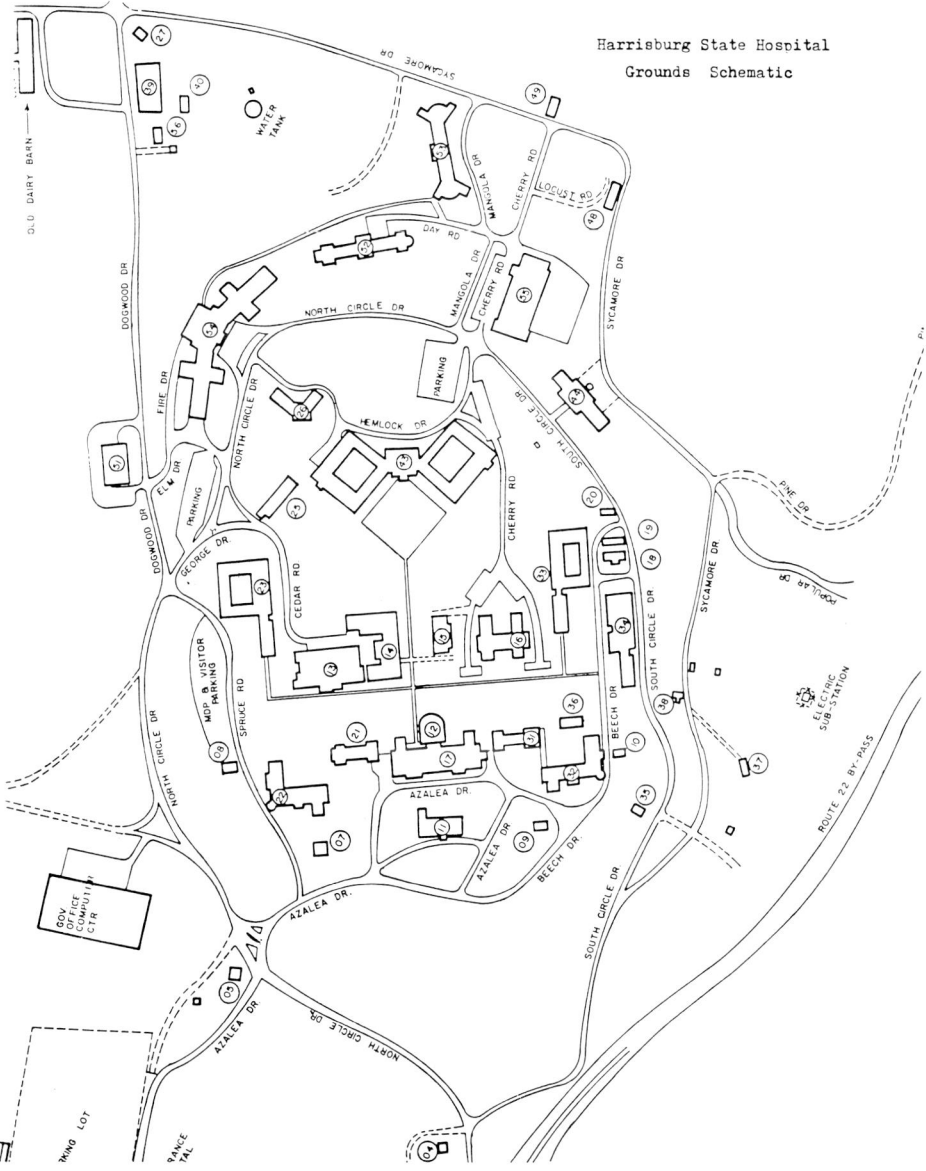

Harrisburg State Hospital
Grounds Schematic

GLOSSARY

alienist—[obs.] psychiatrist; one who assists those with "alienated minds" (who were known as "mental aliens") in the reconstruction of their brain tissue by use of moral management methods.

asylum—a place of refuge or shelter—a term which fell into disfavor with mid-nineteenth-century physicians as it implied, to them, a custodial rather than a treatment facility.

bedlam—[vernacular] for a mental institution or for being in a state of frenzy or tumult. Corruption of the name Bethlehem, the site in England of a widely known mental hospital.

blistering—to shave and blister the head; a treatment intended to let "vapors" trapped in the brain escape.

Bright's disease—[obselete] kidney disease.

cupping—process of "bleeding" a patient by the use of a small glass cup (approximately two inches in diameter) which, when heated and placed over the skin, created a partial suction. Dry cupping; cupping without cutting the skin, wet cupping; the application of a cupping glass to a cut surface.

delirium—a reaction consisting of alternating states of consciousness and mental disorientation—often caused by intoxicants or drugs but also sometimes by metabolic disturbances such as diabetes or an organic brain disorder.

delirium tremens—syndrome caused by use of alcohol; tremors and delusions of persecution are common manifestations.

dementia—reduction or loss of mental capabilities or control over impulses. Also personality changes or impaired judgment. Synonymous with madness, insanity, and lunacy in the nineteenth century.

dementia praecox—nineteenth-century term for schizophrenia; found occasionally, however, in hospital electro-shock records at Harrisburg as late as 1948.

douche—technique that made use of various types of water sprays (fan, jet, vapor, rain and Scotch) as a form of patient therapy. [vernacular] a patient term for a bucket of cold water thrown in the face to quiet them down.

elope—[vernacular] leaving the hospital without permission,

or not returning from an authorized furlough.

epilepsy—a temporary disturbance of brain function sometimes accompanied by convulsions and the sudden loss of consciousness.

feebleminded—a general term used to cover all grades of mental deficiency [idiot, imbecile, moron].

gyrator—device invented by Benjamin Rush which consisted of a chair in which a patient was strapped and then spun rapidly. The rotary motion was designed to give a centrifugal direction of the blood toward the brain and thus cure the patient.

hallucination—abnormal misinterpretation of perceptions where there is no stimulation of the sense. In an illusion, on the other hand, there is a stimulation of the sense but an erroneous interpretation by the individual. In a delusion there is no misinterpretation of the facts presented to the sense but rather an error in judgment as to its meaning.

hydrotherapy—use of douches, electric light, hot air, wet sheet packs and turkish and sitz baths as a form of therapy.

hysteria—derived from the Greek word for uterus; based on the former belief that hysterical women were afflicted due to a "moving" uterus.

idiot—feebleminded individuals who evidence a mental age of 0 to 2 years.

imbecile—feebleminded individuals who evidence a mental age of 3 to 7 years.

inmate—a person confined in a prison or a hospital—although by early in the nineteenth century, many physicians had rejected the term as applying to mental patients, its use continued among the general public and officials such as State Legislators and State Hospital Trustees until well into the twentieth century.

insanity—any deranged state of mind [dropped by physicians by the early twentieth century—now used to denote persons incapable of rational actions in a legal sense].

lunatic—insane person; from the belief that the moon [latin: "luna"] affected the changing behavior of the mentally ill [obsolete today].

mania—[obsolete] any mental disorder, especially one accompanied by symptoms such as general excitement, great loquacity, gesticulation, a disposition to tear off one's clothes, or any other violent behavior. Now used only as a prefix with other terms, e.g. manic-depressive.

maniac—lunatic or a madman; one suffering from "fits," "ebullitions of passion" or "paroxysms."

melancholia—a mental condition characterized by extreme depression, listlessness, or silence; often accompanied with bodily complaints, hallucinations and delusions.

Millerism—a cause of mental illness associated with the disillusioned followers of William Miller, a Protestant revivalist, who preached that the Second Coming would occur on October 22, 1844.

monomania—a condition in which an individual who shows no evidence of insanity in general conversation or behavior, but whose delusion surfaces if the subject comes up, e.g. the patient expresses the belief that he is Napoleon whenever France is discussed.

moron—an individual who manifests the highest level of feeblemindedness; one who evidences a mental age of 8 to 12 years.

morphine—a derivative of opium that, by 1840, physicians reported was yielding great benefits (without opium's side effects) in all cases of insanity. [Thomas Kirkbride, for example, prescribed it for 80 percent of his patients receiving medical treatment.]

neurosis—a disorder of the nervous system for which no physical disease or injury is found.

opium—used to treat delirium tremens and melancholia before the early nineteenth century—its serious side effects on the digestive system, however, made it unsuitable for extended use.

paralysis—a symptom rather than a disease, the term covers a wide variety of disorders of the nervous system (including Parkinson's disease) in which attacks [of paralysis] may last from a few hours to several days; frequently given in the nineteenth century as the cause of death, some of which may have been due to heart disease (strokes), with which it probably was confused.

paresis—the most malignant form of neurosyphilis; it produced a variety of both mental and neurologic symptoms.

parole—an authorized leave or furlough of the patient from the hospital; trial return to original surroundings—periods ranged from a month or two up to one year. The term has fallen into disfavor in recent years because of its similar use for early release programs for prison inmates.

pleasure grounds—the gardens around a nineteenth-century mental hospital where the patients could exercise and socialize; especially those filled with paths, streams, trees and other plant life.

purging—to cause evacuation from the bowels.

restraints—used to physically prevent patients from harming themselves or others; among the devices used were chains, bars, straitjackets, anklets, wristlets, muffs, restraining sheets and utica cribs.

saddle—patient term for the bedstraps used as restraints.

"stomach pump"—patient term for the tube used to force feed those who refused to eat—many attendants would initially try inducing the patient to swallow by pinching their nostrils shut.

utica crib—a small, completely enclosed, low-lying crib used for restraining patients. (One woman reportedly was confined in a utica crib in an Illinois institution for fourteen years.)

ADMISSIONS AND DISCHARGES

Year	Total	Admitted Male	Female	Total Treated	Recovered	Improved	Unimproved	Died
1851	37	24	13	37	—	—	—	1
1852	118	65	53	154	13	16	12	7
1853	163	95	68	269	28	15	28	17
1854	144	93	51	326	28	22	39	22
1855	164	98	66	378	19	30	43	29
1856	129	74	55	379	25	35	54	32
1857	143	76	67	376	25	32	44	25
1958	151	97	54	401	36	30	54	14
1959	143	83	60	410	31	39	43	23
1860	144	73	71	418	31	40	48	8
1861	134	84	50	425	30	50	49	16
1862	109	64	45	389	34	30	42	16
1863	134	78	56	401	21	49	27	23
1864	135	77	58	416	40	31	35	29
1865	153	67	86	434	40	38	15	35
1866	187	115	72	493	47	45	41	33
1867	170	99	71	497	51	39	33	34
1868	180	103	77	520	47	37	55	25
1869	212	103	109	568	40	42	48	28
1870	168	86	82	578	30	39	36	39
1871	206	103	103	640	37	37	85	31

APPENDIX E

Year	Admitted Total	Admitted Male	Admitted Female	Total Treated	Recovered	Improved	Unimproved	Died
1872	212	119	93	663	51	43	56	46
1873	158	87	71	625	40	31	112	34
1874	149	75	74	557	41	31	77	28
1875	178	111	67	558	36	28	43	35
1876	159	97	70	583	38	41	55	33
1877	148	97	62	575	27	34	35	32
1878	147	77	71	595	30	45	64	30
1879	121	74	73	573	29	31	58	29
1880	199	70	51	547	28	49	104	33
1881	199	54	145	532	23	21	93	32
1882	160	75	85	523	23	29	25	34
1883	164	83	81	576	24	38	77	39
1884	128	71	57	526	23	22	20	36
1885	139	79	60	564	27	25	37	45
1886	145	82	63	575	20	20	24	50
1887	150	77	73	611	31	24	13	44
1888	272	125	147	769	30	17	5	52
1889	210	130	80	975	35	40	7	59
1890	188	99	89	922	31	32	8	70
1891	228	117	111	1009	64	49	11	82
1892	226	118	108	1029	65	11	7	82
1893	144	94	50	1008	52	43	56	68
1894	270	177	93	1058	57	104	12	69

ADMISSIONS AND DISCHARGES

Year	Total	Admitted Male	Female	Total Treated	Recovered	Improved	Unimproved	Died
1895	262	142	120	1077	66	76	11	78
1896	218	119	99	1063	48	46	6	60
1897	221	126	95	1123	41	86	9	69
1898	179	94	85	1096	36	70	19	63
1899	225	122	103	1132	36	71	16	81
1900	199	104	95	1126	20	87	3	74
1901	175	92	83	1116	29	65	15	71
1902	163	81	82	1098	31	12	2	66
1903	139	80	59	1123	34	20	9	47
1904	201	118	83	1163	32	15	6	82
1905	198	117	81	1225	24	17	4	74
1906	212	122	90	1315	58	47	8	93
1907	189	118	71	1298	41	84	7	71
1908	271	142	129	1364	29	10	11	59
1909	217	140	77	1470	46	112	7	82
1910	271	158	113	1489	55	11	7	96
1911	207	107	100	1524	19	7	5	87
1912	222	132	90	1595	12	11	5	116
1913	270	152	118	1718	11	38	7	105
1914	222	123	99	1775	29	207	23	102
1915	218	125	93	1630	44	30	14	127
1916	243	144	99	1655	43	13	5	138

Year	Total	Admitted Male	Female	Total Treated	Recovered	Improved	Unimproved	Died
1917	234	140	94	1676	63	87	2	105
1918	229	136	93	1644	50	38	7	163
1919	337	178	159	1720	73	37	10	282
1920	228	141	87	1568	67	42	16	143
1921	206	109	97	1553	76	67	31	124

Note: Commencing in 1922 the Harrisburg State Hospital began preparing reports on a biennial basis. Copies of many of these are no longer available. In the 1960s, moreover, the state Department of Welfare took over all reporting. These departmental reports were issued on a state-wide basis, not by individual hospital. Howard K. Petry reported, however, in 1947 that the population of the hospital was 3398. This figure included 511 who were on parole at the end of that year.

No. 288
AN ACT

To establish an asylum for the insane poor of this commonwealth, to be called "The Pennsylvania State Lunatic Hospital and Union Asylum for the Insane."

SECTION 1. *Be it enacted by the Senate and House of Representatives of the Commonwealth of Pennsylvania in General Assembly met, and it is hereby enacted by the authority of the same,* That Jacob M. Haldeman, Luther Reily, Hugh Campbell, Charles B. Trego and Joseph Konigmacher, be and they are hereby appointed commissioners to select and purchase a tract of land of not less than one hundred acres, situated within ten miles of Harrisburg, which said tract of land shall not cost more than ten thousand dollars; shall have a never failing supply of water on the premises, and be conveniently situated for receiving supplies of fuel; *Provided,* That the said commissioners shall receive no compensation for their services, other than their necessary expenses: *And Provided also,* That if any person or persons shall make a gift of such a tract, the said commissioners are hereby authorized to receive a deed for the same, in trust for the Pennsylvania State Lunatic Hospital, and the sum of fifteen thousand dollars is hereby appropriated for the purpose of erecting and constructing the hereinafter described building and buildings: *Provided,* That the said fifteen thousand dollars shall not be paid until the conveyance of the aforesaid tract of land shall have been made as provided for in this section: *Provided also,* That the sum hereby appropriated shall be retained by the state treasurer out of the amount of relief notes, to be cancelled on the thirty-first of July, one thousand eight hundred and forty-five.

SECTION 2. At any time after said site shall be obtained by the said commissioners, not exceeding three months, they shall contract for the erection of said asylum, on the most approved plan, on such terms as are just and prudent: *Provided,* That said hospital buildings shall be constructed in the most approved manner, of brick or unhewn stone; the foundations to be substantial and of rough mason work; the basements above ground to hammered stone; water-table,

APPENDIX F

window and door sills, window and door caps, and door steps of the same material; partition walls to be of brick, and to contain flues for ventilators, furnace flues for heating, and also water pipes if necessary; the roof to be of slate or tin plate fire proof.

SECTION 3. Said commissioners shall, on or before the first day of January, one thousand eight hundred and forty-six, and on the first day of January annually therafter, until the buildings are completed respectively, render to the proper accounting officers of the commonwealth, an exact account of all the contracts, expenses and liabilities which they shall have incurred, or authorized in the execution of their commissions, with vouchers for the same; and in case of their failure so to do, their authority to draw on the state treasurer for such sum or sums of money as shall hereafter be specified shall cease; and said commissioners shall so build, finish and furnish said asylum, that the whole cost of said buildings and furniture, with suitable apparatus for heating the rooms, for cooking, and for furnishing water for all the uses of the establishment, to accommodate two hundred and fifty patients, and the necessary attendants, shall not exceed fifty thousand dollars: *And provided also*, That the commissioners appointed by this act, before entering upon their duties, shall give bond with such security as may be required by the executive for the faithful and proper application of the funds placed in their hands and performance of their duties.

SECTION: 4. The treasurer is hereby directed to pay to the said commissioners, on the warrant of the governor, out of any moneys in the treasury not otherwise appropriated, such sum or sums of money as they may require for building said asylum, together with the necessary out-buildings, and the complete finishing and furnishing of the same, not exceeding in the whole the said sum of fifteen thousand dollars, at such times as they may be wanted, the expenditure thereof to be accounted for to the auditor general of the commonwealth.

SECTION 5. The governor shall nominate, and by and with the advice and consent of the senate, appoint nine persons to be trustees of the said institution, who shall be a body politic and corporate, by the name and style of the "Trustees of the Pennsylvania State Lunatic Hospital and Union Asylum for the Insane," and shall manage and direct the concerns of the institution, and make all necessary by-laws and regulations not inconsistent with the constitution and laws of the commonwealth; and shall have power to receive, hold, dispose of, and convey all real and personal property conveyed to them by gift, devise or otherwise, for the use of the said institution, and shall serve without compensation; of those first appointed three shall serve for one year, three for two years, three for three years, and at the expiration of the respective periods the vacancies to be filled by appointments for three years; and should any vacancy occur by death, resignation or otherwise, of any trustee, such vacancy shall be filled by appointment for the unexpired time of such trustee. The said trustees shall have charge of the general interests of the institution; they shall appoint the superintendent, who shall be a skillful physician, subject to removal or re-election no oftener than in periods of ten years, except by infidelity to the trust reposed in him or for incompetency—said physician shall always reside in the asylum, he shall be a married man, and his family shall reside with him; the trustees, by and with the consent of the governor, shall make such by-laws and regulations for the government of the asylum as shall be necessary; they shall appoint a treasurer, who shall give bonds to the commonwealth for the faithful discharge of his duties; they shall determine his compensation for services; also the salaries of the other officers and assistants, who may be necessary for the just and economical administration of the affairs of said hospital.

SECTION 6. The superintending physician shall appoint and exercise entire control over all subordinate officers and assistants in the institution, and shall have entire direction of the duties of the same.

SECTION 7. The said trustees, and their successors in office, shall have power to take and hold in trust, for the use and benefit of said asylum, any grant or devise of land, and any donation or bequest of money, or other personal property to be applied to the maintenance of insane persons, in or to the general use of the asylum.

SECTION 8. The admission of insane patients from the several counties of the commonwealth, shall be in the ratio of their insane population: Provided, That each county shall be entitled to send at least one insane patient.

SECTION 9. Indigent persons and paupers shall be charged for medical attendance, board and nursing, while resident in the hospital, no more than the actual cost; paying patients, whose friends can pay their expenses, and who are not chargeable upon townships or counties, shall pay according to the terms directed by the trustees.

SECTION 10. The courts of this commonwealth shall have power to commit to said asylum any person, who having been charged with an offence punishable by imprisonment or death, who shall have been found to have been insane, in the manner now provided by law, at the time the offence was committed, and who still continues insane; and the expenses of said persons, if in indigent circumstances, shall be paid by the county to which he or she may belong by residence.

SECTION 11. That it shall be the duty of the court, in all cases where they shall commit any person to the asylum, to certify to the trustees the legal settlement of such person, if he or she have any legal settlement in this commonwealth; and if such person shall have no such settlement, then to certify the place of residence of such person at the time the offence was committed, on application made, and the poor district so certified to be the place of settlement or residence of such person, shall be chargeable with the expenses of his or her care and maintenance, and removal to and from said asylum: Provided, That the settlement or residence of any such person shall not be so certified, until after due notice shall have been given to the constituted authority having charge of poor in the district to be charged thereby.

SECTION 12. The several constituted authorities having care and charge of the poor in the respective counties, districts and townships of this commonwealth, shall have authority to send to the asylum such insane paupers under their charge as they may deem proper subjects; and they shall be severally chargeable with the expenses of the care, and maintenance, and removal to and from the asylum, of such paupers.

SECTION 13. If the guardian, directors, or overseers of the poor, to whom any patient who shall be in the asylum is chargeable, shall neglect or refuse, upon demand made, to pay to the trustees the expenses of the care, maintenance and removal of such patient, and also, in the event of death, of the funeral expenses of such patient, the said trustees are hereby authorized and empowered to collect the same as debts of a like nature are now collected.

SECTION 14. That if any person shall apply to any court of record within this commonwealth, having jurisdiction of offences which are punishable by imprisonment for the term of ninety days or longer, for the commitment to said asylum any insane person within the county in which such court has jurisdiction, it shall be the duty of said court to inquire into the fact of insanity in the manner provided by law; and if such court shall be satisfied that such person is, by reason of insanity, unsafe to be at large, or is suffering any unnecessary duress or hardship, such court shall, on the application aforesaid, commit such insane person to said asylum.

SECTION 15. In order of admission, the indigent insane of this commonwealth shall always have precedence of the rich; and while the finances of the state do not permit ample provisions for all cases of insanity, recent cases shall have preference over those of long standing.

SECTION 16. The governor, judges of the several courts of record in the commonwealth, and the members of the legislature, shall be ex officio visitors of the institution.

SECTION 17. That the commissioners appointed by the first section of this act, are hereby authorized and required to appoint a committee of five, in every city and county of this commonwealth, to solicit and receive private subscriptions for this laudable and benevolent object, and from time to time pay the same over to the state treasurer; and the state treasurer is hereby directed to pay to the commissioners aforesaid all such sum or sums of money thus received, to aid in the erection of said asylum.

FINDLEY PATTERSON,
Speaker of the House of Representatives
WILLIAM P. WILCOX,
Speaker of the Senate

Approved—The fourteenth day of April, one thousand eight hundred and forty-five.

FRS. R. SHUNK

BIBLIOGRAPHY

Ackerknecht, Erwin H., *Short History of Psychiatry*, Hafner Publishing Company, New York, 1968.

Ahmed, Paul I. and Plog, Stanley C., *State Mental Hospitals*, Plenum Medical Book Company, New York, 1976.

Alexander, Franz G., M.D. and Selesnick, Sheldon T., M.D., *The History of Psychiatry*, Harper and Row, New York, 1966.

Ballou, Mary and Gabalac, Nancy W., *A Feminist Position on Mental Health*, Charles C. Thomas, Springfield, Ill., 1985.

Barton, Michael, *Life by the Moving Road*, Windsor Publishing Inc., Woodland Hills, California, 1983.

Beers, Clifford W., *A Mind That Found Itself*, Doubleday & Co., Garden City, N.Y., 1921.

Biddle, Elizabeth, *Addison Hutton: Quaker architect, 1834-1916*, Art Alliance Press, Philadelphia, 1974.

Bliss, Sylvester, D., *Memoirs of William Miller*, J. V. Himes, Boston, 1853.

Bond, Dr. Earl D., *Kirkbride and His Mental Hospital*, Philadelphia, J. B. Lippincott Company, 1947

Caplan, Ruth B., *Psychiatry and the Community in Nineteenth-Century America*, Basic Books, Inc., New York, 1969.

Clark, Philip Michael, "Bedlam in Penn's Woods," article in *Pennsylvania Heritage*, Summer 1989.

Cohen, Neal L., editor, *Psychiatry Takes To The Streets*, The Guilford Press, New York, 1990.

Commonwealth Fund, *Mental health in the United States; a fifty-year history*, Harvard University Press, 1961.

Cope, Thomas P., *Diary, 1800-1851*, Gateway Editions, South Bend, Ind., 1978.

Corson, Hiram, *The Corson Family, A History of the Descendants of Benjamin Corson*, Henry Lawrence Everett, Philadelphia, 1906.

Curwen, John, *History of the Association of Medical Superintendents of American Institutions for the Insane*, Cowan Printers, Warren, Pa., 1885.

Curwen, John, *A manual for attendants in hospitals for the insane*, William S. Martien, Philadelphia, Pa., 1851.

Dain, Norman, *Clifford W. Beers, Advocate for the Insane*, University of Pittsburgh Press, 1980.

Davis, Patricia Talbot, *A family tapestry, five generations of the Curwens of Walnut Hill*, Livingston Publishing Co., Wynnewood, Pa., 1972.

Deutsch, Albert, *The Mentally Ill in America*, Columbia University Press, New York, 1937.

Dickert, Thomas W., *Life of the Rev. Calvin S. Gerhard, D.D.*, Sunday School Board of the Reformed Church, 1904.

Dix, Dorothea L., *Memorial to the Senate and the House of Representatives of the Commonwealth of Pennsylvania*, Harrisburg, Pa., February 3, 1845.

Dunn, Waldo Hilary, *The Life of Donald G. Mitchell, Ik Marvel*, C. Scribner's sons, 1922.

Foley, Henry A. and Sharfstein, Steven S., *Madness and Government*, American Psychiatric Press, Inc., Washington, D.C., 1983.

Foucault, Michel, *Madness and Civilization, a history of insanity in the age of reason*, Pantheon Books, New York, 1965.

Gilchrist, Agnes Addison, *William Strickland, Architect and Engineer: 1788-1854*, Da Capo Press, New York, 1969.

Goodman, Alvin S., "Harrisburg State Hospital Then and Now," article in *The Challenge*, September-October 1976.

Graham, Thomas F., *Medieval Minds, Mental Health in the Middle Ages*, George Allen & Unwin Ltd., London, 1967.

Grob, Gerald N., *Mental Institutions in America, Social Policy to 1875*, The Free Press, New York, 1973.

Grob, Gerald N., *Mental illness and American society, 1875-1940*, Princeton University Press, Princeton, N. J., 1983.

Hall, J. K., editor, *One Hundred Years of American Psychiatry*, Columbia University Press, New York, 1944.

Hartz, Fred R. and Hoshino, Arthur Y., *Warren State Hospital, 1880-1980, a psychiatric centennial*, Maverick Publications, Bend, Oregon, 1981.

Haviland, John and Bridgeport, Hugh, *The Builder's Assistant*, John Bioren, Philadelphia, 1818.

Heffner, William Clinton, *History of Poor Relief in Pennsylvania, 1628-1913*, Holzapfel Press, Cleona, 1913.

Horwitz, Elinor Lander, *Madness, Magic, and Medicine, The Treatment and Mistreatment of the Mentally Ill*, J. B. Lippincott Company, Philadelphia, 1977.

Jones, Maxwell, *The Concept of a Therapeutic Community*, article from the *American Journal of Psychiatry*, Vol. 112, pages 647-650, 156.

Kirkbride, Thomas Story, *On the construction, organization, and general arrangements of hospitals for the insane*, J. B. Lippincott Company, Philadelphia, 1880.

Kittrie, Nicholas N. *The right to be different; deviance and enforced therapy*, Johns Hopkins Press, 1971.

Laverty, George Lauman, *History of medicine in Dauphin County*, The Telegraph Press, Harrisburg, Pa., 1967.

Levinson, Daniel J. and Gallagher, Eugene B., *Patienthood in the mental hospital; an analysis of role, personality, and social structure*, Houghton Mifflin Company, Boston, 1964.

McGovern, Constance M., "The Community, The Hospital, and the Working-Class Patient: The Multiple Uses of the Asylum in Nineteenth Century America," article in *Pennsylvania History*, Vol. 54, No. 1, January 1987.

Marshall, Helen E., *Dorothea Dix, Forgotten Samaritan*, University of North Carolina Press, 1937.

Morrissey, Joseph P. and Goldman, Howard H., *Cycles of Reform in the Care of the Chronically Mentally Ill*, article in *Hospital and Community Psychiatry*, Vol. 35, No. 8, August 1984.

Neaman, Judith S., *Suggestion of the Devil: the origins of madness*, Anchor Books, Garden City, N. Y., 1975.

Peterson, Dale, editor, *A Mad People's History of Madness*, University of Pittsburgh Press, 1982.

Petry, Howard K., *A Century of Medicine, 1848-1948*, privately printed for The Medical Society of the State of Pennsylvania, 1952.

Porter, Roy, *A social history of madness: the world through the eyes of the insane*, Weidenfeld & Nicolson, New York, 1988.

Rosen, George, *Madness in Society*, The University of Chicago Press, Chicago, Ill., 1968.

Rothman, David J., *The Discovery of the Asylum: Social Order and the New Republic*, 2 vols., Little, Brown & Company, Boston, 1977.

Scott, W. Richard and Black, Bruce L., *The Organization of Mental Health Services*, Sage Publications, Inc., Beverly Hills, California, 1986.

Sears, Clara Endicott, *Days of Delusion: A Strange Bit of History*, Houghton Mifflin Company, Boston, 1924.

Showalter, Elaine, *The Female Malady: Women, Madness and English Culture, 1830-1980*, Pantheon Books, New York, 1985.

Silverstein, Max, *Vital Connections*, Lexington Books, Lexington, Massachusetts, 1990.

Simon, Bennett, M.D., *Mind and Madness in Ancient Greece*, Cornell University Press, Ithaca, N. Y., 1978.

Singer, Erwin, *Key Concepts in Psychotherapy*, Random House, New York, 1965.

Stroup, Atlee L. and Manderscheid, "The Development of the State Mental Hospital System in the United States: 1840-1980," article in the *Journal of the Washington Academy of Sciences*, Vol. 78, No. 1, March 1988.

Talbott, John A., *State Mental Hospitals, Problems and Potentials*, Human Sciences Press, New York, 1980.

Tiffany, Francis, *Life of Dorothea Lynde Dix*, Houghton Mifflin Company, Boston, 1890.

Tomes, Nancy, *A generous confidence, Thomas Story Kirkbride and the art of asylum-keeping, 1840-1883*, Cambridge University Press, 1984.

Tulipan, Alan B. and Heyder, Dietrich W. *Outpatient Psychiatry in the 1970's*, Brunner/Mazel, New York, 1970.

Ullman, Leonard P., *Institution and outcome; a comparative study of psychiatric hospitals*, Pergamon Press, New York, 1967.

Valenstein, Elliot S., *Great and Desperate Cures*, Basic Books, Inc., New York, 1986.

White, James, *Sketches of the Christian Life and Public Labors of William Miller*, Steam Press of the Seventh-Day Adventist Publishing Association, Battle Creek, Mich., 1875.

Wilson, Dorothy Clarke, *Stranger and traveler: the story of Dorothea Dix, American reformer*, Little, Brown, Boston, 1975.

INDEX

Addison's disease 88
alcohol 8, 10, 148, 217
Allegheny County jail 24
American Psychiatric
  Association 71, 225
Anderson, Julius H. 173
anesthesia 21, 203
Asclepius of Prusa 2
Association of Medical
  Superintendents of American
  Institutions for the
  Insane 17, 71, 101, 117-118
Atlee, John Light 102, 125, 130-131
Awl, William McClay 110
Bangs, Edward 34
Bedlam 3, 5
Bell, Luther V. 37
Belleville, Nicholas 15-16
Bigler, William 28, 30
blood-letting 8, 10
Bombaugh, Aaron 48, 51, 68
Bosch, Hieronymus 3
Boughton, Thelma 206
Brueghel, Peter 3
Burnside, James 27, 30
Butler (Kirkbride), Eliza 20
Calder, William, Jr. 84
Cameron, Simon 84
Campbell, Hugh 45, 51, 75
Camp Curtin 55, 95, 97, 99
Cervantes 3
Channing, William Ellery 33, 37
Chapman, Nathaniel 7
Cleaves, Margaret A. 115, 123, 166
  The Autobiography of a
  Neurasthene 116
Cotton Mill hospital 96
Cope, Thomas Pym 42, 44, 47, 52
Corson, Hiram 103, 108-109, 112,
  114-115, 120, 166
Covenant Presbyterian Church 70
Curwen, John 30, 51, 58, 65-71,
  69, 73-74, 75-86, 88-91, 94-101,
  104, 108-110, 112-113, 118,
  122-123, 125, 127-128, 198, 229
  charges against 113-114
  comments on education 86
  Journal 75
  on origins of insanity 83
Dauphin County poorhouse 25, 112
Dempwolf, Augustus 150-151,
  156-157, 175
DeWitt, William R. 106
diagnosis 15, 88
Dickens, Charles 23, 29-30

diphtheria 163
Dix, Dorothea L 23-28, 31-41, 42
  45, 47, 51, 54, 67, 84, 97, 104,
  111, 135, 225, 229-230
  Conversations on Common
  Things 35
  Evening Hours 35
  Meditations for Private Hours 35
Dix, Dorothy Lyne 32
Dix, Joseph 32
Earle, Pliny 12-13, 120
Eastern State Penitentiary 49, 89
Eaton, Hamblen C. 187, 196,
  202-210, 215
"eighth" ward 19, 21
electroconvulsive therapy 196-199,
  206
Elmer (Curwen), Martha 70, 84
Emerson, Ralph Waldo 31, 33
epilepsy 2, 87, 126, 197
Female Medical College of
  Pennsylvania 114-115
Flatley, John 222-223, 228
Fleming (Curwen), Mary 71
Fox, James 48
Franklin, Benjamin 11, 13
Franklin and Marshall College 125
Friends
  Asylum at Frankford 11, 17, 100,
  226
  Society of 9, 14, 21, 84
Fyler, Jared D. 15
Gallaudet, Thomas H. 31
Garver, Jane K. 116-117, 149,
  153, 161, 165-166
Gerhard, Jerome Z. 58, 102, 113,
  122-136, 139, 148, 229
Gerhard, William W. 17
Gettysburg, Pennsylvania
  Poorhouse 24
Gheel (Belgium) 6, 139
Gillette, Claude W. 165
Goodman, Charlotte E. 165
Green, Edward M. 168-169, 171-173,
  183, 200
Gummere, John 15
Haldeman, Jacob 45, 50
Harper, L. B. 200
Harrisburg Academy of Medicine 138
Harrisburg State Hospital (see
  Pennsylvania State Lunatic
  Hospital)
Haskell, Ebenezer 103
Haviland, John 48-50, 51, 74, 80
Heim, Herbert E. 202

INDEX

heridity 129
Hicksites 14, 21
Hippocrates 2, 6
Holman, Samuel 48-49, 69
Hooper, Fred B. 201-202
Howe, Julia Ward 33
Howe, Samuel Gridley 36, 40
Hummel, Betty S. 217
Hutton, Addison 131, 141-146, 150, 156-157, 180, 192
hydrotherapy 157-158
insulin therapy 197-198
Johnston, William 51, 67, 74
Kiefer, Walter E. 164-165
Kindred, J. J. 139
Kirkbride, Thomas S. 7-8, 11-12, 14-22, 47, 51, 52, 67-68, 71, 73, 80, 83, 88, 102-103, 110, 113, 117-118, 204, 230
    on hospital construction 18, 20, 47, 73, 92, 119, 139, 141
Konigmacher, Joseph 38, 42, 44-45, 50-51, 74, 81-82
Krohn, Edith 228
Kunkel, John C. 84
Laucks, S. Philip 119, 155, 215-216, 220-221
Lebengood, Spencer S. 228
Leopold, Joan Y. 228
Lesley, James 45-46
Livingston, J. B. 152, 160
Logan, John B. 199, 206, 220, 222
Malleus Maleficarum 3
Mann Horace 37-38, 41
masturbation 10, 77
Mentzer, John H. 218
mercury 16
Miller, J. A. 96, 99
Millerism 31, 83, 85, 93
Mitchell, Donald G. 66
"moral treatment" 6, 7-13, 9, 12, 17-18, 108-119
More, Sir Thomas 3
morphine 10
Mott, Lucretia 31
opium 8
Orth, Henry L. 131, 138-142, 146, 148-150, 152-153, 156-158, 160-167, 183, 215
    hospital management 167
    as surgeon 138-139, 150
panic of 1837 26
patient labor 19, 219
patient's "bill of rights" 218-219
Penn, William 4

Pennsylvania Board of Public Charities 103-105, 113, 117, 135, 141, 171, 210, 220, 223
Pennsylvania Citizens Association 209
Pennsylvania Department of Welfare (see Pennsylvania Board of Public Charities)
Pennsylvania Hospital 5, 11, 13, 17
Pennsylvania Hospital for the Insane 20, 47, 68, 69, 81
Pennsylvania legislature 25-28, 42-43, 47-48, 89, 111-112, 127, 162, 214, 221-222, 229, 251-255
    appropriations 82, 141, 172, 229
    Committee of Ways and Means 82
    hospital's debt recovery 98
Pennsylvania Mental Health, Inc. 209
Pennsylvania State Medical Society 115, 123, 201-203
Pennsylvania State Lunatic Hospital
    amusements 153, 171
    appearance 76
    Band 59, 171
    Board of Trustees 50-51, 73, 75, 81, 102, 140, 152, 203, 208-209, 212, 220
    causes for admission 85, 129
    Chapel 84, 161, 175, 201
    chaplaincy program 73-74, 207
    construction 127, 160, 175, 192
    dairy herd 147
    farming 90-91, 98, 132, 152, 161-162, 219-220
    food service 133, 152, 158-159, 164, 193, 200-201
    fire 101-102, 131, 134, 141, 167
    grounds 94, 218, 229
    investigations of 112
    laboratory 149, 164, 206
    library 171
    natural disasters 90
    parole 169, 195
    patient labor 91, 130, 132-133, 160, 162-163, 170, 219
    patient occupations 85, 152, 219-220
    patient treatment 105, 126, 157-158, 164, 168, 172-173, 195, 196-199, 201-202, 204-206, 216-217, 227
    piggery 91, 140
    staff 172-173, 229
        standards 100, 173-174
        training 170, 216

INDEX

Sun Parlor 156, 159, 175
surgery 150, 158, 173, 211
Unit System 216-217, 219
ventilation 76, 140
Petry, Howard K. 187, 194-196, 203-204, 208, 229
A Century of Medicine 203
Philadelphia Fund 97
Philadelphia Medical Society 115
Physick, Phillip Syng 15
Pierce, Franklin 91
Pinel, Philippe 6, 8, 9
"pleasure grounds" 10, 19
Pope John XXI 3
Pope Innocent 3
Porter, David 27, 29-30
psychotropic drugs 203, 206
purging 10, 16
Ray, Isaac 12
Reily, George Wolf, Jr. 209
Reily, Luther 45-46, 50-51, 53, 73, 81, 138, 209
Robespierre 8
Rush, Benjamin 5, 15
schizophrenia 197, 227, 230
Shakespeare 3
Shapiro, Harry 209-210, 214
Ship of Fools 3
Shultz, S. S. 96, 99
Slaymaker, William 68, 78

Slothower, Martha 212, 240
Smith, Harlan 199-201
Stanton, Edwin 38
Stanton, Elizabeth C. 31
Strickland, William 44, 52
surgery 17, 21, 150, 158, 173
Thompson, Ford S. 223
tobacco 10
Tristan and Isolde 3
Tuke, William 6
tuberculosis 147-148
typhoid 146
University of Pennsylvania Medical School 7, 16, 67, 125, 168, 227
Walnut Hill 65, 70, 71
Warren State Hospital 113, 116, 128, 195
Washington County, Pennsylvania alms-house 24
Weir, John A. 48, 51, 52, 90, 98, 105
Whittier, John Greenleaf 33, 40
Williamsburg, Virginia 11
Wills Eye Hospital 67
Wilt, Mary Ann 78-79
Wintersteen, Grace 165
witchcraft 4
Wright, W. E. 165
Wyeth (Curwen), Anna 70
Yale College 66, 67, 138